THE GREATEST IN

THE GREATEST INVENTION

TAX AND THE CAMPAIGN FOR A JUST SOCIETY

Foreword by John Christensen

Introduction by Dan Hind

A Tax Justice Network Production

Commonwealth Publishing

First published by Commonwealth 2015

Typesetting and layout Ray Davies
Cover design Kieran McCann
Cover image © Edgar L. Owen, Ltd, edgarlowen.com
Printed in the UK by
TJ International Ltd, Padstow, Cornwall

Contents

THE CRISIS, 2007-2010

2007

2008

Foreword
A Mission to Change the World

The Tax Justice Network can trace its genesis back to the European Social Forum in Florence in November 2002. A message posted to the Forum website by alter-globalisation activists a month earlier invited anyone with an interest in tax havens and offshore financial flows to meet at a marquee in the grounds of the magnificent Fortezza da Basso close to the city's historic centre. I expected, at best, a dozen or so people to show up. To my astonishment, over eighty joined the session which started mid-afternoon and continued, after a pizza break, until midnight when some of us agreed to reconvene the following day.

I had arrived in Florence on an early-morning flight from London, accompanied by my research partner, Dr Mark Hampton (author of *The Offshore Interface: Tax Havens in the Global Economy*, 1996, MacMillan), and War on Want's Pete Coleman. We had a joint mission. Two weeks earlier at a War on Want meeting in London, we had agreed that a new global movement was needed to push tax justice onto the global agenda. Our proposal was for a new research and activist network to create the conditions for building such a movement.

When we arrived the Fortezza da Basso was buzzing. Tens of thousands of activists had convened for the Forum and the city was swamped with riot police. A year earlier at the 2001 G8 summit in Genoa, Italian Prime Minister Silvio Berlusconi, keen to impress world leaders left reeling by anti-globalisation protests in Seattle, had unleashed a brutal police attack on anti-G8 protesters. Hundreds of protesters and police were injured and two protesters killed. In the run up to the 2002 ESF in Florence, Berlusconi's newspapers and TV channels ran lurid stories about violent anarchists targeting the city. Not surprisingly, local businesses hurriedly boarded up their shops, cafes and pensiones – which was slightly inconvenient since neither Mark, Pete nor I had anywhere to sleep that night.

By day three of the Forum we'd agreed that a new network, to be called the Tax Justice Network, would be launched in London in March 2003. Pete Coleman and I were instructed to draft a founding declaration to lay out the network's values and goals. The Swiss research advocacy organisation Berne Declaration chipped in 400 Swiss francs towards website design. Mission done, we left Florence with high hopes, almost no funding, and the seed of a new global movement for systemic change.

A Long Gestation

At the core of the network when we launched it in 2003, was a handful of veterans who had been investigating financial market deregulation, secrecy jurisdictions, tax havens and illicit financial flows for decades; Jo Marie Griesgraber, Sol Picciotto, Prem Sikka, Jack Blum, David Spencer, Richard Murphy, and Ronen Palan, among others. We were multi-disciplinary, inspired by a variety of intellectual traditions, pluralist in outlook, and committed to opening up a critical discussion about the role of tax havens in the globalised economy.

My own interest in tax havens goes back to 1978 when a group of Oxfam volunteers convened at London's School of Oriental and African Studies (SOAS) to discuss systemic causes of poverty. Public disenchantment with development aid had built up during the 1970s, and many people, myself included, were interested in shaping exit strategies from aid and debt dependence. Despite the almost complete lack of official data it was clear that huge sums of money were disappearing from Africa, South-East Asia and Latin America, stifling development and corrupting governance in many countries. We also knew that much of this wealth was headed for London, Geneva and New York via complex networks of offshore companies and trusts located in secrecy jurisdictions. What wasn't clear, however, to any of us meeting at SOAS in 1978, was why politically powerful organisations like the IMF, or World Bank, or successive governments in Bonn, London, Paris and Washington, were so tolerant of this fast-growing phenomenon.

I was training in forensic audit at that time and sensed an important story here. What really piqued my interest was the almost complete absence of academic research on this subject. Tax havens scarcely got a mention anywhere other than the occasional red-top newspaper article about the latest over-the-hill actor going into 'tax exile' in the Bahamas. A few right wing libertarian oriented think tanks were putting out thought-pieces about the benign effect tax havens had in 'disciplining' high-tax high-spend governments. And that was about it.

The SOAS group sent letters (this was long before the days of email and skype) to researchers around the world, but beyond preparing a diminutive literature review, we found no useful analysis of how billions of dollars were routinely transferred daily via secretive offshore structures. We put a research proposal to Oxfam but their priorities were elsewhere, so I went my own way. In 1980 I finished my training in London, left my job and headed to university to study global trade and investment theory. Reagan and Thatcher had come to power and market liberalisation was underway; tax havens were emerging as the turbo-chargers of a brave new financial capitalism.

During a three year honours degree course covering the economics of world trade and investment, the terms 'tax haven', 'transfer pricing', 'illicit financial flows', or anything related, were never mentioned. Capital flight was hurriedly explained away as the product of bad government policy and unrelated to tax evasion and private sector corruption. Every question I put to lecturers about these phenomena was side-stepped: I had strayed into an economic blind spot. Worse, when I tried to shape a proposal for post-graduate research, the dearth of data and published literature made this an academic no-go area.

In 1985 I was working in Kuala Lumpur preparing a proposal for comprehensive reform of the cooperative sector. I became involved in an investigation into high-level frauds at so-called deposit-taking cooperatives. Hundreds of millions of dollars of personal savings had disappeared into offshore shell companies located in places like Hong Kong, Jersey, London and Singapore, and there was no way of identifying who was behind these companies. In December 1985 I wrote a long article about the systemic and political nature of the scandal, and flew out of Kuala Lumpur on the morning it was published in the Southeast Asian Business Times. Such was the level of corruption among Malaysia's business and political elites that I knew I wouldn't be returning to that country any time soon. Instead, I decided that this was the moment to start looking more closely at how illicit money flows through the offshore circuits, and to do this

I returned home to Jersey, where I grew up, and where the offshore financial centre in Saint Helier was booming.

Initially I worked in the offshore company and trust division of accounting firm Touche Ross & Co (now Deloitte Touche), followed by a decade working as the Economic Adviser to the States of Jersey. Working as an insider provided a unique apprenticeship into both the dark arts of tax havenry, and the relations between tax havens like Jersey and the powerful OECD countries like the United Kingdom, which for decades have protected tax havens from all attempts to close them. Throughout my period of service as Economic Adviser I struggled to maintain a degree of integrity in the face of regular confrontations with politicians and my head of department, the Chief Adviser to the States of Jersey. The tensions were sometimes unbearable, and affected my health, particularly since my section was deliberately kept under-staffed and constantly overworked. Eventually I decided to quit my job, sell my home, leave the island, and re-settle near London, none of which was easy with a young family and an uncertain future.

By the time I left Jersey in 1998, the Washington Consensus was well established and tax havens were booming. So much so that the G7 countries – Germany and France in particular – were raising concerns about what became known as harmful tax competition: and the OECD had been commissioned to work on its seminal report, published in 1998, which triggered a fierce response from tax havens and their supporters in Washington like the Cato Institute (which hosts a pro-tax haven lobbying group called the Center for Freedom and Prosperity). But beyond the pioneering research of academics such as Mark Hampton, Susan Roberts, Ronen Palan and Sol Picciotto, and non-fiction crime books like Jeffrey Robinson's *The Laundrymen*, tax havens were still ignored by civil society, other than as an exotic side-show to the world economy.

Then Jenny Kimmis got in touch. Oxfam was planning to research a report on how tax havens impact development; was I still interested in the subject? You bet I was. Oxfam's report (*Tax Havens: Releasing the Hidden Billions for Poverty Eradication*, 2000) was a game-changer. Despite its conservative estimate of the sums lost to poorer countries, the report began to prick the interest of a handful of researchers and activists across the world. In particular, following the earlier

Asian financial crisis of 1997, it attracted attention from the more militant activists of the international ATTAC movement, who were developing their own critique of financial market liberalisation. It was ATTAC activists Raphael Calvelli and Sven Giegold, along with Swiss economist Bruno Gurtner, who convened the meeting in Florence in November 2002. All cited Oxfam's report as an influence.

For its part, Oxfam took no action at that stage beyond publishing the report, partly (I was later told) because it was felt that the issues raised by tax havens were too complex for a single NGO to tackle. Jenny Kimmis, however, wanted to carry on with her research into tax havens: in 2005 she became the first editor of *Tax Justice Focus*.

Empty Pockets: A Reality Check

Returning to London from the heady discussions in Florence, we took stock of the global situation. Our initial mapping exercises indicated no public awareness and minimal research and activist capacity in Europe and North America. The situation beyond those continents was certainly no better. Through 2003 and 2004 I discussed the possibilities for building a global movement with a wide variety of experts. Their responses were hardly encouraging. Most felt that the international institutions responsible for building cooperation on tax matters, above all the OECD which had recently been forced to backtrack on its 1998 Harmful Tax Competition report, were wholly or largely captive to tax haven interests.

There was also deep scepticism about the possibilities for building public support on such arcane measures as automatic information exchange, especially in developing countries where there was little or no engagement on international tax related matters. (That scepticism has had a long tail: even after the Great Financial Crisis in 2008 and the consequent economic crises in many countries, a British Treasury minister told me that people were unlikely to ever take to the streets demanding public registers of beneficial ownership or country-by-country reporting by transnational companies. Just weeks after the minister said this UK Uncut activists did exactly that.)

In 2003, however, tax havens scarcely registered as an issue among the activist communities. While the ATTAC movement was active on the financial transaction tax, and a sprinkling of activists in Belgium,

France, Germany and Switzerland showed some interest in tax havens, the numbers involved were tiny and there was no sign of anything other than sporadic interest among trade unions, faith movements, anti-corruption organisations, human rights campaigners, or corporate social responsibility advocacy groups. The same applied across the entire spectrum of international media. When we listed journalists who had regularly reported on international tax matters between 1998 and 2003, the list came to fewer than twenty – across fifty or so countries. Today this list would number hundreds, possibly thousands, and investigative journalists from across the world are queuing up to join the specialist training course TJN provides in conjunction with the Centre for Investigative Journalism at London's City University.

The *Financial Times* was among the first of the major newspapers to notice TJN's work, and in November 2004 quoted the OECD's Jeffrey Owens talking about the potentially transformative role that civil society could play:

> *The OECD's Mr Owens thinks that the emergence of non-governmental organisations intent on exposing large-scale tax avoiders could eventually achieve a change in attitude comparable to that achieved on environmental and social issues: 'Tax is where the environment was 10 years ago.'*

But the nature of the subject presented some pretty serious obstacles to building a strong activist movement. First, was the sheer complexity of the issues. Well over ninety-nine percent of those who understand international tax matters work on the Dark Side – and most non-experts would rather nail their ears to the floor than have to endure the dull, technocratic droning of tax professionals. Second, we were working in the twilight, with inadequate data and almost no critical academic literature on the subject. Serious research is also blocked by the *omertà* of the tax haven industry. Third, while our senior advisers were experts in their field, they were understandably nervous about getting involved with grassroots activists who have a disconcerting habit of taking to the streets to face riot police. We had to reassure our experts that they wouldn't find their reputations trashed by association. Fourth, the libertarian and anti-state elements of the neoliberal consensus were defending tax avoidance and the offshore as a means to 'starve the beast' of Big Government. Lobbyists like Dan Mitchell and Andrew Quinlan at the Center for Freedom and Prosperity worked hard to provide the tax havens and their clients a veneer of intellectual plausibility. Freedom sounds so much better than privilege.

Finally, and most seriously, we faced indifference and pushback from some who should have been our allies. They just didn't get it. Across the spectrum of trade unions, public interest watchdogs and international development NGOs there was little discernible interest. During the run up to the global *Make Poverty History* events in 2005, the head of one major development NGO said to me on the sidelines of an international conference – apparently in all seriousness – 'I really don't understand what tax has to do with development'. Worse, she warned, TJN risked alienating the development community by distracting from the goal of raising aid levels to 0.7 percent of GDP. She didn't quite say 'back off', but others did. *En bref,* tax justice was simply not on the agenda in the early-noughties age of Tony Blair, George W. Bush and Gerhard Schröder.

One indication of just how low international tax matters were on the NGO agenda came from the United Nations. In August 2003 I called Dr Ahmed Bouab, secretary to the UN's Group of Experts on International Cooperation on Tax Matters, to request an invitation for TJN to attend the Group's annual session in Geneva later that year. There was a long silence on the phone, followed by a sigh. 'I'm close to retirement.' Bouab explained, 'and I've waited twenty years for civil society to pay attention to these matters.' Over three thousand civil societies attended events around the 2003 G8 Summit in Evian to protest on trade and debt related matters. Tax justice scarcely featured,

Months later, across Lac Leman in Geneva, Richard Murphy and I represented TJN as observers at the Group of Experts session, sitting alongside the only other registered NGO, the International Chamber of Commerce, represented by the tax director of a major Swiss bank. Waves of curious diplomats and tax officials, expecting to see ponytailed activists in leather jackets, were visibly disappointed at seeing two middle-aged, greying men in suits.

While potential allies were either lukewarm or sceptical, our opponents were patronising or downright hostile. I wouldn't even hazard a guess at how many times tax accountants, bank directors, lawyers and government officials have told me that TJN doesn't understand the complexity of tax issues, or that tax avoidance improves 'efficiency', or that company directors have a statutory right and duty to avoid tax. The first time I publicly challenged companies to report on their tax positions, at a corporate social responsibility conference at Chatham House, London, in 2004, the audience animosity was palpable and the session moderator looked as if I had dropped a dog turd on the table.

To complicate matters, the finance sector in Jersey had heard about my involvement with TJN and hired a public relations firm in London to warn journalists against me. I got wind of this when a contact at the BBC told me she had been approached and warned that I was 'personally motivated', apparently driven by a grudge against my former employers because I hadn't been appointed Chief Adviser to the States of Jersey (the PR people failed to mention that I never applied for the post). However, what appears to have been a more serious attempt at intimidation came later, in October 2006, when British government security and airport police arrested me while travelling to the annual UN Tax Committee session in Geneva. Was this a clumsy attempt at smearing TJN's reputation? It certainly felt so at the time. I took the experience of a few hours in a chilly Luton police cell as a telling sign that we were treading on the toes of politically powerful players.

Despite the headwinds, we ploughed ahead. We had no funding, forcing me to live off personal savings until a small group of activists from Jersey made a grant to keep TJN going. Campaigning accountant Richard Murphy also freely provided his time to the project, and we had support from a range of senior advisers including Jim Henry, Sol Picciotto, Prem Sikka and David Spencer. Guided by an international steering committee chaired by German economist and activist Sven Giegold, I set out to build the network outside Europe.

It was hard going to start with. In 2005, twelve months ahead of the World Social Forum (WSF) in Bamako, Mali, I contacted academics, activists, government officials, journalists and others across the West African region. They broadly confirmed what we had suspected: there was some awareness of illicit financial flows, trade mispricing via offshore companies, tax cheating by multinational companies, and dodgy deals to secure tax exemptions, but no African-based researchers or NGOs were working on these issues. Nonetheless, meeting in Bamako in January 2006 we agreed to launch an all-Africa network at the WSF in Nairobi, Kenya, the following year. To achieve this we set up a small team, including Matti Kohonen, Roman Kuenzler, Emma Lochery, Jean Merckaert, and me, to check out potential partners, identify the main issues of concern, and recruit someone to help organise events in Nairobi. That was how I first encountered Alvin Mosioma, the young Kenyan economist who, since October 2006, has been devoted to building Tax Justice Network Africa.

The launch of TJN-Africa in Nairobi in January 2007 was a major step forward for TJN, but few people realised how fragile our situation was at that time. A year earlier Richard Murphy and I had met at the pizzeria opposite the British Library to discuss TJN's funding situation, which could be summarised as follows: we had approximately three month's operational funding in hand, and my personal savings were exhausted. Prem Sikka and the Association for Accountancy & Business Affairs financed our annual research workshops at Essex University; but attempts to raise money through membership fees and crowd sourced funding had yielded almost nothing. The situation was so dire that Richard and I agreed that if we had not secured new funding by July 2006, we would (unwillingly) abandon the project.

The Cavalry Rides In

At the eleventh hour the Joseph Rowntree Charitable Trust granted me a bursary for my work, and Christian Aid also offered some research funding to keep us going.

TJN's finances have never been anything other than tight, forcing us to operate on a model we call 'hyper-resilient'. We rent no office space: TJN's international headquarter operates from a studio I built with my sons at the end of my garden in Chesham, Buckinghamshire. Salary levels are still pegged significantly below those in the charity sector; we have little or no reserve capital, and we are exceptionally frugal with our administrative costs. Whatever difference we might have made, we are still too racy for most funder's tastes. They can't bring themselves to recognise the role that the financial architecture plays in preventing 'developing countries' from improving human welfare.

From day one TJN needed to rally public support around demands that were a little more complicated than 'close down the tax havens.' These are not dragons that can be killed with a single well-aimed spear; we are up against multi-headed beasts that constantly transform themselves, reproduce, and have sharp teeth. We needed a set of carefully targeted demands that would pin down the monsters that flourish in globalised financial markets.

We began with country-by-country (CbC) reporting, an accounting standard that would disclose profits-shifting by transnational companies. The idea was originally mooted at a meeting between Richard Murphy, Prem Sikka and myself in Jersey in 2002. Richard worked the idea into a draft international reporting standard, which subsequently formed the basis for a protracted advocacy programme led by the Publish What You Pay coalition. For years the corporate community dismissed the proposal as pie in the sky. The OECD is now working CBCR into a global standard.

We did the same with tax information exchange processes, which are vital if governments are to deter wealthy people from holding their assets offshore to evade taxes. After pushback in 2000/01 from George W. Bush's administration against its 1998 Harmful Tax Competition report, the OECD retrenched around a somewhat useless process known as information exchange 'upon request.' The OECD knew that a swamp needed to be drained, but it was handing out drinking straws. Tax havens merely needed to sign a few bilateral agreements based on an expensive and inoperable standard to be deemed 'cooperative and transparent', even if those agreements were only with places like the Faroe Islands, or Greenland, or other tax havens. In true TJN berserker style we rejected this approach and demanded much deeper information sharing through routine and automatic processes. For years our demands were pooh-poohed by government and OECD officials, some of whom argued that developing countries were not interested in receiving this data from tax havens, and lacked capacity to make use of it. This situation was finally resolved in 2012 when Indian Prime Minister Manmohan Singh told his G20 country partners that India required automatic information exchange to tackle its extensive tax evasion problems. The OECD is currently working up a new multilateral standard along the lines of our original demands, which might seriously dent the criminogenic environment of offshore secrecy jurisdictions, though time will tell whether the lobbyists will successfully derail the project.

A crucial part of the task of rolling back the tax havens lies with tackling the secrecy of offshore companies, foundations, trusts, and, of course, bank accounts. A lucrative global market exists for secrecy, and a vast infrastructure of banks, law firms, accountancy practices works in cahoots with offshore secrecy jurisdictions to supply secrecy to their tax cheating clients.

We set out to confront these powerful players by turning the corruption discourse on its head. While the World Bank has carefully shaped its definition of corruption to target public sectors in the global South, we took a broader view of corrupt practices and focused on the financial infrastructure that enables the cross-border movement of billions of dollars of dirty money. In January 2007, while attending the launch of TJN-Africa in Nairobi, Alex Cobham, Sol Picciotto, Nicholas Shaxson and I mapped out a proposal for a new index to rank countries (and their dependent territories) on the basis of their secrecy laws, their compliance with anti-money laundering regulations, and their willingness to cooperate with information exchange. With initial research funding from the Ford Foundation, Richard Murphy and Markus Meinzer started the dry and laborious process of trawling through laws, regulations, and an array of international reports, to create the Financial Secrecy Index. Economists Alex Cobham and Petry Jansky did the groundwork of ranking the results according to each country's share of the global market for offshore financial services. Since its first publication in 2009 the FSI has transformed the corruption debate: ranking major OECD countries like Luxembourg, Switzerland, U.K., and the U.S.A. as the most important secrecy jurisdictions, has made it possible to reconfigure the geography of corruption, bringing the role of offshore companies and trusts and suchlike into prominence. On the back of this we shaped our demand for public registers of beneficial ownership: penetrating the true identities of the warm-blooded owners of the secretive shell companies and offshore trusts. Without public access to beneficial ownership information the automatic information exchange processes will not deter sophisticated tax cheats and other crooks. In 2013 the G8 presidency finally acceded to our demand.

Winning the Arguments

On a wall of my office in Chesham hangs a cartoon of Don Quixote that I bought from a street vendor in Moscow in the dying days of the Soviet Union. It serves as a reminder of the pitfalls of tilting against windmills like the OECD or the IMF. Through TJN's early years there was a shared feeling that we were engaged in a valiant but hopeless struggle against the most powerful people on the planet and the all-pervading ideology of financialised liberalism that backed their interests. But the banking crisis that emerged in 2007 marked a turning point, beyond which TJN's mission seemed less quixotic – though more urgent. The banking bailouts of 2008 and the subsequent collapse of public finances in many countries had various roots, but a major factor was the rising share of global income going to the 1 percent and the falling contribution they make to government revenues. Another, less obvious underlying cause of the crisis was the role of tax havens – and particularly the archipelago of British islands linked to the City of London – in fostering lax financial regulation and the aggressive, race-to-the-bottom deregulatory dynamics that prevent effective oversight of the shadow banking system. The so-called shadow banking system is cast by onshore banks onto their countless offshore subsidiaries and affiliates.

In November 2007 the *Guardian* newspaper, following consultation with TJN, published a lengthy exposé of how banana trading companies use offshore subsidiaries to shift profits to tax havens. The article attracted interest across the world, and was followed shortly afterwards by Christian Aid's seminal report 'Death and Taxes' which adopted a hard-hitting approach to show how corporate tax avoidance literally causes deaths in poorer countries. When asked to pinpoint a tipping point moment in TJN's development I highlight that *Guardian* article and Christian Aid's report as major steps. TJN's position was further boosted in 2009, when Richard Murphy was invited to blog live from within the G20 summit hall in London as finance ministers and heads of state discussed measures to tackle offshore secrecy.   The subsequent publication of *Treasure Islands,* (2011) Nick Shaxson's brilliant exposé of tax havenry, also played a big role in explaining to the public and to opinion-formers why tax havens are a core rather than peripheral issue.   A prominent pro-tax haven lawyer based in London subsequently told me that *Treasure Islands* was so well-researched and compelling in its arguments, that attempts at counter-argument were doomed.

From 2009 onwards it was clear that tax justice was rising up the political agenda. Public opinion was stacked in our favour in many countries, crisis-hit governments were scrambling for revenues, and inequality was seriously harming any prospects for a sustained recovery.

Global media coverage of tax havens and tax cheating was rising steadily. It skyrocketed in 2012 when we published Jim Henry's estimate that up to $32 trillion of private wealth was stashed offshore. Reacting to public anger, G20 leaders were now regularly talking about the need for measures against tax havens. And the tiny team at TJN – just four staffers at that time – was swamped by enquiries from journalists, general public, and NGOs around the world. Nick Shaxson jokes about this deluge of demands as being like drinking water from a fire hose, but joking aside we urgently needed to reorganise the global network to separate TJN's core research and communications activities from the hustle and bustle of campaign and advocacy work. Brilliant new research ideas were being discarded daily because we lacked capacity and, with steam coming out of our noses, the pressure just kept building.

We finally succeeded in launching the Global Alliance for Tax Justice in 2013 to take on all the tasks related to coordinating regional and global advocacy and campaigns. This has allowed TJN more time and space to widen its thematic coverage. For now, we have selected two themes that we feel should become core tax justice themes in the coming years: firstly, confronting the rise of the politics of 'competition' between states leading to the lemming-like race-to-the-bottom on taxing capital. The beggar-thy-neighbour practices of countries like Ireland and the U.K. need to be recognised for what they are: economic warfare. Tax wars is a far more accurate term for this phenomenon. Secondly, making links between tax justice and human rights is a no-brainer when you stop to think about it, but much of the human rights community has been studiously looking the other way for decades.

Human rights activists rightly demand that states fulfil obligations relating to security, education, health and other services. They now need to start paying attention to where the money comes from. Equally, they need to be more critical of corporate claims about being human rights 'compliant' when companies are purposefully setting up complex offshore structures to avoid paying taxes where they're due. As the UN's special rapporteur on extreme poverty, Magdelena Sepúlveda wrote in a special edition of *Tax Justice Focus* in June 2014, when governments choose to cut crucial services to poor people in the name of austerity, more often than not they are making a choice between raising the tax contribution of rich people and corporations, or imposing cuts on the poorest and most vulnerable people. In Sepúlveda's own words:

> *In nearly every country of the world it is not a question of lack of resources, but rather of a lack of political will to collect and marshal these resources in a manner that is compliant with human rights.*

In 2014 TJN's team, led by Liz Nelson, partnered up with the Center for Economic and Social Rights in New York to collaborate on a programme to put tax justice at the heart of the human rights community. Reframing human rights in this way will hopefully bring a new focus to the human rights agenda, drawing attention to how tax havens deliberately deprive other countries of the resources they need to fulfil their human rights obligations, and investigating how powerful banks and accounting firms assist clients with dodging taxes while claiming to be human rights compliant.

Given more resources we'd love to go further. The austerity measures imposed across the world have impacted more heavily on women than on men, partly because the fiscal cutbacks have hit benefits to carers and single mothers. The gender dimensions of tax injustices need far more research to highlight how different tax regimes discriminate against women. We'd also love to collaborate in research and campaigning on tax and the environment: everyone knows how the energy market, for example, is rigged in favour of the hydrocarbon industry, with billions of dollars of subsidies supporting the big oil companies, far outstripping the subsidies paid to the renewables sector. All these issues need to be brought to the surface and turned into effective campaigns. We still have our work cut out: back to that firehose!

John Christensen
April, 2015

Introduction
What is Necessary is Possible

As Peter Coleman notes in the first article in this collection, tax is an ambiguous thing. As individuals we often experience it as a burden, even a criminal raid on funds painstakingly secured from an indifferent world. But much of what we are, and everything we have, would be lost without the systems of law and social coordination that taxes fund. However much we dislike paying up, tax really is the price of civilisation.

Indeed, as the title of this collection makes clear, tax is in a sense our greatest invention. For good, and all too often for ill, it has been the means by which we have funded our collective endeavours. From war and domestic repression to health programmes and moon shots, tax has been the great enabler. Here, too, then, an almost crushing ambiguity.

When the Tax Justice Network was created a little more than a decade ago the conventional wisdom had settled around the assumptions of the so-called Washington Consensus. Globalization left nation-states no choice but to compete with one another to attract both capital and talent. A predatory race to the bottom on regulation and social protection was presented as the inevitable outcome of titanic historical forces. Tax revenues adequate to pay for social services were an unaffordable luxury. Politicians ruefully told voters that nothing could be done.

Widespread resentment of tax and what Adam Smith called our 'disposition to admire, and almost to worship, the rich and the powerful' were artfully combined.[1] If society's winners were able to keep more of their money, surely they would spend it wisely. Investment would flow into new industries. Pretty soon we'd all be rich enough to hire our own tax accountants and join our betters on the beach.

Wealthy individuals and large companies managed to avoid paying the tax they owed even as nominal rates on income and profits fell. The same process of deregulation that allowed widespread tax avoidance permitted tax evasion and money laundering on an unprecedented scale. Grand corruption and transnational crime have grown to the point where they now constitute business as usual. Just as crime exploited the resources of the banking sector, the banking sector exploited the business models made possible by systemic fraud. The globalised financial system piled up unsustainable debts offshore and then collapsed.

Slowly and unsteadily public discussion has begun to include an acknowledgment that something is amiss. Tax – and more specifically, the ability of powerful public and private actors to avoid, evade, or legislate away, their obligations to pay it – is moving back to the centre of our programmes for reform. In the words of Thomas Piketty, if you want to reduce inequality and poverty 'you can't expect everything from fiscal redistribution, but that nonetheless is where you have to begin'.[2] And if we are serious about fiscal redistribution then we have to take into account the institutional mechanisms that have made the payment of tax for the wealthy an increasingly optional matter.

The Tax Justice Network has been integral to the rediscovery of tax as an instrument of policy, and to the wider effort to restore some degree of rationality to debates about economic management. Long before the credit markets seized up in 2007-8 its members were warning that the global financial architecture was unsustainable, and that the many pathologies in the modern economic and political settlement met offshore.

In the pages that follow I have sought to trace the development of the Network's own ideas and its engagement with other debates and reform initiatives in civil society. The very first edition of the *Tax Justice Focus* in 2003 carried a piece by Peter Coleman on the professional enablers of tax avoidance, a piece by Prem Sikka on one of the accounting mechanisms ('transfer pricing') used to minimise tax payments, and a piece by Lucy Komisar on the need for Americans to develop a tax system capable of paying for public services. Since then the Network has developed new lines of inquiry, and it has reached out to find common ground with others. But these early themes continue to inform the Network.

In 2005 the Network began publishing regular editions of the *Focus*. The role of tax havens in perpetuating under-development in the global south rapidly emerged as a central pillar in the Network's thinking. Articles by Olowabi Bakre, Bob Awuor, Patrick Smith and others highlighted how both Francophone and Anglophone Africa had suffered from decades of depredation by despotic regimes working in concert with European corporations and financiers. The major offshore centres, including New York and London, were indispensable in this process of parasitic extraction.

It was from this perspective that the Network began to push for a new approach to corruption that took seriously its enabling infrastructure in the legal and financial sectors. In a 2006 article 'Corruption and the Role of Tax Havens' John Christensen pushed back aggressively against the notion that corruption was a developing world problem that Europe and the United States would nobly solve. Corruption was a problem for the core states in the global economy, Christensen argued. At the time it was an uncomfortable position to take. But, as the fallout from the financial crisis has demonstrated, it is substantially correct.

When a global economy predicated on rapid credit expansion and low taxes first faltered then fell apart in 2007-8 the Network began to address the root causes of the crisis in an unregulated financial system. Philip Sarre's 'Financial Flows: The Big Picture' was typical. Meanwhile Nicholas Shaxson's blunt 2007 editorial 'Donors, Wake Up', 'Waking the Slumbering Giants' by Alex Wilks and 'Making the Link: Tax, Governance and Civil Society' by Olivia McDonald marked a shift in the attitude of development NGOs towards capacity building in the developing world. The links between financial volatility at the centre and persistent poverty on the periphery were becoming increasingly obvious.

The mainstream media began to pay closer attention to the dynamics of offshore finance. Heather Stewart and Ian Griffiths' *Guardian* piece 'How Multinationals Avoid the Taxman' was something of a breakthrough in this regard. This period also saw a programme of reform in the global financial architecture beginning to emerge. In 2007, for example, Richard Murphy set out proposals in the *Focus* for his 'country-by-country reporting' standard, a change in accounting protocols that he had first outlined in 2003. Country-by-country reporting makes large-scale tax avoidance substantially more difficult, without requiring new global institutions of the kind that can set nerves in North America jangling. The Network also highlighted the role that land value tax can play in a progressive tax regime.

The years 2011 and 2012 saw a series of books and articles published that led to an astonishing breakthrough in public awareness of the Network's agenda. Nicholas Shaxson's *Treasure Islands* in January 2011 helped shape popular resistance to austerity in the UK and has now been translated into more than twenty languages. The business press had also begun to look more carefully at the tax affairs of the multinational companies. Tom Bergin at Reuters and Jesse Drucker at Bloomberg worked on groundbreaking investigations into the arrangements that Starbucks, Google and others used to reduce their overall tax liability way below the rates paid by most companies and individuals. This new attention to tax evasion by large corporates helped shape the response to the financial crisis in both Britain and the United States.[3]

In 2012 James Henry's online report *The Price of Offshore Revisited* put a number on offshore balances and brought home to a mass audience the sheer scale of fiscal crime. That same summer 'Where the Money Lives', Shaxson's *Vanity Fair* investigation into Mitt Romney's tax affairs, made the offshore system a major issue in a US presidential election for the first time.

In the last two years or so the Network has worked to connect its central concern for tax justice with a number of complementary campaigns and social movements. The *Focus* has run issues where guest editors including Richard Wilkinson and Kate Pickett, Adrienne Margolis, Liz Nelson, and Will Snell approached issues like economic inequality, the abuse of human rights, gender justice and the privileges of the professional class in a frame that also took fiscal policy and tax justice into account.

Over the course of the decade the *Focus* has published a great number of technical pieces on specific aspects of tax policy or particular episodes. Space constraints mean that we have only been able to reproduce a few of them here – 'Pulp Reality, Tax Fiction' by Jorma Penttinen, 'Taxing Thoughts' by Sheila Killian, for example. I would like to take this opportunity to thank Luis Flávio Neto, Tatiana Falcão, Kerry Sadiq and Vikram Vijayaraghavan and all the writers for the Tax Justice Network who have given so generously of their time and expertise.

The flipside of our disposition 'to admire, and almost to worship, the rich and the powerful' is our tendency 'to despise, or, at least, to neglect persons of poor and mean condition'. The guardians of the current organization of the world skillfully exploited our power worship during the boom. After the bust they have been equally adept in manipulating our contempt for the weak. But throughout the successful imposition of austerity the Tax Justice Network has continued to insist that it is the rich and the powerful who must take responsibility for the problems we now face. The facts support the Network's perspective.

The facts alone will not bring about the changes we need in the years ahead. Those who benefit from the prevailing inequality and those who are hungry for their share of the spoils will not meekly give way to the force of the better argument. But they have lost their claims to embody the unstoppable force of what has to happen. They stand exposed as dangerous fantasists at best and criminals at worst. A great deal now depends on whether we can bring our natural inclinations into line with reality, whether we can shake off the temptation to defer to the rich and powerful, no matter how absurd and sinister they become.

We can either commit to a kind of Soviet capitalism, where none of our assumptions stand up to reasoned scrutiny and no one believes a word they say. Or we can pay attention to the facts and recognise the need for fundamental reform. If we choose the latter course then the Tax Justice Network can claim some part of the credit. Its work will become part of a programme that brings sustainable prosperity and liberty to the generations that follow us. If not the Network can take some consolation and great pride in the fact that they did their best.

Dan Hind
July, 2015

ESTABLISHING TERMS, 2003-2006

Pinstripe Outlaws

Pete Coleman

Once upon a time in the west...

Despite capitalism's tendencies to favour the rich above the poor, all mainstream theories of efficient taxation in a capitalist economy excuse only the poorest from a contribution. In many developing countries, ravaged by unequal relations with the heartlands of capitalism, this can be large sections of the population – rural communities and informal sector workers – but in the industrialised countries, few people have income or consumption so low that the state does not extract at least some tax. The rapid spread of consumption taxes across the world in the last three decades means that even where workers do not pay direct taxation, pretty much everything above (and sometimes including) the barest means of survival requires a tax payment.

Taxation brings with it two competing obligations. Usually, a human being's first reaction is a desire to minimise tax. The tax transaction is experienced as the forces of bureaucracy taking something away; not exactly pleasant for any of us. After all, we possess legitimate motives to generate and protect resources for ourselves, for our families, and for our businesses. This is one of the great unifying experiences of modern life, a gripe of truly global proportions.

The second, competing obligation is the social contract, an obligation to contribute to public revenue, arising from the individual's or the corporation's status as a beneficiary of the broader society around it. We accept that to have a legal system, education, healthcare, national defence, infrastructure, and even government itself, then this has to be paid for. Only if the state takes an income, a cut of the economic activity occurring within its territories, can it organise these kinds of public goods and services. Thus we also accept this second obligation, despite its apparent contradiction to the first.

These competing obligations are mediated by legislation. The first impulse is restrained by the state, to allow the realisation of the second. As individuals, we are relieved of the contradiction when we accept legislation as being in our social interest. In general terms, the law sets out what is intended and consensual. In this regard, tax legislation is no different from other legislative restrictions on our individual actions, such as laws against theft and violence. Such laws are accepted by consensus, because despite reducing one freedom, they help shape society around us to provide different freedoms, to our net benefit.

In principle, if the social contract's worth more than the paper it should be written on, then what is intended and consensual is also morally just. Most of us accept we will contribute what is legally due, and no more. High-tax enthusiasts don't voluntarily pay more than the minimum just to make their point, and proponents of lower taxes don't usually resort to criminal tax evasion just to make theirs.

Desperado

So what is wrong with this picture? When we minimise our taxes according to legislation, but then pay up what we owe, is this not tax justice? Why do we need a campaign, a democratic intervention, a social movement?

The answer lies within the current nature of tax legislation – put simply, in key areas, it is now failing the majority of citizens. The tax burden is shifting, away from the wealthy, and onto ordinary people. National tax legislation has failed to remain effective in the 21st century global economy, and has not been replaced or sufficiently strengthened by effective international legislation. This is not a point of view – this is a matter of fact, proved by trends in aggregate tax figures, and proved by the massive capital flows passing through tax havens that dwarf the real economic activity occurring there.

In a world of nation states, the social contract has been most effective when working on a national basis. Indeed, as citizens, we still accept our side of the contract by reference to national legislation. Capital though has gone international. Big Money faces no immigration controls, it needs no passport, no state to call its home. Capital is free to roam the world at practically no cost – this is the key change of the last two decades. This means that all too often, capital can simply duck out of the national social contract. Meanwhile, at the global level – despite international law and international institutions, despite tax treaties and OECD initiatives – the international social contract (if such a thing exists at all) fails to prevent massive global tax avoidance. Some might say it positively encourages it.

By failing to keep pace with changes in the global economy, tax legislation now helps to undermine the very social contract that it is charged with upholding. Wealthy individuals and corporations run rings around national legislation to avoid paying taxes in the countries in which they operate. Capital zooms in and out of tax havens at the touch of a button. Economic activity is often recorded as occurring wherever taxes are low, irrespective of where it actually takes place. Specialist accountants and lawyers are highly rewarded for imaginatively and deliberately subverting the intended, consensual levels of tax in those states where the real economic activity happens. A quick trawl through the web reveals how brazen such advisors are, shamelessly advertising their ability to help dismantle the social contract in return for a big fat fee.

Of course, the terms of the social contract – what is actually intended or consensual – are only a vague ideal. However, there are certain obvious indicators, such as the comparative rates of tax actually paid by different sections of society, or standard legislative rates of tax, or recent historical rates of tax. All such indicators suggest the inescapable conclusion that the low effective tax rates enjoyed by some of the world's wealthiest individuals and corporations are neither intended, nor consensual. In this respect, Big Money now operates outside of any meaningful social contract, beyond the scope of the intended and consensual rates of tax in the economies from which it draws its profits. Beyond a certain point, modern tax avoidance is actually legislation-avoidance. Capital has – quite literally – become an outlaw.

Hang 'em high

Although society may encourage some tax allowances and tricks – particularly to encourage certain social policies or economic activities – it is also obvious when these tricks are pushed too far. As described in Lucy Komisar's article elsewhere in this edition, studies from the US revealed a shockingly large number of giant corporations paying little or no tax throughout the mid-1990s. The most famous individual study of the same period revealed that News Corporation paid around 7% on profits, even though the three countries in which most of its activities occurred had standard corporation tax rates averaging around 30%. Such low corporate tax payments are neither intended by the legislation, nor consensual within the societies where News Corporation carried out its business. On the contrary, they undermine the social contract. Such corporations have become freeloaders, successfully externalising the cost of maintaining the public goods and services – indeed, the broader socio-economic frameworks – on which their business relies.

Similarly, wealthy individuals who organise their affairs through offshore trusts and secret accounts are also freeloading, departing from what is intended and consensual. If the law appears to allow it, it is only because it's not up to the job of preventing it. At no time has the question been put to democratic electorates, 'should the super-rich pay tax at rates lower than the average working family?' In recent decades, the social contract for taxation has been re-written, largely by just one party – the wealthy themselves. *This has occurred not through democratic legislation, but through its exact opposite – the undermining of democratic legislation.* That's what's wrong with the simplistic picture presented by those who defend the world's worst tax avoiders, those who seek moral refuge in their legally sanctioned tax assessment, no matter how low. In east and west alike, civilisation's great legends have always taught us that you don't have to be a criminal to be an outlaw.

The Tax Justice Network seeks redress. We are voices from the other party to the social contract. It seems to us that capital's been running the show, governments have either gone along with it or done a pretty poor job of resisting it, and the ordinary folk haven't had much of a say. The TJN exists to enable a response. Through social justice movements, through citizens' groups, through trade unions and NGOs, through the institutions of democracy, we seek to facilitate political action, and to promote research and education. Our declaration describes the problems, and begins to search for solutions. Our proposals are intended to strengthen the social contract for taxation, both at national and international levels.

Despite the balance of power in the world economy, we have one advantage that the wealthy tax avoiders don't – we are a network drawn from civil society, from ordinary people. The wealthy are few in comparison. Capital's not quite as self-reliant as all the bluster and bravado would have us think. On both micro and macro levels, history shows what happens when capital withdraws too far from the social contract on which it relies. One way or another, recent global tax trends carry grave risks. We intend to stop these pinstripe outlaws from stitching up their deals with compliant states, leaving the rest of us to pick up the bill. Maybe everybody cheers an outlaw when they're a lone figure fighting the forces of oppression, but not when it's the bank manager himself who's emptied the safe and skipped off into the desert with the whole town's cash.

September, 2003

Why the U.S. Needs Tax Justice

Lucy Komisar

'Only the little people pay taxes.' That is the famous statement uttered by tax cheat and hotelier Leona Helmsley, as reported by her maid. She ended up in prison for tax evasion. But she was an exception. Today, the U.S. administration and Congress work together to remove tax burdens from the rich and shift them to the middle class and the poor. Here's how that has happened.

The U.S. income tax dates to the 16th Amendment to the U.S. constitution, ratified by the states in 1913. It was adopted because of a Supreme Court decision in 1895 that ruled that the attempt of Congress the year before to tax incomes uniformly throughout the United States was unconstitutional. Before that, most revenue came from 'excise' taxes on liquor, tobacco, and the like.

Until World War II, only the rich paid income taxes. As a result of war expenses, Congress broadened the base, increasing the number of taxpayers by ten million between 1939 and 1945. They also established a highly progressive rate structure, with rates reaching 94 percent for the richest taxpayers.

Progressive taxation as a part of the 'social contract' in the U.S.

Joseph J. Thorndike, Director of the Tax History Project[4], explains that the U.S. could have adopted a national sales tax, or other alternatives, but President Franklin Roosevelt decided – impelled by the wartime need for a progressive tax seen to be just – to create a broader, steeper income tax, part of a longer political process beginning at least a decade earlier.

Thorndike said, 'the 1930s witnessed the growth of an intellectual consensus for mass-based income taxation.' He cited the impact of the 'New Deal' electoral coalition, which came during 'the class-charged 1936 presidential election,' Roosevelt's commitment to tax fairness and his high-profile campaigns against wealthy tax avoiders, the views of the technocrats in the Treasury Department, headed by Treasury Secretary Henry Morgenthau, and the fiscal needs of World War II at a time when the Depression had reduced other federal income. (Morgenthau was the father of Robert Morgenthau, the Manhattan District Attorney who is the U.S. law enforcement official most committed to attacking tax havens.)

What's changed and why

Between then and now, there has been a sea change in American politics, due largely to the decimation of the political power of the American trade union movement. Unions in the early 1950s represented 35 percent of workers but in 2001 counted only 13 percent (9 percent of private sector and 35 percent of public sector workers). Political power has shifted to the corporations, which buy administrations and members of Congress through campaign contributions.

Under Roosevelt, the U.S. initiated 'withholding taxes' – deductions made by employers from workers' paychecks. There was little chance workers could cheat when they filed their annual 'tax returns.' But owners and professionals were not subject to withholding. And they found it easy not to report income.

Tax burden for the rich, poor, and middle classes

In the 1980s, the rightwing Ronald Reagan administration and a compliant Congress drastically slashed taxes on wealth and corporations. In 1981, the top tax bracket – the amount charged on the very rich – dropped from 87 percent to 50 percent. Then in 1986, it was cut again to 28 percent, while the corporate tax rate was reduced from 50 percent to 35 percent. Changes in 1990 and 1993 (the last under Bill Clinton) raised the top individual rate to 39.6 percent. The George Bush 2001 tax cut – skewed in favor of the very rich – dropped the top rate again, to 33 percent. But, of course, that number is not actually paid by the rich, who hire armies of accountants to invent tax shelters and hide their money offshore.

And in the 1990s, an orchestrated campaign accusing the

US Internal Revenue Service (IRS) of 'unfair practices' led to legislation that banned the agency from getting tough on tax cheats. To make the IRS less effective, Congress cut its budget. So even while the rich had seen their legal taxes cut, the IRS lost interest in seeing that they paid even those sums. The IRS shifted the focus of its audits from the rich to the middle class and poor. And it has taken only limited action against institutional cheating though tax shelters and tax havens.

One example is legal action in 2000 that got 1998 and 1999 American Express and MasterCard records for U.S. taxpayers with accounts in Antigua and Barbuda, the Bahamas, and the Cayman Islands. It is not illegal to have such accounts, but they must be reported on tax returns. They rarely are. Based on what it discovered, the IRS began hundreds of cases to recover back taxes. It said, "If the MasterCard information is representative of the industry, there could be 1 to 2 million U.S. citizens with debit/credit cards issued by offshore banks. This compares with only 170,000 Reports of Foreign Bank & Financial Accounts being filed in 2000 and only 117,000 individuals indicating they had offshore bank accounts (tax year 1999). The search was expanded in 2002 to get records of MasterCard payments for Americans' accounts in more than 30 offshore havens.

However, IRS attempts to go after offshore tax evasion are inadequate. Senator Carl Levin, author of legislation against shell banks adopted by the U.S. in 2001, in May 2003 wrote the IRS that 'abusive tax shelter transactions and offshore tax avoidance schemes entered into primarily by corporations and high income individuals, result in tens of billions of dollars in lost U.S. revenues each year, with estimates ranging from $40 to $70 billion annually.' He said while the IRS demands that poor citizens provide documentation of tax claims, 'no equivalent requirements exist for taxpayers claiming millions of dollars in tax benefits involving undocumented domestic and offshore trusts.'

He cited a study by the Transactional Records Access Clearing-house (TRAC) at Syracuse University, which showed that that the vast majority of 2002 IRS audits were aimed at low and middle income taxpayers. The study found that in 2002 audits of corporations totaled only 3 percent of total IRS audits, but accounted for over 80 percent of the additional taxes recommended, with most resulting from audits of corporations with assets exceeding $250 million. The TRAC statistics also indicate the IRS is auditing a much smaller percentage of corporations than ten years ago.

The result is that the burden of taxes has shifted increasingly from the wealthy and the corporations to the middle class and the poor.

Robert S. McIntyre, director of Citizens for Tax Justice (Washington D.C.) and a member of the steering committee of TJN, said 'during the 1950s, U.S. corporations paid 28 percent of federal revenues. Now, corporations pay just 11 percent.' A study by the CTJ's Institute on Taxation and Economic Policy found that although big corporations are supposed to pay 35 percent of their profits in taxes, 250 of the nation's largest and most profitable corporations paid only 20.1 percent in 1998, down from 22.9 percent in 1996, and far below the 26.5 percent that a similar group of large companies paid back in 1988.[5] Among companies that actually got rebates yielding tax rates in 1998 of less than zero, were Texaco, Chevron, PepsiCo, Pfizer, J.P. Morgan, Goodyear, Enron, Colgate-Palmolive, MCI Worldcom, General Motors, Phillips Petroleum and Northrop Grumman.

McIntyre, who wrote the study, said, 'with significant help from Congress, corporations appear to be finding ways around the tax reforms adopted in 1986.' He said, 'if big corporations actually paid 35 percent of their U.S. profits in federal income taxes, as the tax code ostensibly requires, corporate income taxes this year would total at least $308 billion. But actual corporate-tax payments this year are expected to be only $136 billion.' He said, 'Microsoft, in fact, actually paid no tax at all in 1999, despite $12.3 billion in reported U.S. profits. Microsoft's tax rate for the past two years was only 1.8 percent on $21.9 billion in pre-tax U.S. profits.'

How tax havens contribute to problems in the U.S.

Tax havens are an important avenue for tax evasion by the rich and by corporations. A major reason why many major corporations pay little or no federal income tax is the use of tax havens for transfer pricing, estimated to cost U.S. taxpayers some $43 billion in 1999.

A new tactic is corporate inversions, whereby a U.S. company creates a new parent corporation based in a tax haven like Bermuda. The company and any foreign subsidiaries become subsidiaries of the new parent, and the entire corporation then benefits from tax reporting and regulations that are often significantly less demanding and expensive than those in the United States. In the past few years, about two dozen publicly traded companies have reincorporated in Bermuda or announced they would do so. Rich individuals also set up phony offshore residences.

The IRS thinks that the country loses $75 billion a year because U.S. corporations and rich people set up phony headquarters or residences in offshore tax havens. Among the corporate offshore tax dodgers are Harken Energy, which set up an offshore tax evasion while President George Bush was on its board, and Halliburton, which went from nine to 44 offshore havens while Vice President Dick Cheney was running it. Are tax evaders patriots?

Trade unions, workers' pension funds and state officials are taking the lead in a campaign to prevent the move offshore – and to bring back those who've already gone. They have filed legal suits and shareholder resolutions. Several members of the U.S. Congress have introduced legislation to end the offshore tax advantages. Senator Charles E. Grassley, the Iowa Republican who is the chairman of the finance committee, would narrow or eliminate the gap between the effective tax rates of these tax cheats and their onshore competitors.

Legislation in Congress and several states would ban the governments from signing contracts with expatriate American companies. However, the Republicans blocked a measure that banned companies with offshore mailboxes from getting contracts from the Homeland Security Department. Apparently they think getting less revenue makes the U.S. stronger.

Some NGOs such as Citizen Works, Taxpayers for Common Sense and The Bermuda Project are attacking the corporate inversions and the use of offshore havens to escape taxes. Citizen Works lists the corporate tax dodgers with information about their estimated tax savings, U.S. government contracts and product descriptions.[6]

How tax practices impact on economic and social development in the U.S.

The failure to collect revenues has had a devastating impact on the ability of the federal and state governments to pay for social programs.

The Bush administration said would cut child care subsidies for 200,000 children over five years. Its budget also cuts housing aid and other social spending.

Most states have had to close budget deficits of $40 to $50 billion. As a result, they have cut back on social programs. For example, the state of Missouri, to save more than $360 million, eliminated health insurance coverage for about 36,000 low-income parents. It reduced health services for new mothers, including family planning and postpartum services. It ended dental services for low-income adults, affecting about 300,000 people. Similar moves were taken by other states to cut health and welfare services.[7]

The Portland, Oregon police budget has been cut by more than 10 percent in the last three years. Station houses now close at night, and 64 officers have been cut from the 960-member force. There's no overtime pay; so, undercover drug agents may stop following suspects or executing search warrants when their shifts are over. The city can't pay much for public defenders, but the U.S. Supreme Court says people can't be kept in jail without access to lawyers. So, police tell suspects in nonviolent crimes that if they can't afford lawyers, they will be freed. Not surprisingly, crime is rising: car thefts up 19 percent and home burglaries up 21 percent over last year.

Prospects for progressive taxation in the future

With corporate control of U.S. government increasing and influencing both the Republicans (traditionally the party of business) and now also the Democrats (who once represented the interests of labor), the chance for tax 'reform' to shift the burden back to the wealthy is very small.

The only chance to reduce the gap between what the rich pay and what they should pay is to end their use of tax havens. Though the U.S. anti-corporate inversion campaigns are targeting use of tax havens for phony registrations, there are not yet campaigns in the

U.S. that broadly attack the use of offshore centers to help people and corporations cheat on taxes. The Tax Justice Network provides a rallying point around which individuals and groups can work with each other to build such campaigns.

September, 2003

Transfer Pricing: How to Get 160 Missile Launchers for the Price of a Ballpoint Pen

Prem Sikka

Would you buy any of the following? How about plastic buckets from the Czech Republic at $973 each, or fence posts from Canada at $1,854 each? Perhaps a kilo of toilet paper (about four rolls – unused) from China for $4,122; a litre of apple juice from Israel for $2,052; a ballpoint pen from Trinidad for $8,500; or maybe a pair of tweezers from Japan at $4,896 each? Not persuaded by such brilliant bargains? Then would you like to sell a toilet (with bowl and tanks) to Hong Kong for $1.75, prefabricated buildings to Trinidad at $1.20 each, bulldozers to Venezuela at $388 each, or missile and rocket launchers to Israel for just $52 each?

You won't find such dodgy prices in your local market, but these are the actual prices charged by some of the world's biggest multinational corporations, all authorised by some of the best accountants, and by political friends in high places. Their game is to shift the tax burden onto somebody else. It is played through 'transfer pricing'.

'Transfer pricing' is the accountant's term for purchases and sales that take place within the same group of companies. Because the transactions are within the same company, management has enormous scope to ignore commercial, 'arms-length' prices, and trade at arbitrary prices instead. This affords opportunities to shift capital and taxes without any questions being asked.

Although many national tax authorities treat such tricks as tax evasion, they often do not have sufficient resources to scrutinise companies' books in enough detail to identify such transactions. This gives enormous scope to companies and accountants to bend or break the rules. Indeed, with multinationals often the only suppliers of many goods and services, they are even in a position to rig the perceived commercial prices – effectively setting their own laws for what they can get away with.

Suppose a multinational company has a factory in country 'A'. The factory produces a television for £200 and 'sells' it to a subsidiary of the same group, based in tax- haven 'B.' The price of this transfer is arbitrarily defined by accountants as the cost of production, £200. This tax haven subsidiary then sells it to another foreign subsidiary in country 'C' for another arbitrary transfer price of £375. The television is then sold to a consumer in country 'C' for £350.

The multinational company reports a real worldwide profit of consumer price less cost of production, ie £350 – £200 = £150; this ignores the transfer prices. But this global profit is not liable to tax, since tax systems are nationally-based. In each of the 3 countries through which the television has passed, the profits declared in each have been artificially defined.

The subsidiary in tax haven 'B' reports a large profit, equal to the difference between the two transfer prices: £375 – £200 = £175. Being declared in a tax haven jurisdiction, little or no tax is paid on this 'profit'. The subsidiary in country 'A' reports a profit of zero, since it transferred the television at the cost of production. The subsidiary in country 'C' has actually managed to record a loss of £375 – £350 = £25, which it can offset against tax arising from other operations in country 'C'. As if by magic the multinational has ended up generating a net tax loss, despite real global profits. Armies of accountants legitimise these figures, and tax authorities have little practical choice but to accept them. Indeed the big accountancy firms devise the schemes, audit them and then say that the resulting company accounts are 'true and fair'. The fact is, by doing so they organise and legitimise the dishonest shifting of the tax burden away from these giant companies, onto the rest of the population.

Although this kind of simplistic and arbitrary transfer pricing may risk being declared an illegal sham, there is little doubt that variations on the theme are common. You only have to look at the miraculously low global tax payments by many multinationals through the 1990s, or at the vast amounts of crude oil which are traded in a mountain village in landlocked Switzerland, to suspect that this is both well organised and widespread. The aggregate figures for world trade confirm it: around 60% of all trade takes place within multinational corporations, and around 50% appears to pass through tax havens, even though there is scant productive activity occurring there. Evidence from the USA suggests that accounting practices masquerading as transfer pricing 'policies' are having a bigger impact on wealth transfers from ordinary people to corporations than any of the headline financial scandals (e.g. Enron, WorldCom). A recent study estimated that due to the transfer pricing policies of major multinational companies, for the years 1998 to 2001, the US Treasury lost more than $175 billion of tax revenues. That is an extraordinary figure, even by American standards.

September, 2003

The Africa Question: Where Do All the Profits Go?

Pierre Guindja and John Christensen

Whilst all eyes are turned this year on how to make better use of development aid flowing into Africa, attention is also turning to the question of what has been happening to the continent's own financial resources in recent decades. And increasingly people are looking to the major companies, banks, oil producers, mining giants and food multinationals and their subsidiaries that dominate the African business scene.

In late February 2005 Chairman of the Nigerian Economic and Financial Crimes Commission (EFCC), Mallam Nuhu Ribadu, announced that his commission had already started investigations into allegations that some of the world's largest oil exploration and production businesses have been engaging in tax evasion and aggressive tax avoidance practices that have defrauded the Nigerian government of billions of dollars.

Ribadu also suggested in his speech to senior managers of the Nigerian National Petroleum Corporation, that unnamed oil companies have been evading taxes and excise duties over many years and have connived with Nigerian revenue officials in this process. Evidence of such connivance had previously come to light in 2004 when US construction and oil services giant Halliburton, formerly run by US vice-president Dick Cheney, submitted a filing to the Securities and Exchange Commission which revealed that its subsidiary Kellogg Brown & Root had paid US$2.4 million in bribes to a Nigerian government official in order to reduce its tax bills in 2001 and 2002.

But according to Ribadu the problem of tax avoidance, which is endemic across Africa, goes beyond the extractive industries. EFCC has also initiated investigations into the banking sector, and according to *AllAfrica.Com*, several senior bank officials have been arrested in Nigeria in recent weeks and are expected to face trial on charges of corruption and tax evasion. Ribadu said that EFCC has already recovered some money from banks and that 'bank executives have been directed to make available regular reports on their transactions to the commission.'

Similar concerns have also been raised on the other side of the continent. In January the Kenyan Revenue Authority (KRA) revealed that it is currently owed a staggering US$1.32 billion in unpaid taxes, much of which, according to KRA commissioner-general, Michael Waweru, is probably unrecoverable. US$1.32 billion represents approximately fifty percent of total state revenue in a country which currently has an external debt of around US$6 billion.

According to Waweru some of the tax debts are held by businesses that are no longer trading in Kenya or no longer in operation. KRA has intensified efforts to raise revenue, partially through broadening the tax base and improving tax compliance, but discussions between Tax Justice Network and a senior Kenyan tax official in late 2003 revealed that despite recent institutional improvements in the revenue service, KRA remains under-resourced when it comes to taxing multinational businesses which typically operate their accounts through offshore accounts created to conceal true operational costs and profits.

The problem of how to tackle transfer pricing and overloading of intra-company costs is particularly pressing for African countries, many of which are dominated by extractive industry multinational businesses. Whilst recent initiatives by the governments and NGOs have focused on transparency of revenue flows into government coffers from the oil and mining sectors, little attention seems to have been paid to how much profit has been generated by the oil companies themselves, and what tax is being paid, and where, on those profits.

Charles McPherson of the Policy Division of the World Bank has warned that the expected increase in sub-Saharan African oil revenues arising from production increases in countries such as Nigeria, Angola, Sudan, Chad and Congo-Brazzaville provides a 'lightning rod for corruption' in Africa. Without greater accounting transparency by the major businesses which dominate the African extractive industries, revenue officials are forced into an uneven struggle to obtain the information they need in order to tax the national subsidiaries of multinational businesses that are virtually at liberty to declare whatever profits they choose.

British Prime Minister Tony Blair has taken the political lead in promoting greater revenue transparency through the Extractive Industries Transparency Initiative, but this initiative is at best a partial solution since it focuses on government receipts without considering what sums ought to be being paid on the profits and income flows generated in the private sector.

This is, of course, the major question facing Africa. Whilst corruption amongst state officials rightly attracts attention, the problem of illicit capital flight, frequently linked to tax evasion and aggressive tax avoidance is of greater consequence to a continent that has seen staggering sums, probably amounting to hundreds of billions of dollars annually, disappear offshore into the western banking system in recent decades.

The role of western banks, many of which operate throughout Africa and offer offshore banking and financial services both to their multinational clients and to the national business elites, remains under-researched and almost beyond scrutiny. A full investigation into how the western banking system encourages and sustains tax evasion, tax avoidance and illicit capital flight might reveal why, despite the huge increase in output of minerals and commodities in recent decades, Africa remains a largely impoverished continent.

March, 2005

Pulp Reality, Tax Fiction

Jorma Penttinen

The benefits of foreign direct investment are more or less taken for granted. The transfers of technology, employment opportunities, direct money flows, and revenues for local and state government are seen to benefit the host country. It was no surprise then that Uruguay was more than keen to accept the building of huge pulp factories on the banks of river Uruguay, on the other side of which is Argentina. The Finnish-owned Botnia factory would produce one million tonnes of pulp when operating, and the Spanish-owned Ence would be half that size.

Botnia's plant will be the biggest ever foreign investment in Uruguay's history, and according to the calculations produced by Botnia, the factory would increase the country's GDP by 1.6 per cent. Botnia's investment is explained by the lower costs: fast growing eucalyptus trees and cheap labour mean that production costs are half those in Finland. The pulp is not destined for South American markets; it will be transported to Europe and China.

There are, however, dark clouds over the Botnia project. Civil society organisations in Uruguay and Argentina share concerns about the environmental impact of the mills. Protest has been particularly strong in Argentina, where the president has also voiced opposition to the pulp mills on environmental grounds. According to an opinion poll carried out in August 2005, just over half of Uruguayans opposed the pulp mills. The issue will be referred to International Court of Justice by Argentina, and the presidents of both countries will meet in the near future to discuss the two pulp mills.

As well as the environmental concerns, there is another more complex question of whether the Botnia investment will bring any real benefits to the Uruguayan economy. In Finland, Botnia currently has five pulp mills. Their combined production is 2.7 million tonnes – only three times that of the Botnia mill in Uruguay – and they employ directly some 1,600 people. The mills are situated mainly in small towns and are very important to the surrounding communities. To the local municipality, the personal income tax of the company employees is the most important benefit; and in a good year the company taxes equal this. There is also a property tax which goes directly to the local municipality. The benefits from dividend taxes and VAT are paid mainly to the state.

In Uruguay, Botnia has been able to negotiate itself free of these kinds of obligations. The land area was rented for $20,000 for 30 years, which is practically nothing. The special legislation of the *Zona Franca* free trade area will guarantee that Botnia does not have to pay any customs duty on machinery and equipment imports; which equals nearly one hundred million euros tax relief in a billion euro project. The majority of the equipment is manufactured in Finland.

Furthermore, the company will not pay income tax under the free trade area contract. It will pay source tax on dividends, services and assembling work. The profits will mainly be given in the form of dividends to foreign shareholders and thus exported out of the country. Even though the production costs are half those of Finland, the pulp will be sold at the world market price.

It has been estimated that pulp mill will add $200 million per year to Uruguayan GDP, and that it will generate some $25 million annually in taxes. During the construction period the project will employ around 4,500 people, and later there will be some 300 people working in the mill. It is estimated that the pulp mill will generate 8,000 jobs indirectly, mainly in the eucalyptus plantations. According to Botnia, the project is already the biggest private employer in Uruguay.

But when Ricardo Carrere of the World Rainforest Movement was asked what financial benefits the pulp mill will provide, his answer was 'none'. He had seen pulp mills in Indonesia, South Africa, Brazil, Chile and Finland, and argued that the vast Uruguayan mill will diminish into a small one when all tax exemptions and subsidies are taken into account.

Basically, the pulp mill will not pay any taxes. As Carrere explained, the harvesting of eucalyptus trees is supported by tax relief and the state is building roads, port facilities and other infrastructure for the company.

Carrere does believe, however, that the increase in GDP will indirectly benefit Uruguay. The growth of GDP and major foreign investment will improve the image of the country in the eyes of international monetary institutions, banks and investors. The problem is that future investors will certainly demand equal treatment from the state and the companies will continue to avoid paying taxes. A factory of this size is a powerful economic agent in a country like Uruguay; granting tax exemptions to encourage foreign investment means that this power is transferred to foreign companies. This is a great loss to democracy

The Finnish state is selling itself short by supporting this kind of investment. Free trade areas and the many tax exemptions available give transnational firms a green light to avoid their social responsibility by not paying taxes. Until now, trans- national companies that are at least seen as Finnish (for example, only 10 per cent of Nokia shares are actually held by Finns) have been able to use their financial power to influence policy on foreign investment.

A big political issue in Finland at the moment is the announcement by paper company UPM-Kymmene that it plans to reduce its workforce in Finland by 3,600 people over the next two years. It seems particularly odd that the Finnish embassy in Uruguay should be vigorously supporting the Botnia investment at such a time. The project is seen in Uruguay and Argentina – and also in Finland – as 'a Finnish project', yet the benefits for the Finnish state and people are very questionable.

March, 2006

Corruption and the Role of Tax Havens

John Christensen

Transparency International has played a lead role in shaping the global campaign to counter corruption and has highlighted the huge cost to business of doing business in countries where bribe taking is regarded as the norm. Africa in particular has come under the Transparency International spotlight, accounting for almost half of the bottom 20 per cent of the TI 2005 Corruption Perceptions Index (CPI). Famously, Chad, a small land-bound state which has recently joined the ranks of the hydrocarbon exporting economies, was ranked as the most corrupt country in 2005. Nigeria held that illustrious position for many years, but now comes sixth from the bottom, scoring a mere 1.9 on an index which ranges between 10 (highly clean) to 0 (highly corrupt). Small wonder then that US and European politicians feel entitled to lecture African leaders on the need to get their house in order. But before doing this they should turn the spotlight through 180 degrees and take a closer look at the other end of the corruption spectrum.

Only one African country, Botswana, is ranked amongst the least corrupt 20 per cent of the CPI for 2005. Almost all the remainder are OECD states. And 40 per cent of the countries ranked as least corrupt according to Transparency International's vision of the world are tax havens, including major centres such as Singapore (ranked 5th overall), Switzerland (7th), United Kingdom (11th), Luxembourg (13th), Hong Kong (15th), USA (17th), and Belgium and Ireland (jointly 19th). For good measure Barbados and Malta, both tax havens, rank 24th and 25th respectively. Iceland, also a tax haven though only a minor player, ranked as least corrupt country in 2005.

In focusing on the 'demand side' of 'petty' corruption, i.e. the extortion of bribes by public officials, as the main indicator of corruption, TI has played a key role in distorting public perceptions of corruption thereby reinforcing negative images of Africa whilst distracting from the higher level corruption of major companies and governments from the North. This is not to downplay the harm caused to Africa by bribery, but the steady growth of petty corruption in recent decades has at least in part been driven by IMF and World Bank conditionality, which pegs civil service salaries at an arbitrary percentage of wholly inadequate government budgets. However, as Raymond Baker has so convincingly demonstrated in *Capitalism's Achilles Heel*, bribery represents only around 10 per cent of the massive dirty money flow out of developing countries, with proceeds of crime and illicit commercial transactions being of far greater importance. By widening the definition of corruption to include embezzlement, larceny and crimes involving illicit commercial transactions used for facilitating capital flight and tax evasion, we gain a far more complete picture of corrupt practices in action, and of the importance of the 'supply side' in encouraging and facilitating global corruption.

According to the recently published report of the Africa All Party Parliamentary Group (AAPPG) of the UK government, the supply side covers both the persons and institutions offering the bribes, and – crucially – the financial systems which launder the proceeds of corruption.[8] Companies from the industrialised countries have been guilty of offering bribes to secure contracts and special treatments, including tax incentives, and frequently this happens even when bribes have not been solicited. But more importantly, international banks and other financial intermediaries have played the key role in establishing and maintaining the offshore financial systems which enable dirty money to flow from South to North with relative ease and impunity. According to Baker, illicit commercial transactions involving mispricing, abusive transfer pricing, and fake transactions, account for approximately 65 per cent of cross border dirty money flows originating from developing and transitional economies. In the case of Africa:

> *As much as 60% of trade transactions into or out of Africa are estimated to be mispriced by an average of 11%, which translates into annual capital flight in excess of $10 billion. Fake transactions are estimated to account for a further $150-200 billion*[9].

The vast majority of this illicit trade is laundered via tax havens linked to the international banking system, and it generally remains offshore to be managed by the plethora of banking businesses (largely from the North) offering wealth management services to their high net-worth clients. With 2005 seeing record growth in the numbers of people in Africa and Latin America with liquid assets exceeding US$1 million, largely on the back of surging commodity prices, it is not surprising that the offshore financial services industry turns a blind eye to what the AAPPG report describes as 'rampant kleptomania'.

Like many who have studied corruption in Africa, I have concluded that the problem is largely stimulated by the supply side. The ease with which proceeds of crime and illicit commercial activities can be laundered into secret bank accounts and offshore companies owned by offshore trusts inevitably encourages criminal behaviour and protects it from investigation. Working with corporate investigators and journalists covering major crimes in Africa and elsewhere in the South, I have noted how investigations have almost invariably led to accounts held in Switzerland, Luxembourg, the British Crown Dependencies, the Cayman or similar tax havens. This is typically where the investigations have ended, because, despite all the international conventions put in place in recent years, these offshore territories do not cooperate with legitimate investigations and refuse to publicly disclose even basic information about ownership or basic financial accounts. This determination to protect secrecy, even in the light of massive evidence of abuse, suggests that western governments are still not serious about wanting to remedy endemic corruption, despite ample evidence of its inevitably harmful social and economic consequences. As one witness told the Parliamentary Group during the course of its enquiry:

> *With one hand, the West has pointed the finger at corrupt African leaders, with its other hand, its bankers, lawyers, accountants, art dealers, health authorities, universities, estate agents and embassies have been actively or passively encouraging wealth out of Africa into the West's economies.*[10]

June, 2006

Capital Flight and Africa

Patrick Smith

Nigeria's anti-corruption czar, Nuhu Ribadu, tells of the multi-billion dollar losses suffered by his country from corrupt deals, tax evasion and pricing scams. He held the World Bank and IMF annual meeting in Singapore spell-bound with his accounts of billions of Nigeria's oil wealth which have been siphoned into western accounts and tax havens over the past three decades. Ribadu was feted by World Bank President Paul Wolfowitz who is working hard to convince everyone that the Bank is getting serious about corruption –within his organisation, and within both western and developing country governments, and within the transnational companies that dominate the global economy.

Wolfowitz is using tougher language than his predecessors and has appointed a high-powered lawyer, Suzanne Rich Folsom, to head up the Bank's new investigation unit, the Department of Institutional Integrity. Wolfowitz's anti-graft blitz comes as a raft of new books highly critical of foreign aid and the growth of state corruption have been written by former World Bank officials such as Robert Calderisi and William Easterly.

Such books and at least some of Wolfowitz's rhetoric openly question the wisdom of the big new foreign aid push promoted by British Prime Minister Tony Blair's government last year alongside proposals by American economist Jeffrey Sachs to end global poverty by 2025 with a massive transfer of wealth from the world's richest economies to the poorest.

There is, however, one critical issue missing from the arguments of both the pro and anti-aid camps, and indeed missing from much serious economic analysis by the World Bank and the IMF. There is in fact already a massive transfer of wealth in the global system but the transfers – amounting of several hundred billion dollars a year – are overwhelmingly from the world's poorest countries to the richest.

This is not just the corruption, more narrowly defined by Wolfowitz, it is a range of global financial transactions – both legal and illegal – that are starving the treasuries of some of the world's poorest states.

Call it 'dirty money' or flight capital, it's the money that is illegally taken out of developing countries each year through a combination of pricing and tax scams, and the plain theft of state resources. The cost of corrupt contracts currently is one of the smaller elements of this outflow, according to experts such as Raymond Baker based at Washington's Brookings Institution. Current estimates are that it is over US$30 billion a year from Africa alone. These losses easily eclipse the value of the aid and debt promised to Africa by the rich countries at their annual G8 summit.

No one can put a precise figure on volume of dirty money but in 1998, Michel Camdessus then Managing Director of the IMF said in Paris that 'estimates of the present scale of money laundering transactions are almost beyond imagination – 2 per cent to 5 per cent of global GDP would probably be a consensus range'. Applied to global GDP of US$32 trillion a year, that indicates a range of US$640 billion to US$1.6 trillion a year.

This figure is just part of the dirty money equation. 'Laundered money' is money that breaks anti-money laundering laws. It doesn't cover the billions of dollars of tax-evading funds – the revenues from commercial crime on transactions that are deliberately mispriced to move money, mainly out of developing countries, to offshore tax havens.

So where does all the money come from? First, there are the proceeds from crime: global organised crime, which is rapidly infiltrating Africa, makes around US$1.5 trillion a year of which the drugs trade – again much of it originating or transiting through Africa – makes around US$400 billion a year.

Counterfeit goods, many of them coming from Asia but again increasingly produced in Africa, are reckoned by Interpol to account for about US$450 billion of current world merchandise exports of US$6.5 trillion a year. Also important are the illegal arms sales: these cover most of the small arms used in Africa's wars, either by rebel movements or governments such as Sudan's which are sub-ject to international sanctions. Illegal sales of small arms alone are put at over US$1 billion a year, with illegal sales of all conventional weapons at as much as US$10 billion.

Growing in importance, too, are illegal sales of oil as the world price spirals. Unrecorded oil sales come mainly from Saudi Arabia, Russia and increasingly from Angola and Nigeria. More than a million barrels a day are illegally extracted and traded.

Shell reckons Nigeria is losing more than 100,000 barrels a day from various forms of oil theft, known locally as 'illegal oil bunkering' where the stolen oil is clandestinely loaded onto tankers and the trade documentation is elaborately forged. This trade deprives Nigeria of several billion dollars of oil revenue a year, and many of the gangs behind the violence in the Niger Delta buy their arms with the proceeds from bunkering.

Commercial and state corruption are important not just for the volume of funds that are shifted out but also because of the damage they do to the integrity of judicial and political institutions. If officials can be easily bribed, they allow corporate criminals and drug barons to operate with impunity. 'Government corruption creates a permissive environment, and this magnifies criminal activities and financial shenanigans in the rest of the economy,' says Raymond Baker.

Those financial shenanigans, Baker says, are the biggest components of 'dirty money': the transfer pricing and mispricing that allow corporations to take out hundreds of billions of dollars each year from developing countries and into tax havens.

How does it work? The basic principle is to use mispricing to take the money out: over pricing the goods that a country imports or underpricing the goods that it exports. For decades, in Cote d'Ivoire, President Houphouet-Boigny and commodity traders deliberately underpriced the country's cocoa exports. The difference between the price officially recorded and channeled through Cote d'Ivoire's central bank and the real market price of the exports was shared between the politicians and the traders involved in the scam, and then banked offshore.

The scam also works the other way around: researchers have found that Nigeria pays as much as ten times the market price for many of its finished good imports such as generating sets: the central bank remits the money overseas in payment of the grossly inflated invoice. Again the proceeds are shared between the foreign trading company and the local corrupt officials facilitating the payment and order.

The other key technique is transfer pricing. This can only happen within a multi-national corporation with a headquarters organisation, usually in Europe or the USA, and several subsidiaries, usually in Africa, Asia and Latin America. The headquarters of the multinational sells components and services 'internally' to its affiliate company in Africa at a hugely marked up price thus ensuring that the local entity makes only a minimal profit and minimising its tax liabilities.

Researchers such as Baker put the volume of mispriced trade at between 5 per cent and 7 per cent of the US$4 trillion of world trade each year: that's over US$200 billion each year. Common to all these transactions – mispricing, drug smuggling or corrupt payments – is the use of the West's pin-striped army of lawyers, accountants and company formation agents and the experts who hide the ill-gotten gains in offshore tax havens.

Attempts to improve international cooperation on tax and regulate offshore operations are moving painfully slowly. At least US$11.5 trillion is currently held in offshore tax havens. Incredibly, tracking such huge illicit outflows is not regarded as a priority by international financial institutions.

September, 2006

The Spoils of Oil: How Multinationals and Their Professional Advisers Drain Nigeria of Much Needed Resources

Owolabi Bakre

Fifty years of oil and gas exploration that should have transformed Nigeria into a prosperous country have brought only misery and extreme poverty to the country's people. Successive Nigerian governments have failed to provide basic infrastructure, public services and much-needed development programmes to stimulate wealth distribution. The evidence shows that almost all the transparency and good governance-preaching multinational oil companies operating in Nigeria – in collaboration with the erring Nigerian rulers, politicians and public officials – have been partly responsible for the country's economic woes.

Trade liberalization, forced on Nigeria by multilateral institutions such as the World Trade Organisation (acting under the pressure being exerted by the multi-national oil companies), has had the effect of shifting the tax burden from the oil companies onto local consumers who are already burdened by extreme poverty.

Despite the existence of exploitative tax rules, the oil multinationals have been further heavily involved in criminalising the Nigerian business culture, compromising the nation's policymakers, contaminating national institutions and subverting the nation's due process. The oil companies have also been implicated in environmental pollution, have refused to cooperate with the Nigerian regulators, and have also consistently disobeyed a series of court orders to compensate the victims of pollution, especially in the Niger Delta.

Almost all the oil multinationals were found to have been using fraudulent means to obtain public subsidies, tax incentives, export credit guarantees and reserve additional bonuses from the Nigerian government. These companies employed armies of accountants and auditors to effect tax evasion and illegal capital flight from the Nigerian economy. The companies benefit from Nigerian infrastructure and public utilities, but consistently refuse to pay their share of the democratically agreed taxes on the huge profits they make in the country every year.

The case of the Shell Petroleum Development Company (SPDC) provides one example. It was only after its failure with the Federal Inland Revenue's Appeal Commissioner, the Federal High Court, Court of Appeal – and knowing full well that it would also fail to get what it deemed as a favourable verdict at the Supreme Court – that the company finally agreed to settle out of court its disputed tax liability of US$17, 857,142.86 (owed to the Federal Inland Revenue of Nigeria). Nigerians are eagerly waiting to see if this out of court settlement initiated by SPDC actually takes place.

In addition, a recent value for money audit carried out by the Nigerian House of Representatives Committee on Petroleum Resources accused SPDC of colluding with the Nigerian Minister of State for Petroleum Resources, Edmund Dau-koru, to underpay the Nigerian government by US$3.2 billion for the crude oil extracted there.

Another example is provided by the case of Chevron Nigeria Limited. After investigations of tax evasion, the Nigerian House of Representatives Committee on Petroleum Resources has ordered the United States oil producer to refund to the Federal Government of Nigeria a total sum of US$492 million. This is money that Chevron failed to pay as a part of its tax obligations.

Another United States oil servicing and engineering company, Halliburton, on interrogation by the Nigerian Economic and Financial Crime Commission (EFCC), admitted that its officials paid US$2.4 million to some erring Nigerian public officials to gain tax favours and receive tax cuts from its liability totaling more than US$14 million. Halliburton is also currently under investigations in the USA and Britain for illegally paying about US$180 million to the former military ruler, the late General Sani Abacha, and some other top officials of his regime to secure contracts to build a natural gas plant in Nigeria.

These scandals of the transparency, accountability and good governance-preaching multinational oil companies have been carried out using the professional services and expertise of their accountants and auditors. These professionals helped the companies to evade taxes and effect illegal capital flight from Nigeria in the first place, then helped them to deny that these corrupt practices took place – even after investigations had confirmed that they did.

The corrupt attitudes of Nigerian rulers, politicians and public officials and the collaboration of the oil multinationals operating in the country have contributed greatly to the impoverishment of the Nigerian economy and the country's 70 per cent poverty rate.

September, 2006

Tax Justice and the Oil Industry

Nicholas Shaxson

There has been much recent discussion about two complementary transparency initiatives: one, backed mainly by non-governmental organisations (NGOs), is called Publish What You Pay (PWYP), while another, backed by NGOs and governments and oil and mining companies, is known as the Extractive Industries Transparency Initiative (EITI). It is possible that a Tax Justice approach might be relevant for considering the big gaps in both approaches.

These two initiatives originated, in large part, from NGO campaigns on Angola, where it had become clear that large amounts of oil revenues were 'disappearing', at the behest of the presidency, meaning that the IMF, and Angola's own finance ministry, among others, could not make sense of national accounts. With a history of war and hyper-inflation, Angola made a vivid case study for the problem. Oil company reports require disclosure of amalgamated data by region or globally, making it theoretically impossible to unpick it and find out BP's Angola data, say, and construct an independent picture of how much money Angola really earns.

When BP said in February 2001 that it would publish its payments to Angola unilaterally, Angola threatened it with contract termination, and the British company stepped smartly back into line. The NGOs, as a result, launched PWYP, partly as an effort to level the playing field. Instead of asking oil companies to publish data unilaterally, it advocated a mandatory approach: western regulators, legislators, and/or international bodies would require companies to disclose disaggregated data for their worldwide operations. But ExxonMobil, Chevron and Total, in particular, and several governments, resisted this, arguing (among other things) that since state oil companies are responsible for a large share of poor oil-producing countries' revenue, you would still not get the full picture even if all western companies operating in those countries disclosed disaggregated data.

So the EITI was born. This takes a voluntary approach to disclosure of data: governments like Angola's or Congo's would voluntarily disclose data, giving a clearer picture of their revenues than ever before. EITI has had some success, albeit a bit patchy.

Both these approaches have relative and shared strengths and weaknesses. One shared weakness is that they both deal with the issue of a country's oil revenues after costs have been deducted. They do not touch the cost base of the oil industry at all. This is quite an omission – for example, Angola has eleven or twelve major oil projects under development, several of which have involved investment costs worth US$3 billion or more, which form part of the cost base of the industry. Three billion dollars here, three billion there – and soon you are talking real money.

This is a murky terrain, which under Production Sharing Contracts (common in the oil industry) corresponds to what is known as 'cost oil' –that portion of each barrel of oil that is paid back to the oil companies to cover the initial investment costs they put in.(The remainder, 'profit oil' is split between the government and the companies on a sliding scale formula.)

This cost base is hard to monitor for reasons that will be familiar to people in the Tax Justice Network: tricks like mispricing and thin capitalisation enable companies to shift money around through subsidiaries to maximise their costs and tax deductions. Audits can help countries get a better grip on these, and the Angolan state oil company Sonangol has also taken the step of taking large stakes in local joint venture partnerships with a wide array of big international companies providing helicopters, catering, shipping, drilling equipment, and the like, helping Angola get a better grip on what exactly is going on inside the cost base of its industry.

In 2004, Sonangol tried to go a step further – telling the oil companies that they would be required to route all their payments related to their Angolan operations through local banks. There were several reasons for attempting this: it would provide more money to local banks (and hence local vested interests) in fees, and it would theoretically enable them to provide more credit to the local economy.

Another reason was what one Angolan official described as "the flip side of transparency" – to enable the Angolans to see more clearly how the money really flows through their industry. Everyone is asking them to be transparent, the official said; why can they not ask the oil companies to be more transparent to them? In a rare show of solidarity, the oil companies came together to oppose this initiative, which appears to have been dropped, at least for now. (However, independent Angolan media reported in June this year that Deputy Prime Minister Aguinaldo Jaime said at a meeting in Hanover that he was still angered by the fact of oil companies' financial flows related to Angola were 'offshore' and should be routed through local banks.)

An important point here is that Angola, or at least some important people or factions in Angola, seem to have interests aligned with those of the Tax Justice Network. This is not to say that an alliance between TJN and Angola is necessarily feasible (given the billions of dollars gleefully salted away offshore by Angolan politicians, it seems rather unlikely), but that the Angolans' concerns are generic, and that it is possible that the TJN might, in future, find allies in the most surprising places.

September, 2006

Hooray Hen-Wees[11]

John Christensen

Returning to my native island of Jersey in the 1980s after a long absence, I found the island transformed into an offshore finance centre. The combination of deregulation and technological change had opened up new markets. International banks and accountancy firms were queuing up for a slice of the action. The old town houses and merchant stores of Saint Helier were giving way to office blocks and car parks, and the island's labour market was so overheated that unqualified school-leavers were being paid higher salaries than graduates on mainland Britain. Porsches, Jaguars and BMWs were the favourite cars on an island that measures nine miles by five.

I took a job in a trust and company administration business, where I had to follow instructions faxed daily from banks and law firms across the world. This was a world of smoke and mirrors, in which a Jersey registered company might be owned by a trust based in Luxembourg, with nominee trustees living in Switzerland. This procedure, involving secretive arrangements spanning three or more tax havens, is regarded as good practice in the tax planning industry, which goes to extraordinary lengths to inhibit investigation of what it does and on whose behalf.

One of my jobs was to set prices for goods and services traded within multinational companies in a way that minimised the amount of tax they had to pay. This process of 'transfer mispricing' has allowed plastic buckets to be imported to the US from the Czech Republic for a nominal price of $972.98 each, and rocket launchers exported from the US to Israel for $52.03 each. The resulting profits are allocated to a tax haven. Transfer mispricing is possible only within a multinational corporation, however. Companies without a global reach can achieve the same result by dealing through an agent in a tax haven, who pays part of his mark-up into the offshore account of the vendor or purchaser. I did a fair bit of this 'reinvoicing', too.

A lot of my work related to trade with Asian or African countries. In some cases a special purpose vehicle – a company, trust, partnership or other legal entity set up for a particular purpose (often tax-related) during a transaction – would be used to make a one-off payment to an apparently unrelated third party for 'consulting' or agency services. Other companies were used for operating insider-trading scams. I was bored and angered in equal measure.

Any concerns about the origins of this money, much of which came from African states, were brushed aside. One Friday evening, before our habitual office binge-drinking session, my section supervisor, with characteristic bluntness, told me that she didn't want to discuss these things and didn't 'give a shit about Africa anyway'. Her attitude was typical. Profitability was sky-high and no one made the connection between their actions and criminality and injustice elsewhere.

Appointed in 1987 as an economic adviser to the States of Jersey, I quickly saw that the banking and finance regulatory regime was, shall we say, light-handed. Local politicians lived in fear that scandal would harm the island's international reputation and lead to intervention from the UK government. The preferred solution of leaving no stone turned lasted for a surprisingly long time, but when scandal finally came in 1996 – a currency trader called Robert Young, working in cahoots with Cantrade Bank, a Jersey subsidiary of the Swiss banking giant UBS, defrauded investors of $26 million – the *Wall Street Journal* concluded that Jersey was an offshore hazard 'living off lax regulation and political interference' and offering an invitation to money-laundering. Politicians responsible for financial regulation sat on the boards of the banks that they were appointed to regulate, and senior civil servants interpreted laws and regulations so as to further the personal interests of senior politicians and their cronies.

There have been several international initiatives aimed at tackling financial irregularity since the late 1990s, but the offshore economy has scarcely changed since I left Jersey in 1998. Shortly after taking power in 1997, Labour commissioned a former Treasury official, Andrew Edwards, to review the regulatory arrangements of the Crown Dependencies. Key recommendations from his report were simply ignored, however, and the fundamentals of secrecy remain largely unchanged. Offshore companies are now required to provide regulators with details of ultimate (or 'beneficial') ownership, but this information is not in the public domain and is obfuscated by a web of trusts and special purpose vehicles spread across several other jurisdictions. There remains no requirement to file annual financial statements. Offshore trusts are not required to provide any details about settlors or beneficiaries and have no requirement to file any financial records.

Banking compliance officers tell me, off the record, that due diligence procedures, even when 'politically exposed persons' (PEPs) are concerned, are largely box-ticking exercises. According to a US Senate report, Riggs Bank described one of its PEP clients as 'a retired professional who achieved much success in his career and accumulated wealth during his lifetime for retirement in an orderly way'. The PEP in question was General Augusto Pinochet, who held between $6 and $8 million in offshore accounts established by Riggs, and is now being investigated for fraud and embezzlement.

Jersey became an offshore finance centre as a result of pressure from local law firms, some with strong political connections, and from the major City of London banks which had begun migrating offshore in greater numbers after Labour took power in 1964. Noticing that the Cayman Islands had successfully turned themselves into a tax haven, the States of Jersey decided to create a regulatory and judicial climate that was more attractive to the offshore finance industry. The boom of the 1980s and early 1990s saw the number of offshore tax havens increase from about 25 in the early 1970s to 72 by the end of 2004, as new laws were passed to encourage the use of offshore trusts, international business companies, tax-exempt special purpose vehicles and limited liability partnerships.

In the wake of the 1980s international debt crisis, banks shifted to targeting the world's eight million or so high net-worth individuals (HNWIs, or hen-wees), believing they provided the most profitable growth area. In 1995 I was told that the industry target was to move the majority of hen-wee financial assets to offshore accounts and trusts within a decade. To judge from a recent study showing that $11.5 trillion of hen-wee assets are currently placed tax-free or minimally taxed offshore, the banks have made significant progress towards this goal. Were the returns on that sum taxed at an average rate of 30 per cent, the $255 billion additional revenue would cover the financing needs of the UN Millennium Project, which aims to double aid to poor countries by 2010.

In the 1980s much of the money coming into Jersey originated in the Middle East, sub-Saharan Africa and South-East Asia, but the fall of the Soviet Union led to a rapid growth of new business from Russia and Eastern Europe. In the early 1990s, an acquaintance with a small trust business in Saint Helier told me that he had signed up a Russian client with assets of more than $100 million. No one could really have believed that this wealth was obtained legitimately. Jersey has been a popular destination for Russian money, which is estimated to have flooded into Western banks at a rate of $20 to $30 billion annually since 1989. In 2002, the Institute for Information and Democratisation in Moscow concluded that the total outflow of corrupt and illicit funds, including losses due to customs corruption, 'would effortlessly climb to $400-$500 billion'. Of this amount, probably $300 billion rests in Western and offshore accounts.

Microstates and small island economies, isolated and economically vulnerable, provide an ideal environment for the secretive world of offshore finance. Largely autonomous in domestic political, fiscal and judicial affairs, they act in a way that amounts to selling their sovereignty: in other words, they enact legislation favourable to those seeking to minimise both tax and regulation. They provide, as a result, an interface between the world of furtive money movements and the circuits of the global financial markets.

Many in the global justice movement think that increasing aid to poor countries will be ineffective unless it's accompanied by measures to tackle the causes of poverty, which include the problems of capital flight and tax evasion. In *Capitalism's Achilles Heel*, Raymond Baker probably errs on the conservative side in his estimate that the flows of dirty money from poorer countries into offshore accounts managed by Western banks are currently $500 billion annually. Corruption, which attracted so much media attention in the run-up to the G8 Gleneagles summit, accounts for only 10 per cent of this total.

Some of this money might be round-tripping: going to an offshore company, before being re-invested in the country of origin under the guise of foreign direct investment, thus attracting tax breaks and subsidies for the 'beneficial' owners of the investing company, who may well live in the country being invested in. Most flight capital, however, leaves its country of origin permanently, much of it destined for the financial and property markets of the major Western economies.

The current global aid budget of $78 billion is insignificant alongside these massive wealth transfers in the opposite direction. It's anyone's guess how much dirty money has accumulated offshore, but at least $5 trillion has been shifted out of poorer countries to the West since the mid-1970s.

The outflows of domestic financial resources and the wholesale tax evasion that goes hand in hand with capital flight have had a devastating impact on developing and transitional economies. Deprived of domestically based private investment and tax revenues to fund public services, many governments have been forced into dependence on foreign direct investment and expensively serviced external debt. Both impose strict conditions on recipient states.

By and large, Western governments and multilateral agencies have downplayed concerns about dirty money except when drugs and terrorism are involved. James Wolfensohn provides the exception: during his presidency of the World Bank, he suggested that illicit financial dealings might partially account for the bank's failure to achieve its goals. For the most part, however, the political and media focus has been on looting by despots and their cronies rather than on the workings of a global financial system that encourages and facilitates the movement of dirty money. Astonishingly, neither the World Bank nor the IMF has tried to investigate or quantify capital flight and tax evasion.

More than 50 per cent of the total holdings in cash and listed securities of rich individuals in Latin America is held offshore. Data for Africa are sparse, but the trend shows a huge increase in the rate of capital flight from sub-Saharan Africa in the 1980s, with about 30 per cent of the GDP of that region disappearing offshore in the second half of the 1990s. The situation in the Middle East and North Africa is even worse, which helps to explain the chronic unemployment and social tension throughout the region. Earlier this year, Tony Blair's Commission for Africa proposed an additional $25 billion in aid to Africa by 2010, a sum dwarfed by the amounts coming out of Africa's porous banking system.

Drawing on his time running businesses in Nigeria in the 1960s and 1970s, and his subsequent research into money laundering as a guest scholar at the Brookings Institution, Baker dispels any notion that offshore corporate lawlessness began with Enron, WorldCom and Parmalat. Things may have got worse since the 1980s, but Baker compellingly demonstrates the extent to which international trade and investment patterns have been constructed around elaborate tax evasion schemes in use since colonial times. With at least half of all world trade now being conducted on paper via tax havens, the opportunities for fraud and skulduggery are immense.

The ability of multinational businesses to structure their trade and investment flows through tax-haven subsidiaries provides them with a massive financial advantage over nationally based competitors. Local firms, regardless of whether they are technically more efficient or more innovative, find themselves competing on an uneven basis. In practice this market distortion favours the large business over the small, the international business over the national, and the long-established business over the start-up. The outcome has been that both in theory and in practice the use of tax havens by virtually every major global bank and multinational business has nullified David Ricardo's doctrine of comparative advantage. Fundamentalist advocates of a no-holds-barred approach to free trade have persistently turned a blind eye to this problem. For those like Baker – and myself – who believe that free and fair trade can generate viable economic growth and spread its benefits across society, the blatant unwillingness of key players like the IMF, the World Bank and the UK government to tackle these global market failures says a lot about their real intentions.

Having suffered decades of venal dictatorship, Nigeria is a world-beater when it comes to dodgy financial practices. But the looting of the country's resources, which reached its peak during Sani Abacha's presidency in the 1990s, happened with the connivance of an extensive pinstripe infrastructure of banks, lawyers and accountants who provided the means for tens of billions to be shifted offshore. Some of these aiders and abetters came from Jersey. They would have been aware of the source of the funds and must have profited magnificently from handling this stolen property.

Challenging the view that financial scandals and tax dodging are isolated cases in an otherwise robust system, *Capitalism's Achilles Heel* shows how these 'negative externalities', as economists describe them, have generated a spirit of lawlessness that threatens the integrity of the market system and the finance industry as a whole. A British tax accountant was quoted in the *Guardian* last year as saying that 'no matter what legislation is in place, the accountants and lawyers will find a way around it. Rules are rules, but rules are meant to be broken.' The victims of this predatory tax-dodging culture include the poorest and most vulnerable people on the planet.

Much of the growth of the offshore economy has been driven by British lawyers and accountants. As early as the 1920s, they pioneered the use of trusts, shell companies, transfer mispricing, re-invoicing, dummy wire transfers – which give the impression a company is operating out of a tax haven rather than its actual location – and special purpose vehicles. Dodging tax was the prime motive, but inevitably, as Baker explains, laundering narco-dollars and paying off corrupt officials involve the same processes as tax evasion.

There's little doubt that secrecy drives the offshore economy. This was acknowledged by members of the Swiss Banking Association when, in a rearguard action in the wake of the Nazi gold scandal, they took out half-page ads in various broadsheets to propose, unconvincingly, that 'secrecy is as vital as the air we breathe.' But secrecy has a cost. In most countries of the South, there is general public resentment that the proceeds from national resources have been expropriated and exported wholesale to Western bank accounts. The corrosive outcome of poor education, failing infrastructure and entrenched unemployment is widespread discontent and an increase in poverty and crime. 'Crime flourishes in weak states, those that have millions in poverty, often accompanied with vast inequality,' Baker writes. 'Poverty fosters crime, and crime is in business with terrorism. Terrorism feeds off crime and poverty. It is the middle link in this chain – crime – that unites poverty and terrorism, a linkage that needs to be well understood.'

With no concern for justice and equity, fundamentalist utilitarian theories have been deployed to justify expropriation and lawlessness in the name of efficiency and freedom. The result has been an economic order that cannot and does not meet the world's welfare and security needs.

October, 2006

The Great American Job and Tax Scam

Greg Leroy

Tax competition is an international blight, but it is also a plague within the borders of the United States. In fact, competition for jobs and tax receipts within the United States has been an 'economic war among the states' for more than three decades.

Economic development – defined as spending by states and cities for job creation or retention – now finds the average state with more than 30 subsidy programmes: property tax abatements, corporate income tax credits, sales and excise tax exemptions, tax increment financing, low-interest loans and loan guarantees, free land and land write-downs, training grants, infrastructure aid – and just plain cash grants.

The bottom of the iceberg – in every sense of the word – is tax breaks. Those granted by states – income, sales and excise – are the least visible, least accountable, and most corrosive ways states fund economic development. Those granted locally – especially property tax abatements and diversions – are especially harmful to schools.

This system has a long history and many moving parts. It traces back to at least the 1930s and the Great Depression, and really matured by the 1970s. By then, most of the key actors were in place: secretive site location consultants who specialise in playing states and cities against each other; 'business climate' experts with their highly politicised interpretations of tax and jobs data; and an organised corporate network orchestrating attacks on state tax systems.

Today, this industry has spawned a more elaborate cast of characters: rented consultants packing rosy projections about job creation and tax revenue; subsidy-tracking consultants who help companies avoid leaving money on the table; and even an embryonic industry to help businesses buy and sell unused economic development tax credits, now legalised in at least four states.

States and corporate lobbyists justify economic development tax breaks by claiming job creation and tax base enhancements. But they routinely fail to deliver on both counts. Investigative journalists, non-profit researchers, and state auditors routinely find companies – many companies – that have failed to create or retain as many jobs as they said they would. Companies that are paying poverty wages or failing to provide healthcare to their employees. Companies that are abandoning the cities and sprawling onto farmland and natural spaces. Even companies that are out-sourcing jobs offshore. It is not unusual to find companies that have not created any new jobs, even some that have actually laid people off since receiving the subsidies. Others that got subsidised just to move existing jobs from one place to another, where they are proclaimed to be 'new.'

Less well known is the corrosive effect job subsidies have on state and local tax revenue. There is a growing body of evidence, from national statistics and from individual states, that over the past 25 years corporations – especially big ones are getting lower tax rates and paying a smaller share of the cost for public ser-vices. The evidence is especially disturbing on income taxes: in many states a large share of big companies are paying zero state income taxes, or tiny mini-mum taxes.

University of Iowa Professors Peter Fisher and Alan Peters use a 'representative firm' computer model to take a hypothetical new factory – with an average-size capital investment and rate of profit – and project the tax result if the factory is built in a state's enterprise zone, which bundle multiple tax breaks.

In 20 industrialised states, they find that 'incentive wars have proceeded to the point that state corporate income taxes are on the verge of disappearing in some states, at least with respect to new investment.' In other words, new factories generate such large tax credits, they pay little or no income tax. In fact, for 12 of those 20 states, their model indicates that typical companies building new factories can actually generate net tax credits – that is, the deals create negative income taxes.

Analysing by 16 industrial sectors (such as food processing, transportation equipment, etc.) they found that for Texas, in 9 out of 16 sectors, companies are get-ting negative income taxes; in Ohio, it's 13 out of 16; and in Kentucky, 15 out of 16. In three states – Iowa, Michigan, and South Carolina – they found that in all 16 sectors, companies are getting negative tax rates!

The aggregate evidence of revenue corrosion comes from government studies of state revenue, academics, taxpayer watchdog groups, studies of large publicly traded companies – even from a few angry governors and state treasurers. Experts conclude that tax breaks enacted in the name of economic development are a major problem, along with surging corporate use of loopholes like Delaware Passive Investment Companies.

First, the national evidence. The Congressional Research Service (CRS) – a non-partisan body that works exclusively for Members of Congress – tracks long-term trends in state and local corporate taxes. It reports that the effective corporate rate for all state and local taxes – in other words, income, property, sales, excise, utility taxes, etc. – has declined sharply over the past two decades. In the 1980s, companies paid an average of 6.93 per cent of their profits in all state and local taxes. In the 1990s, the average rate was 5.12 per cent, and by 2002, the last year studied, the rate had declined to just 4.99 per cent. That's an overall rate decline of 28 per cent.

Why are corporations paying less? 'Perhaps the most obvious explanation is the tax competition among states to attract business,' the CRS concludes.

More evidence comes from the Center on Budget and Policy Priorities. In the second half of the 1990s, when the U.S. economy was sizzling, federal corporate income tax revenues grew an average of six per cent a year. But state corporate income tax collections rose at just half that rate. Same companies, same profits, same years, half the tax.

It's not just the rate of corporate taxes, it is also the share of revenue companies provide. In 1980, corporate income taxes accounted for 9.7 per cent of state tax revenue; by 2000, it was down to 6 per cent, and for the next three years, it averaged only 5.2 per cent.

Put another way: if corporations contributed the same share to state treasuries in income taxes in 2003 as they did in 1980, the states would have received $27.3 billion more to help pay for smaller school-class size, public safety, healthcare and infrastructure. Or they could have avoided raising that much in taxes, especially the regressive consumption taxes that many states enacted.

To give a state-specific example, in Florida, the St. Petersburg Times found that 98 per cent of companies in the state paid no income tax in 2002, including cruise-ship giant Carnival Corp., with 4,220 employees in the state, more than $1 billion in 2002 profits – and a corporate registration in Panama.

Despite such findings, progressive state budget advocates are cautiously optimistic about their chances for reform. Already, 12 states have some form of annual, company-specific disclosure of costs and benefits (including four that disclose on the web); 19 states use money-back guarantee 'clawbacks,' and one state, Illinois, has enacted a mandatory Unified Development Budget that will help expose the 'bottom of the iceberg' – corporate tax breaks.

December, 2006

Export Processing Zones: The Kenyan Experience

Bob Awuor

The use of export processing zones (EPZs) as a regional or national development strategy extends back to the 1920s when the first zone was established in Spain. More recently, the UK Thatcher government was a leading advocate of 'enterprise zones' and Kenya also started to experiment with the idea in the 1980s.

EPZs represent a direct form of tax and regulatory competition in which special laws provide for a range of incentives to attract offshore investment for export production. The packages of incentives vary from zone to zone, with some common features including: tax holidays, duty-free import and export, unrestricted repatriation of profits and exemption from national labour laws. Some countries and regions also offer exemption from environmental laws and regulations. Critics of EPZs argue that tax incentives shift the tax burden onto local businesses and labour, and the regulatory exemptions undermine hard-won measures to protect labour and the environment. Supporters of tax incentives regard them as necessary for countries wanting to attract mobile capital.

Kenya enacted its EPZ Act in 1990. This made it possible for EPZs to be established with incentives such as a 10 year corporation tax holiday, subsidised credit, state sponsored infrastructure and exemption from trade tariffs on imports. At that time the Kenyan government anticipated that EPZ programmes would create jobs, attract new types of higher value-added processing and manufacturing activity, and diversify export earnings away from reliance on unprocessed agricultural produce.

EPZs are now an established feature of the Kenyan economy. Approximately 40 zones have been gazetted, and according to the Kenyan Human Rights Commission (KHRC), over 35,000 Kenyans are employed by businesses offshored in this way. The majority of these workers are women.

At face value the EPZ policy appears to have created a lot of jobs and the businesses established in these zones have recorded profits. Export volumes have also risen, particularly since the US government negotiated the African Growth and Opportunity Acts (2000 and 2002). More recently there has been a huge growth in trade with China. But Chinese interest in investing in Kenya appears to be motivated by the possibilities for using Kenyan quotas for textile exports to the US market.

The apparent success of the EPZ policy was challenged in 2003 when a series of wildcat strikes by mainly women workers exposed a pattern of exploitation and harsh working conditions. These strikes were organised in Nairobi and Athi River in protest against subsistence wages, non-payment of overtime, summary dismissals, sexual harassment and failure to observe health and safety standards. The workers were not supported by the Central Organisation of Trade Unions and the Trade Minister branded the strikers as 'hooligans'. However, subsequent research by the KHRC has revealed a pattern of companies pressuring workers to achieve production targets by working long hours of frequently unpaid overtime. The outcome, according to KHRC, was high staff turnover, stress, fatigue, absenteeism and labour unrest. The government responded in 2004 by calling for freedom of association for workers in EPZs but few companies have since recognised trade unions.

As well as degrading the rights of Kenyan workers, it appears that EPZs have contributed little to the economy. For starters, the great majority of businesses established in EPZs are engaged in labour intensive, low value-added garment assembly. The cloth is largely imported in finished form (increasingly from China) for assembly and export. The technologies involved are basic and require few skills. Furthermore the government has not followed a strategy of targeted incentives to promote links between EPZ firms and the onshore economy. The result being that economic links largely consist of employment for an underpaid workforce forced to work exceptionally long hours to subsist. Some Kenyan businesses also fear that leakage occurs as EPZ output seeps across the porous border between the EPZ economy and the domestic economy.

Even the apparent success of the EPZ policy in creating employment is questionable as not all EPZ jobs are new. As happened in Mexico during the 1990s when a process of 'maquiladorisation' occurred as local companies shifted to the EPZ sector, Kenyan companies have re-established themselves in EPZs in order to take advantage of the fiscal incentives and lower unit labour costs. Kenya's unemployment problem remains acute.

And the picture is no rosier on the revenue side. EPZ companies are generating profits, but there is no evidence of profits being re-invested in the Kenyan economy. The majority of profits appear to be being shifted offshore through transfer pricing arrangements. Some companies have relocated after the expiration of their tax holiday. Needless to say the workers employed in EPZs do not earn sufficient income to pay higher yields of tax revenue, and the trade tax exemptions have probably led to a net decrease in tax revenues arising from the introduction of the EPZ policy.

Speaking recently in London, Kenyan Finance Minister, Mr Amos Kimunya, said: 'We have sealed loopholes through which people previously evaded tax, and have instituted reforms and legal measures that broaden the tax dragnet, so that financing for public expenditure is largely drawn from internal resources.' I hope that the tax dragnet will be ex-tended to target EPZ enterprises be-cause the real cost of the EPZ programme far outweighs any benefits. The question we must now ask is whether there are any grounds for continuing to subsidize big, non-tax-paying foreign business through the EPZ programme.

December, 2006

Tax Competition: A Case of Winner Takes All?

Richard Murphy

At taxation and economic seminars all over the world it is suggested that 'tax competition' is a good thing. But, as Professor Michael Devereux of Oxford University admitted at the EU tax competition conference in September 2006, this is more a statement of faith than proven fact.

The Tax Justice Network does not accept that tax competition is benign. We consider it harmful because it is designed and promoted by political and commercial interests acting on behalf of a tiny minority in society.

This claim requires justification. First it is important to define what tax competition is. It is a variety of processes involving preferential treatment whereby governments compete to attract mobile capital to locate in their country. This might involve minimal or zero tax rates, as are offered by tax havens, but it also includes tax holidays and the subsidies offered through export processing zones, and other forms of direct and indirect subsidies which serve to attract mobile capital. The biased nature of tax competition is demonstrated by the fact that it seldom manifests in the form of lower rates of sales tax, which are regressive in nature: indeed in the majority of low income countries sales taxes have been increased, typically without exemptions, to compensate for lower tax yields from capital.

Next it should be noted that those who promote tax competition do so for four reasons:

Firstly, they argue that individuals and companies spend more wisely than government, the logic being that government is not subject to market mechanisms in making choices and is not therefore receptive to consumer preferences.

Secondly, they assume that, in the absence of competitive pressure, government is inherently inefficient, a trend exacerbated by their belief that all governments are prone to spend for the aggrandisement of politicians or civil servants. This tendency, they claim, is so pervasive that even the ballot box is unable to curtail it.

Thirdly, they claim that business efficiency is undermined by the administrative and financial burdens that taxation imposes.

Fourthly, they suggest that taxation gives inappropriate price signals to markets and as such all taxation should be reduced to minimise market distortions.

In combination these arguments demonstrate that tax competition lies at the heart of the Neo-Conservative agenda. Because Neo-Conservatives believe that democratic governments are unable to contend with these issues, they support the use of tax havens to encourage the relocation of mobile capital and to exert pressure on the governments of populous states to reduce their tax rates.

There is no evidence to support the case for tax competition. Firstly, taxation exists because societies want the State to act as a provider of key services, including law enforcement and defence. In addition, most societies recognise that there are other services which only the State can supply because they must be provided for the benefit of their whole population or the greater cost of not doing so will be borne by all members of society and not just those that fail to receive them. These services include the provision of health and education services and the supply of the complex physical and societal infrastructure which enable modern commerce to function. Access to these services needs to be available to all irrespective of their means. The greatest overall beneficiary of this public provision is business, which as a result of these services enjoys the advantage of having a healthy and productive workforce with the financial means to enjoy the products companies seek to supply.

Second, in practice markets cannot function efficiently in sectors such as health care, education and pension provision. The need to ensure service provision for the benefit of all means there will never be sufficient capacity to provide significant choice in these sectors. Consequently, private supply would result in private monopoly which is universally considered abusive. The ballot box is therefore the best regulator available to avoid abusive market structures and indicate society's preferences. The resulting services may be less than perfectly efficient, but as has been shown by the experience of privatisation, the market frequently does worse. This is especially true when markets are used to provide welfare services to ensure that people live free from fear of destitution or unemployment. Freedom from fear is fundamental to the success of markets be-cause fear discourages people from spending and is an impediment to investment.

Third, the assumption that government is inherently inefficient is wrong, as is the assumption that market signals are needed in the supply of all services. In many cases those signals transmit misinformation and misallocate resources or result in unmet demand. Market based arguments for tax competition are therefore not valid when electorates can make a genuine choice between centre-left and centre-right political actors.

Finally, the argument that low tax states are needed to 'correct' the result of such ballots reveals contempt for the concept of democracy. This contempt can only be based on the belief that some in society deserve preferential treatment, which is the belief at the core of the Neo-Conservative argument for tax competition.

The tax justice argument is based on the simple proposition that it is preferable to protect the well-being of the majority through regulation and taxation rather than to allow capital to roam without constraint and untaxed. This proposition recognises that the burden imposed by tax competition arises from the deliberate actions of players pursuing self-interest. As an example, PricewaterhouseCoopers recently wrote a report for the World Bank in which they asserted that:

> *If, for example, [taxes] are used for transfer payments, then the net impact on long-term economic growth may be negative.*

Transfer payments are the pension and benefit payments which old, disabled, sick and unemployed people – as well as the providers for many children – rely on to avoid absolute poverty. In the same report PWC also asserts:

> *Attempts to impose internationally uncompetitive tax rates on these forms of mobile capital may be particularly damaging to an economy in the long-term.*

Neither assertion is referenced or supported by data. Both are statements of preference indicating a bias towards the rich and powerful.

Our job is to offer alternative choices which provide balance in this debate. Our prime motive is a concern for poor people, especially in the developing world, but we also argue that effective markets are as important for society as effective governments. Without the security provided by public services there are compelling grounds for believing that markets will fail due to a crisis or crises of confidence. Tax competition that undermines state revenues could precipitate such a crisis.

With public services crumbling in many developing countries – and with even developed countries being forced to switch the tax burden increasingly away from capital and onto middle and lower income earners – the case for combating tax competition to protect markets and societies from predatory practices is compelling.

December, 2006

Tweedledum and Tweedledee Go Offshore

The following unpublished extract from Alice in Wonderland was recently found in a Jersey attic...

'It's obvious,' said Tweedledum, adopting a rather condescending tone.

'Self-evidently true,' snapped Tweedledee, peering at Alice over his reading glasses.

'If you don't cut our taxes,' continued Tweedledum, 'profits will fall and you will have even less money in the treasury.'

Alice sighed. She had heard this before, but it still didn't make sense. Taxes on profits were already low, businesses paid far less tax than in the past, but they just wanted more tax cuts and subsidy.

'We need the money to invest in health and education ... ' Alice began, but before she could finish her sentence, Tweedledee jumped up from his chair and strode to the window.

'Privatise.' he snapped. 'Let business do it more efficiently.'

Nonsense, thought Alice. Look at the mess that business had made of the trains and the water industry. And how many people can afford to pay the rates charged by private schools?

Gazing out the window, Alice saw the expensive motorcars in the executive car park and thought about how many of her constituents could barely afford to pay their rent.

Whilst these thoughts crossed her mind, Alice heard Tweedledee and Tweedledum muttering in an agitated way about how business needed lower taxes and less regulation.

Listening hard, she heard words like 'globalisation' and 'deregulation' and 'share options'.

'Gentlemen,' she interrupted, firmly but politely, 'for many years business has been demanding subsidies and tax cuts. I think business should pay its fair share towards public services.'

But this made them mutter even more loudly, and after a while Tweedledum strode across the boardroom and stood rather too close for Alice's comfort.

'You see, my dear,' he said, and his smile sent a shiver down her back, 'unless we pay ourselves more money, we won't have incentive to invest.'

Alice was not impressed by this line of argument. She knew the gap between rich and poor has kept rising, and with debt spiraling out of control, something needed to be done to redistribute wealth and income, because otherwise the economy would stagnate.

As Alice gathered her thoughts to ask why businesses were paying so little tax when they were making record profits, Tweedledum leant forward menacingly and hissed: 'If you don't give us our tax cuts we will go offshore. And then we won't pay any taxes at all.'

But whilst Tweedledum and Tweedledee marveled at this splendid idea, Alice leant forward to read the tiny badge on Tweedledum's jacket, which said: 'Only the little people pay taxes.'

December, 2006

THE CRISIS, 2007-2010

Gender and Taxation Systems

Caren Grown and Imraan Valodia

Over the past decade most developing countries have significantly reformed their tax systems, prompted in part by trade and financial liberalisation. Several nations have embarked on some form of gender-sensitive budgeting on the spending side. Few of these, however, address the revenue side. It would seem a good idea to start changing this, because tax policies often have important, though unrecognised, gender implications.

In low and low-middle-income countries, the International Monetary Fund has advised governments to rationalise taxes, amend regulations on exemptions and credits and on joint filing of personal income taxes, and to introduce user charges for some public services. Some countries have also introduced new taxes, such as capital gains taxes. These reforms have had far-reaching implications for the level and form of tax revenue, and for how the burden of taxation falls on different groups. In many countries, discussions about tax reform are dominated by the views of economists and financial analysts, and the process of reform is often not subject to full democratic debate. As a result, technical considerations of efficiency and ease of administration often overshadow discussions of social (and gender) equity.

In high-income countries, indirect taxes account for only about a third of tax revenue, while the other two-thirds comes from direct taxes such as personal income or corporate taxation. In low-income countries, however, it is the other way around: about two-thirds of tax revenue is raised through indirect taxes, which include trade taxes (such as import tariffs), excise taxes (such as on alcohol and cigarettes) and broad-based taxes on goods and services (such as General Sales Tax and VAT.) Income tax, however, accounts for just over a quarter of tax revenue in low-income countries.

Trade liberalisation has intensified the pressure to reform systems in many countries, with conflicting effects. On the one hand, corporate profits tax rates have fallen substantially as developing countries compete to attract footloose capital. On the other hand, requirements to reduce trade tariffs have forced governments to compensate for this loss of direct taxes by introducing indirect taxes such as value-added taxes.

This has had two main effects. First, research suggests that these alternative forms of revenue have not replaced the revenue from lower trade taxes, forcing governments to cut spending on public services and social protection programmes. Second, increased reliance on indirect taxation has tended to make the tax system more regressive overall in many developing countries, making it harder for poor countries to use taxes as a tool for redistributing wealth.

A growing body of research suggests that the need for social protection has increased in countries that have liberalised their economies. Employment practices have become increasingly flexible as employers attempt to reduce costs. This has gender implications because the proportion of women in 'flexible' jobs tends to greatly exceed that of men. Many women in developing countries earn their livelihoods through informal employment, and therefore lack formal contracts, work security, and access to leave or health benefits. There is consensus that social protection programmes can improve their lives, reduce their vulnerability and increase their ability to earn a living.

While gender activists have begun to participate in discussions and policy analysis regarding the need for social protection on the spending side in developing countries, few studies address how taxation affects the 'losers' of trade liberalisation. More research is needed here: for example, incidence analyses of indirect taxes will provide insights into whether the burden of taxation has been shifted to poorer households, and particularly to women, as tax reforms that increase sales taxes and reduce corporate taxes are implemented.

Preliminary research suggests that some personal tax policies are explicitly biased against women. In South Africa before 1994, for instance, women were taxed at a higher marginal rate than men, based on the argument that the male was the breadwinner and women's incomes supplemented the household income, so should be taxed more heavily.

Similar – though often less explicit – biases exist in personal income tax systems in other developing and developed countries. For instance, tax exemptions such as car allowances in personal income tax codes typically favour men, who are more likely to own cars (for which tax credits are often allowed), while discriminating against women (who are more likely to incur other forms of travel costs). Although this is less researched, some consumption taxes may be biased against poor women who spend a larger proportion of their incomes on consumption goods.

As noted earlier, there is concern that contemporary tax reforms tend to increase the incidence of taxation on the poorest women while failing to generate enough revenue to fund the programmes needed to improve their lives. The introduction of value-added taxes in many developing countries is a case in point. Even with generous zero-rating of basic foods in South Africa, VAT is a regressive tax, placing an unfair burden on poorer households, who spend a larger proportion of their incomes on VAT compared to higher income households. Women in South Africa tend to be over-represented in lower income households, and consequently pay an unfair portion of the VAT take.

Gender analysis of tax policy can potentially improve reform efforts. Alternative measures (including the mix of direct and indirect taxes, and the structure of rates, exemptions, credits, allowances, and so forth) should be explored to assess whether they address the goals of raising revenue and promoting gender equality objectives.

Tax policy should be part of public discussions about the level of government services and who should pay for them, including the share paid by women and men in their role as investors, consumers, workers, and employers. This debate is particularly important in countries where the pressure to raise revenue is great, but where state capacity to do so has been undermined by trade and financial liberalisation.

March, 2007

Taxing Thoughts

Sheila Killian

Traditionally, countries seeking to attract investment by fostering a low-cost business environment have done it by moderating wage demands, by subsidising infrastructure and fostering human capital, or by maintaining low taxes. Of these approaches, taxes are the easiest to manipulate. Tax competition traditionally involved the simple strategy of reducing tax rates to attract business. Multinationals responded by locating high-profit, highly mobile activities within the target jurisdiction. In general these are low-skill activities such as manufacturing, which can be fairly easily moved to new locations if tax rates rise or if a more attractive proposition presents itself.

Ireland is now finding that low taxes alone will not anchor the multinationals on which it has become so dependent. The inward investment has brought high wages and rising prices, and Ireland has become an expensive country to do business in. It is now losing low-value manufacturing jobs to Eastern European and developing countries. So Ireland has embarked on a second round of tax competition. The government is encouraging multinationals to locate not just their production facilities in Ireland, but their Research and Development (R&D) too. The hope is that intellectual capital is less mobile, less easily replicated, and will root the multinational more firmly in Irish soil.

Ireland offers two main incentives. One is a 20 per cent tax credit for any increase in R&D spending after 2003. Given that the tax rate in Ireland is currently only 12.5 per cent, this effectively allows a 160 per cent tax deduction for qualifying expenditure, which covers a wide range of activities. Naturally, this encourages multinationals with an Irish presence to designate as much as possible of their spending there as R&D. A second 'anchoring' strategy is a total exemption from tax for patent income, where the associated R&D work has taken place in Ireland (see box). So as multinationals increase R&D spending in

92

Ireland, they can patent the resulting technology and charge patent royalties to other divisions of the group. The stream of royalties is not taxed when dividends are received in Ireland, and no withholding tax is imposed where the dividends are paid overseas.

With manufacturing work being moved to lower-cost developing countries, patent royalties can now be charged to (and tax consequently deducted from) these poorer countries for the use of technology developed in Ireland. This 'royalty pipeline' shifts taxable profits first from the developing country to Ireland, then from Ireland to the multinational's home country (such as the U.S.,) free of Irish withholding tax. Multinationals have, unsurprisingly, responded by increasing R&D spending in Ireland and obtaining patents there. While goods formerly produced in the North are now increasingly manufactured in the South, the patent income flows from the poor South to the rich North.

Ireland illustrates how companies are now shifting their priorities away from producing goods towards producing intellectual property. And this has some rather sinister, unforeseen implications for poor countries.

Since patent royalties are paid between subsidiaries within the multinational group, and not on the free market, transfer pricing becomes opaque, which makes it very hard for taxing authorities to challenge the rate paid, because there is no benchmark to compare it with. So companies can use their intellectual property to strip profits out from the developing countries where the goods are manufactured, and repatriate them through countries like Ireland with minimal tax. And, once companies think of product development in terms of intellectual capital rather than trade, low-margin products (on which royalties cannot be recouped like this) are seen as unviable, and research priorities are concentrated on high-margin products – on obesity drugs, for example, rather than on malaria medication. This is one reason why poverty campaigners have had to fight so hard for discounts on items such as anti-retroviral drugs in sub-Saharan Africa. In addition to this, intellectual property rights prevent the process of learning-by-copying, and the production of generic drugs by local companies in the South, which exacerbates the technological divide in all areas protected by intellectual property rights.

The ideological underpinnings of these processes are unclear.

Countries like Ireland set out to achieve a defined objective – attracting and anchoring inward investment, but the measures they have used impoverish developing countries in ways they may not have foreseen.

The system suits multinational firms. As long as their activities are couched in terms of intellectual property rather than the simple production of saleable goods, their taxes are minimised, their transfer pricing is opaque, and their selling prices are high. As more countries join in the second round of tax competition, they will have a wider choice of attractive locations, and even greater bargaining power with the governments of competing countries. The first round of tax competition has been harmful enough. This new game based on intellectual property threatens to be even more damaging.

March, 2007

The Tax Consensus Has Failed

Alex Cobham

The Tax Consensus has been led by economists and tax experts working with the international financial institutions. A look through the IMF's Article IV consultation documents with member countries shows how pervasive it has been in driving recommendations and, ultimately, policy. Unfortunately, this Tax Consensus has failed.

To understand why this consensus has failed, first consider the four clear outcomes of taxation: the four Rs.

The first R is Revenue. Taxes raise money to pay for health, roads and education, or for more indirect things like good regulation and administration. Most people are familiar with, and accept, this function. Not everyone, however, recognises that there is more to tax than this.

The next R is Redistribution: taxation can help reduce poverty and inequality, and spread the benefits of development more widely. Different taxes have different effects: according to a recent survey of two decades of tax studies, income taxes are usually progressive (they reduce inequality;) corporate taxes are regressive (increase inequality) at low incomes but then become progressive; property taxes are progressive; indirect taxes (like value-added tax, VAT) are generally regressive, and the overall picture is mixed, although at low incomes, taxation is often regressive. Many people are familiar with this function of tax, although not everyone agrees with it.

The third R is Re-pricing. Taxes (and subsidies) can be used to change behaviour: taxing tobacco, pollution or carbon-based energy, for example, is accepted by many people as a way to curb potentially harmful activities.

The final R is the one most often forgotten, and it may be as important as the first: Representation. Taxation strengthens and protects channels of political representation: when citizens are taxed, they demand representation in return from their rulers.

Why the Tax Consensus has failed

For developing countries in particular, the Consensus has failed on each one of these four Rs.

First, it emphasises tax neutrality: a tax system should not distort production or consumption decisions, because it is argued that this would reduce economic efficiency. In practice, however, this has meant a shift away from direct taxation (which is generally progressive) and towards more regressive indirect taxation (as well as trade liberalisation, in the name of greater efficiency) and the net result has been that governments in poor countries have been stripped of the essential tools for redistribution – frequently with the effect of worsening inequality, hence often damaging political stability and consequently harming efficiency too. Little political space has been left for re-pricing either.

How the consensus undermines redistribution in poor countries

The Consensus also emphasises that redistribution should happen, if at all, via spending, not via taxation. But this assumes that governments have available a full range of instruments, including – critically – an option to make direct cash transfers to households, which can theoretically be combined with non-progressive taxation to generate the equivalent effects of a progressive (e.g. income) tax. But in low-income countries, including much of sub-Saharan Africa, governments simply do not have the capacity to make these transfers. So following the tax consensus involves giving up most of their power to reduce inequality. This can have disastrous effects.

How the consensus undercuts revenues

Another feature of the Tax Consensus is that governments are supposed to aim for revenues of around 15–20% of GDP – even though revenues in the EU-15 countries average more than 30%, and quite often significantly more than that. Governments are consequently encouraged to limit their revenue targets and constrain their spending. A study by Michael Ross of the University of California, Los Angeles

(UCLA) showed that channels of representation are systematically strengthened when the share of tax revenue in government spending is higher. That is, when governments rely most on tax. Other research has shown that direct taxation (through personal income taxes and corporate profits) is the most important, in terms of strengthening relationships of accountability between rulers and ruled. But the Tax Consensus is telling poor countries to avoid direct taxation, and to reduce revenues, again with potentially very negative effects on the strength of governance and the quality of institutions.

Government is an outcome of taxation

In short, the Consensus holds that governments should focus above all on revenues (with a role also for redistribution and re-pricing). What is missing is this: the system of government itself is one of the most important outcomes of tax. In other words, healthy political representation emerges from the process of taxation, leading citizens to hold governments to account. The Consensus implicitly assumes that the channels of political representation are already strong. For this reason alone it is unsuited to poor countries.

Not only that, but the Consensus has not generated sufficient revenues. One reason is that it tends to ignore massive revenue losses as corporations and High Net Worth Individuals (HNWIs, or Hen-Wees) evade and avoid taxes. I estimate that US$385bn of tax revenues are lost annually by developing countries, and a key part of this is due to international tax evasion. The amount that might be recovered using better tax policies significantly exceeds global aid flows.

Tax is a social act

But more broadly, and not just for these reasons, compliance in poorer economies is particularly low. This raises another issue: paying tax is a social act. People don't pay tax according to raw economic maximisation, as the consensus implicitly assumes – in fact, studies repeatedly show that tax compliance significantly exceeds what you might expect from maximising, rational agents, given the existing levels of fines and (expected) chance of getting caught. The experimental economics literature has found that people's behaviour is more complex than this: compliance depends positively on (i) the perceived or expected level of redistribution, and (ii) individuals' expectation of others' compliance levels (one study refers to 'tax morale' – a belief in contributing to society by paying tax – and shows that the size of the shadow economy depends directly on this.) So it seems that paying tax reflects, to a significant degree, a desire to participate in society, not just economic maximisation. This, then, is the final flaw in the Tax Consensus. Domestically it has undermined redistribution, and internationally it has failed to prevent evasion – and together these perpetuate non-compliance and the continued failure of tax systems in poorer countries.

Conclusion

The Tax Consensus has failed. It has failed to deliver desperately needed revenues; it has little or no place for redistribution; and this, with the absence of international measures to tackle evasion through tax havens and by multinational firms has fostered dismal levels of real (and perceived) compliance. This outdated ideology now needs to be overthrown, so that poor countries can put a range of policies back on the table and be free to choose the tax policies that they really need: tax systems that raise revenue, redistribute and strengthen channels of political representation for genuinely sustainable development.

June, 2007

How To Make Multinational Companies More Transparent

Richard Murphy

The campaign for Country-by-Country (CbC) reporting by multinational corporations (MNCs) arose from two initiatives. First, the Tax Justice Network (in its very early days) wanted to get disclosure of which MNCs were using tax havens and were abusing transfer pricing. I wrote a draft International Financial Reporting Standard for discussion, which was published by the Association for Accountancy and Business Affairs (AABA) in 2003. Then, in 2004, I started advising the Publish What You Pay (PWYP) coalition on the extractive industries (that is, industries based on minerals like oil) and, more specifically, the Extractive Industries Transparency Initiative (EITI). My report, 'Making it Add Up', was published by Global Witness and Save the Children UK in February 2005, highlighting problems with EITI. It suggested, among other things, that:

> *companies in each country [should] publish all their payments to government, in a full and timely manner, which allows for meaningful comparison.*

PWYP then asked me to develop an accounting standard for the Extractive Industries. When it became clear that this avenue for progress was closed for the time being, PWYP and TJN made a submission to the IASB (International Accounting Standards Board, a private Delaware corporation) in March 2006. Eighty organisations supported our submission.

What we're calling for

We are calling for standards that would go beyond the extractive industries and would embrace all companies. These standards would require each MNC to report:

1. In which countries it operates;
2. What it is called in that location;
3. What its financial performance is in each country, identifying third party and intra-group trade, and labour-related information;
4. How much tax (and other benefits) it pays to government locally as a consequence.

This information should be reported for all territories, without exception, where the multinational corporation operates. Anything less will not do. (This does not require every country to agree to accept the standard, as the requirement would be imposed at an international level.)

Why this is important now

In November 2006 the IASB, which is trying to get its standards to converge with U.S. accounting standards, issued its latest standard, known as IFRS-8. They had clearly ignored our submission and we felt it was a backwards step: it not only did not incorporate a CbC requirement, but also moved away from clear geographic reporting and gave huge discretion to management on how to report financial data. We think the old standard, IAS-14, is better.

However, the opportunity to lobby on this increased recently, because the European Commission is reviewing a proposed accounting standard that could be amended to make such reporting mandatory for all European based companies. This opens an opportunity to put pressure on the EU to reject the IASB standard, revert to the old one and go back to basics.

Various EU parliamentarians have expressed concern about IFRS-8, and now we are getting significant support from UK and international financial institutions: the UK's National Association of Pension Funds and the Investment Management Association are behind us, and see the merit of our arguments. Internationally, the International Corporate Governance Network, with $10 trillion under management, has expressed reservations about IFRS-8 in a letter signed by Calpers, America's largest pension fund. (The link with investors does not guarantee victory, but it adds considerable institutional weight to the arguments, and suggests that we are raising questions of broad concern.)

Many people and organisations shy away from things like this, which may seem remote and arcane. Believe me, they matter. Europe must have the right to reject an IFRS, or democratic control of reporting passes to a privately owned Delaware corporation substantially funded by the Big Four accountants. Accounts should be about more than the question of whether to buy or sell shares (the IASB's definition of 'decision usefulness') but should also be about accountability and stewardship. The benefits are hard to quantify, but we believe that CbC reporting could potentially benefit poor countries as much as all foreign aid, and it could substantially bolster democracy and governance in rich and poor countries alike. Here are a few more reasons to be concerned:

1. **Accountability matters.** A company cannot be accountable unless it can be identified. This means that the names an MNC uses locally must be on public record. Too often they are not. CbC reporting names and identifies local subsidiaries.
2. **Corporate governance matters.** Many recent corporate scandals have involved offshore subsidiary companies. These are becomingly increasingly common, but it is recognised that managing them creates severe governance issues for MNCs, resulting in increased risk for shareholders and others.
3. **Corporate social responsibility (CSR) matters.** CSR is about the relationship between a company and its host community. The host community should know the companies operating locally. CbC reporting provides that information.
4. **Corruption matters.** The EITI, for example, seeks to hold companies in the extractive sector to account for tax payments they make, and the governments that receive those payments to account for what they do with them. Many MNCs resist disclosing information because of competitive pressure, contractual

obligations and local political opposition. By making the standards international CbC would overcome these objections, enhancing transparency.

5. **Development matters.** Aid can sometimes help poor countries develop, but it is not a sustainable answer. Local declaration of economic activity by MNCs, with consequent accountability for taxes paid, could help break this cycle and create independent, accountable governments much better able to raise their own taxes.

6. **People matter.** MNC accounts include statements on the number of employees a company has and their aggregate remuneration. CbC would require this statement for every country, providing invaluable information on labour conditions worldwide.

7. **Tax matters.** MNCs have more opportunity than any other group to plan their tax affairs. They can shift profits from state to state, artificially, to find the lowest overall bill. CbC discloses companies' profits and taxes in each country where they operate, so they can be held accountable for what they do and don't pay. If this were tackled, enough tax might be collected to pay for the Millennium Development Goals.

8. **Trade matters.** 60% of world trade is intra-group trade across national boundaries between companies under common ownership or control. Existing MNC accounts encourage transfer mispricing by hiding this trade from public view. CbC shows it all.

9. **Transparency matters**. In many countries a corporation does not have to publish its accounts: so what it does in that country is not a matter of public record. What MNCs do has enormous implication for the wellbeing of the world. CbC overcomes this problem, by putting all MNC activity 'on the record.'

10. **Where you are matters.** Some countries are unstable, politically unacceptable, or subject to sanctions. If a company trades there, shareholders and civil society should know. Where you are matters. Currently, companies can hide where they operate. CbC would expose them to transparency.

March, 2007

Illicit Financial Flows: Will the World Bank Rise to the Challenge?

John Christensen

Raymond Baker is a determined man. At a TJN meeting with the World Bank's governance team in 2006, he politely but very firmly asked: 'What will it take to persuade the World Bank to do a proper job of investigating dirty money flows?' Baker estimates such outflows at $1.0-1.6 trillion per year, half from developing and transitional economies, but he wants the World Bank's experts to do their own sums. At the meeting there were embarrassed smiles and shuffled papers, but no clear indication that the Bank, for all its fine words about tackling corruption, was willing to engage.

How things have changed over the intervening 12 months. Dirty money, capital flight and tax evasion are moving centre stage and were the theme of a major conference in Washington on June 28 which assembled lawyers, policy specialists and investigators, many of whom had not properly thought about the issues before. Paul Wolfowitz had recently left as head of the World Bank, and Norwegian diplomat Bjorn Brede Hansen announced at the conference that his government will commission Wolfowitz's successor, Robert Zoellick, to prepare a forensic study into how illicit funds flow out of developing countries. Ray Baker can take much of the credit for making this happen. Hansen also announced his government's plans to lead an international task force to investigate tax havens and crack down on the abusive practices they enable. TJN and Ray Baker's team at the Global Financial Integrity program will be advisers to this task force.

'We have an integrated global structure in the Square Mile and Manhattan,' Baker said in his introductory speech, 'whose basic purpose is to shift money from the poor to the rich.' Startling evidence was presented at the conference of how this is done, with offshore legal entities evolving to enhance tax haven secrecy in the face of global anti money laundering initiatives. Concerns were raised about how new countries, including Ghana in West Africa (where a large oil discovery was recently announced), are preparing to create offshore financial centres to compete in an already crowded market. The *Economist* also recently described efforts by Sudan to set itself up as a tax haven. According to Ray Baker:

> *A mineral exporting nation serving as an offshore financial center and tax haven is surely the worst combination possible. Ghana's own wealth will inevitably get sucked into this black hole, driving apart rich and poor and forestalling economic development. Opting for such an unwise step should signal the end of any further need for foreign aid.*

Speaking on the World Bank's behalf, global governance director Daniel Kaufmann acknowledged that corruption had received no attention before the 1990s, and agreed that much still needs to be done. Yet he downplayed concerns about tax evasion to a second rank issue, and failed to demonstrate that the World Bank understands how tax havens create enabling environments for grand corruption. Herman Wiffjels, World Bank executive director for the Netherlands, showed a far better grasp of the subject, and spoke of the Bank's failure to act as a truly global institution. 'Zoellick has to take the World Bank to the next level,' he said, "explicitly including the element of illicit financial flows in this equation.'

June, 2007

Africa: The Shadow World of Oil

Xavier Harel

The shenanigans and opulent lifestyles of the offspring of some African presidents make regular headlines. Leader of the pack is the oldest son of Teodoro Obiang Nguema, Equatorial Guinea's dictator, who was given a $35 million villa in Malibu, California, complete with swimming pool and tennis court. Another is Gabonese president Omar Bongo's son, Ali, likewise the happy owner of a sumptuous pad in Malibu, this one valued at $25 million.

Until very recently the affairs of Denis Christel Sassou Nguesso, son of the president of oil-rich Congo Republic (not to be confused with the larger Democratic Republic of Congo-Kinshasa), were handled more discreetly. But publication of bank statements dating from 2004 and 2006 by British NGO Global Witness shows that he enjoys the same taste for high living as his peers: palaces, smart restaurants, top brand clothes and shoes, fine leather goods... Denis has spent up to $48,000 monthly on luxury goods, revealing a particular fancy for Louis Vuitton. Nothing prevents Denis from enjoying the high life: the young playboy directs Cotrade, a subsidiary of the Congolese national oil company – Société Nationale des Pétroles du Congo (SNPC), which is responsible for marketing the country's oil.

While 70 per cent of the Congolese population lives below the poverty line, the hundreds of millions of dollars he has squandered between Paris and Marbella didn't come from hard work on the part of Denis Christel. In fact they consisted of commissions on oil shipments paid into accounts held at the Bank of East Asia on behalf of Long Beach Limited, a company domiciled in Anguilla, with Denis Christel Sassou as sole beneficiary. For example, on 19 March 2005, Long Beach Limited's account was credited with $320,000: a commission arising from a shipment on the tanker Tanabe. The company's account was also topped up with commissions paid by

Sphynx Bermuda and African Oil and Gas, shell companies used by President Sassou to embezzle oil rents for his own benefit.

These embezzlements would never have been revealed had it not been for an American vulture fund. Without the efforts of lawyers acting for Kensington – an American fund holding debt instruments valued at over $100 million – to track Congolese assets, we would still know nothing about who was hiding behind Long Beach Limited. The company was managed by nominees to avoid disclosure of the owner's identity: a handy way to keep dodgy commissions out of sight from prying eyes. Kensington seized $12 million from the accounts of Long Beach Limited and Elenga Investment Limited, another Anguilla registered company established for the benefit of Blaise Elenga, number two at Cotrade.

Oil companies are particularly attracted to the discreet ways of tax havens. SNPC – a public company responsible for marketing Congolese oil on behalf of the national treasury – made a habit of selling oil shipments at way below market price to Bermuda-registered Sphynx Bermuda, a company belonging to... Denis Gokana, president of SNPC. He resold the shipments at market price and pocketed hundreds of millions of dollars, at the expense of the Congolese people. Dozens of tanker cargoes were sold this way, via shell companies, for the sole purpose of embezzling oil rents. Both BNP Paribas, a major French bank, and commodity trader Trafigura, helped along the way.

The British Virgin Islands and Jersey lie at the heart of a scandalous structure apparently created for the sole purpose of disguising ownership of Congolese oil reserves.

But first, we must backtrack slightly. When Denis Sassou Nguesso seized power in 1997 after a bloody coup d'état, he discovered that his predecessor, Pascal Lissouba, had handed control of a number of Congolese oil assets at way below their real value to the oil major Elf, which was omnipotent in Congo. The incoming ruler asked for compensation. In 2003, following a long period of negotiations, Elf, which was taken over by Total in 2000, ceded to the Congo – for a token payment – an old oil field (Likouala) which still held reserves of tens of millions of barrels. But instead of handing management of the field to SNPC, the government immediately sold it to a Congolese company with no experience in the oil industry, Likouala S.A. The

IMF quickly suspected this was a device to fill the coffers of Sassou or one of his cronies. The Congolese argued that the transaction only involved Total, Congo and SNPC. Be that as it may, the proceeds from Likouala cannot be traced. And for good reason: Likouala S.A. is controlled by a trust created in the British Virgin Islands, which in turn is owned by a foundation based in Jersey. This is an obvious way to hide the real owners of the oilfield. As a result, several hundreds of millions of dollars have disappeared into thin air, to the benefit of a mysterious foundation in Jersey. The oil industry feeds unbridled corruption. The Elf Affair revealed how a cut from each barrel of that company's output was paid into the Swiss bank accounts of the rulers of Congo-Brazzaville, Congo and Cameroon. Elf's former chairman, Loïk Le Floch-Prigent was well aware that on top of official payments made for oil licences, unofficial payments were also paid to those leaders' Swiss bank accounts.

The secrecy of tax havens provides perfect opportunities for the oil industry to corrupt dishonest leaders with relative ease.

September, 2007

Revealed: How Multinationals Avoid the Taxman[12]

Felicity Lawrence and Ian Griffiths

Global banana companies supplying the UK are using tax havens to avoid paying tax on their profits here and in developing countries, the *Guardian* has found.

The investigation reveals that large corporations are creating elaborate structures to move profits through subsidiaries to offshore centres such as the Cayman Islands, Bermuda and the British Virgin Islands, to avoid handing money over to tax collectors in the countries where their goods are produced, and in those where they are consumed. Governments at both ends of the chain are increasingly being deprived of the ability to raise tax for development or services.

Dole, Chiquita, and Fresh Del Monte, the three companies that supply several UK supermarkets and between them control more than two thirds of the worldwide banana trade, generated over $50bn (£24bn) of sales and $1.4bn of global profits in the last five years. Yet they paid just $200m, or just over 14% of profits, in taxes between them over that period, our analysis of their financial accounts reveals. In some years the banana companies have paid an effective tax rate as low as 8%, even though the standard rate in the US where they have their headquarters and file their full accounts is 35%.

The banana companies are not alone. Nearly a third of the UK's 700 largest businesses paid no corporation tax in the year 2005-06. A further third paid less than £10m each, according to figures from the National Audit Office.

The use of offshore havens by rich individuals to avoid paying tax was high on the political agenda this autumn, with Gordon Brown matching the Conservatives' pledge to tax 'non doms'. But increasingly, the far bigger challenge for government is how to keep up with the strategies being developed by large corporations to cut their tax bills.

About 60% of world trade now consists of internal transfers within transnational companies, according to the OECD. By weighting their costs towards countries such as the UK or the US that have higher rates of tax, corporations can make little taxable profit in those countries. Instead their profits are weighted towards subsidiaries they have set up in jurisdictions that charge little or no tax. Del Monte Fresh Produce UK, Chiquita UK and Dole's UK business, JP Fresh, report combined sales in the UK of over £400m in their most recently filed annual accounts. Yet between them they paid only £128,000 in UK tax.

Fresh Del Monte, currently the supplier of the vast majority of Asda's bananas and some of Morrisons', is registered in the Cayman Islands and has more than 30 Cayman subsidiaries. The Caymans have a zero rate of corporation tax. It also has subsidiaries in other tax havens including Gibraltar, Bermuda, the Dutch Antilles and the British Virgin Islands. Over the last five years its actual tax paid has been as much as $69m a year less than tax calculated at the standard US corporation rate.

Dole, which supplies bananas to Tesco in the UK, paid actual tax that was $20m a year less than tax at the standard US rate. Its accounts only list its largest subsidiaries, but these include companies in Bermuda, Liberia and Puerto Rico. Chiquita, which also supplies Tesco, lists 11 subsidiaries in Bermuda at the end of 2006. Our analysis of its accounts over five years shows that its actual tax paid is as much as $44m less a year than US standard rates.

In a double blow to the developing countries where the bananas are produced, the fall in tax as a percentage of profit paid by the large corporations has coincided with ruthless driving down of costs. Wages have been reduced on plantations even as working hours have been increased.

Fair trade campaign group Banana Link says Fresh Del Monte sacked all 4,300 of its workers on its Monte Libano plantations in Costa Rica in 1999 and re-employed people on reduced wages and benefits, a model it later rolled out across all its plantations. Chiquita's plantation labour costs meanwhile, which were 5% of its total costs in 2004, had been cut to just 2% in 2006.

Richard Murphy, a tax expert who advised the NAO on its report on the performance of the UK Revenue and Customs, said that large companies are effectively now able to set their own tax rates.

'Corporation tax is falling worldwide as a percentage of profits. Corporations seem to be deciding what they should pay, not as a percentage like the rest of us, but as a sum above which they don't want to go.'

John Christensen, a former economic adviser to the Jersey government and director of the campaign group Tax Justice Network, said the *Guardian* investigation confirmed that the flight of capital was continuing, having reached unprecedented levels in the 1990s. 'The trend in the last 30 years has been to shift the burden of tax away from companies on to the consumer and labour. Capital is increasingly going untaxed.' Dole declined to comment on the *Guardian*'s detailed allegations, saying that they involved confidential and proprietary information. Chiquita said it complied with all tax laws in the jurisdictions where it does business. Chiquita added that 'a significant portion of our earnings occur outside the US where they are subject to taxation at the local tax rate.' Both companies say they are working with the Latin American unions to address workers' rights.

Fresh Del Monte said it too operated in many countries and complied with all local tax law and international tax treaties. It added that it also complied with all local labour laws, was a strong proponent of freedom of association, and that the average wage of its agricultural employees in the countries where it operates exceeds the mandated minimum agricultural wage.[13]

November, 2007

Waking the Slumbering Giants: Why Development NGOs Have Been Slow to Take Up Tax Justice

Alex Wilks

In a piece for the *Financial Times* in March 2008 John Christensen and David Spencer wrote that 'tax, not aid, is the most sustainable source of finance for development'. The article called for civil society groups 'to wake up', implying that they are mostly asleep on their watches. This is harsh, but it is true that too few groups are taking a broader look at South-North capital flows. Of Eurodad's 54 member groups fewer than 10 work on tax and capital flight on a sustained basis, although the number is growing rapidly.

When I ask people why they are not yet working on this, the first reply is almost always that it is very complex and quite abstract. It can be hard for NGO policy and campaigns staff to understand, to communicate across their organisations, and to persuade all team members that this is an agenda to engage with. Some also say that the topic is quite arid and lacks the immediacy of several other topics and campaigns. It is a challenge to think of a campaign recruitment drive where you approach church-goers, festival punters, or neighbours saying 'have you got a moment to talk about tax?' A rival campaigner showing a picture of a landmine victim is likely to have more success.

Then, when people do dive in, they find that solid numbers to build a case are hard to come by – this being the nature of clandestine flows and hidden transactions. Managers and boards in many NGOs require tight business cases to be made for potential new campaigns. Candidate ideas must pass tests not only to prove that the problem is important, but above all that something can be done over the 3–5 years of a typical NGO campaign. Many NGOs may not yet be convinced there is a real chance to make a difference, especially as tax havens and corporations will not give up their gains without a fight. Some NGO managers also fear they may be victims of costly libel suits if they mention companies evading taxes owed to developing countries.

Jens Martens, in his report *The Precarious State of Public Finance* also hints that many development groups worry that the tax justice agenda may let rich country governments off the hook. NGOs, he argued, reacted rather sceptically to the Monterrey Financing for Development Conference outcomes which emphasised mobilising domestic resources. 'They suspected (not without good reason), that governments of rich countries wanted to deflect attention away from their own responsibilities and the necessary reforms of the international economic and financial system.'

TJN colleagues face a more philosophical barrier too. In principle, everyone can agree that taxes are a necessary part of building a civilized society, but many NGO activists are deeply sceptical about building strong states through taxation. It is much easier for people to buy into a critique of rich individuals and companies dodging taxes than it is to swallow a general set of positive proposals on tax. Some may see TJN and its supporters as living in European ivory towers, promoting idealistic Hellenic principles of a functional welfare state responsive to its citizens through an exchange of taxes and services. Many activists spend their time (and risk their lives) trying to carve out space for their communities to eke a livelihood free of government interference and oppression. Why should oppressed groups trust that their government will be a benefit, not a burden?

To summarise, some NGOs have been slow to take up the TJN agenda because they see it as complex, abstract and diversionary – and some have philosophical doubts about the progressive potential of states. But things are moving in the right direction, with more and more development campaigners understanding the arguments and making the case within their organisations to take it up. The complexity and abstraction can be taken care of by the policy wonks and public education specialists, and people are realising that these campaigns absolutely do not let rich countries off the hook.

Similar objections were previously raised about other development finance issues – such as trade and debt. About ten years ago a large number of groups "woke up" to the debt crises afflicting many low-income countries: more and more organisations realised that pouring aid money into countries paying out the same amount or more in debt service was not a strategy that could be maintained. The Jubilee 2000 movement, mass petitions and protests arose from a few determined individuals working to back what groups in Mexico, the Philippines, and many other southern countries had pointed out for ages was a major difficulty they faced.

Now many of Eurodad's member groups who tackle debt want to transition into tackling capital flight. There are individuals in most of the larger NGOs in the UK and several other European countries who would love to work on this issue more. This is likely to supplement, rather than replace, calls for more and better aid – which will remain a constant, partly because it is so close to so many NGOs' core mission and public image.

Richard Murphy recently wrote 'I think that we have passed a tipping point; the occasion when the momentum for change becomes unstoppable'. Is this accurate, or campaigner hyperbole? Tax justice may well become the next big thing among development NGOs, NGOs working on corporate social responsibility and related topics. But TJN will need to keep sounding the alarm.

June, 2008

Global Capital Flows: The Big Picture

Phillip Sarre

For a decade or more, the media have portrayed international financial flows as the leading edge of globalisation, growing ever bigger, faster and less bounded. Activity and movement are certainly mushrooming, but the flows are not quite what was expected, even as portrayed by official figures. There are substantial unreported flows.

Official figures, most of which rest on IMF national accounts collected for 80 countries, portray a world economy highly uneven in space and time.

For example, World Bank data show that high income countries, with 16% of the world's population, have 79% of world GDP (as measured using exchange rates for currencies). Most of the $167 trillion in financial assets are held in just a few countries China has a third of the financial assets of the whole of the less developed world, which total $24 trillion, only 14.7% of the world total – proportionately less than their 21% share of GDP.

Inflows, Outflows, Cross-Border Flows

In 2006 annual net cross border capital inflows totalled $8.2 trillion. The US had the largest inflow, at $1.86 trillion (compared to the outflow of $1.05 trillion); the Eurozone countries totalled inflows of $3.3 trillion (half with each other, half with the rest of the world); the UK received $1.25 trillion. Since 1996, 45% of the growth in inflows was to Eurozone countries, with another 35% to the US and UK. Even after several years of fast growth, less than 10% of the growth in inflows went to Less Developed Countries (LDCs). Yet the $704 billion that they received in 2006 was exceeded by net outflows of over a trillon, making them net exporters of capital to the high income countries.

Rapid Growth

Change over time is also striking. McKinsey data[14] from 2008 shows that from 1990 to 2006:

World GDP doubled, to $48 trillion (thousand billion).
World trade tripled.
World financial assets quadrupled, to $167 trillion.
Cross border investment assets quintupled, to $75 trillion.
Annual net capital flows increased eightfold, to $8.2 trillion.

So cross border flows are growing at faster rates than other economic activities, and financial transactions faster than production or trade. Net annual flows of capital remain quite small in relation to financial assets, however, and more than half of those are still owned and invested in the same national economy.

To make matters even worse, in 2005 the World Bank had reported capital inflows to the less developed world as $571 billion – in a table that also included an 'adjustment line', composed of errors, omissions and acquisition of overseas assets, of $345 billion, indicating a very serious margin of error. (And, amid the $8.2 trillion net cross border inflow figure above, outflows were $87 billion less, suggesting that some exporters of capital do not report it.)

Foreign investment, assets, liabilities

By the end of 2006, foreign investment assets held by Eurozone countries had overtaken those in the US.

In 2006, the difference between countries' net foreign assets and net foreign liabilities ranged between the largest debtor, the US, and the largest creditor, Japan. Interestingly, the two countries regarded as being at the forefront of financial innovation – the United States and the United Kingdom – are among the largest debtors (along with Mexico and Brazil, whose economies have grown slowly since the late 1970s), while the two major economies that have been regarded as in trouble over the last decade, Germany and Japan, are amongst the largest creditors – along with the big oil exporters and new growth phenomenon China.

Phillip Sarre

Financial integration, discrepancies, and outflows from poorer countries

Lane and Milesi-Ferretti[15] use a range of official data and academic studies to build the most comprehensive database on the financial assets and liabilities of 145 countries. Their data reveals some rather interesting features in the international financial landscape.

First, financial integration – measured as combined assets and liabilities – among 'More Developed Countries' (MDCs) tripled from 1970 to 2004, but for LDCs it grew by only 50 per cent, leveling off in the 1990s.

Second, there was an overall cumulative discrepancy between reported assets and liabilities, reaching 6 per cent of world GDP in 2002, or about $2 trillion. More than half the overall discrepancy was accounted for by foreign owned portfolio equity holdings in the USA, Luxembourg and Ireland, for which no other jurisdiction claimed ownership. More detailed analysis showed that International Financial Centres were among the worst under-reporters of foreign asset ownership.

There were substantial unrecorded inflows to Switzerland, the UK and US, running at about $100 billion each, and outflows from Russia, Italy, China and Norway. High percentages of GDP were lost to countries including Mozambique, Oman, Ethiopia, Bolivia, Zambia, Kuwait and Lebanon.

There have been various studies and estimates of unreported movements of capital, most recently by the European Network on Debt and Development.[16] These studies both identify the nature of these flows and suggest that they outweigh the flows of aid (about $90 billion a year) and investment into less developed countries.

The disparity in treatment of flows is stark. Past loans and investments are meticulously recorded and payment demanded, while transfers by dictators, money laundering of drugs profits and manipulation of internal prices between divisions of MNCs move even larger sums – without attribution. Unrecorded flows use offshore financial centres, with low taxes and bank secrecy, to obscure flows, but assets end up being held in mainstream institutions in developed countries. Recent estimates suggest that twice as much capital was spirited out of Africa between 1970 and 2005 as the total debt recorded for that continent.

To sum up, the open capital markets that were expected to make investment available to less developed countries have in fact operated to concentrate capital in more developed countries, using both legal and illegal transactions, often through a network of offshore financial centres. Forays of finance into some less developed countries have been small and volatile, contributing to crises as much as to development.

September, 2008

In Need of a Fix: Double Tax Avoidance Rules as the Institutional Foundation of Tax Competition

Thomas Rixen

Tax competition is generally taken as given; a 'natural' corollary of economic globalisation. Of course, economic globalisation is a necessary condition for tax competition: if production factors were immobile, it could not happen. Yet it is not a sufficient condition. Whether there is tax competition at all, and how it is structured, depends on the rules governing how trans-border movements are taxed. These rules are laid down in the double tax avoidance regime. Analysing how these rules work, and how they generate today's particular structure of harmful tax competition, could open up tax policy debates to co-operative international approaches, rather than sinking into ultimately self-defeating national responses.

The double tax avoidance rules constitute the structure of tax competition

The original purpose of international tax co-operation was to avoid double taxation, and to co-ordinate overlapping tax claims of nation states on international trade and investment. In the 1920s, when the League of Nations drafted the first principles of double tax avoidance, the intention was to liberalise the international economy. The principles and rules of double tax avoidance were codified in a non-binding model convention that developed into a de facto standard. Since the 1960s, the model convention has been sponsored by the Organisation for Economic Cooperation and Development (OECD), which has become the central forum for discussing and co-ordinating international tax issues. The model convention's fundamental principles have not changed, though its technical details undergo ongoing modification. Governments have now concluded more than 2000 bilateral tax treaties based on this model convention.

The double tax treaties preserve sovereignty. They merely allocate rights to tax among the jurisdictions involved, without prescribing how they should exercise these rights (including the right not to levy taxes at all). National governments have exclusive formal authority to determine the tax base, tax rate, and tax system, independently from other governments. So double tax avoidance rules operate only at the interfaces of national tax regimes. There is no attempt to harmonise tax systems between countries.

The rules for allocating the taxable profits of multinational enterprises (MNEs) between jurisdictions are emblematic of this sovereignty-preserving principle. Under a 'separate entity' approach, allocations are the same as would result if the different entities of a multinational group were independent actors transacting in a market – the 'arm's length' standard. Governments can define the tax base and the tax rate as they wish.

Unintended Consequences

This setup does achieve market liberalisation, but its sovereignty-preserving aspect has unintended consequences in the form of tax evasion, avoidance, and competition. Explicitly, the rules only tell states how to avoid international double taxation. Implicitly, however, they also tell taxpayers how they can 'optimise' tax payments. For example, taxpayers can use the indeterminacy of the arm's length standard to manipulate transfer prices (legally), or they can use shell or 'letterbox' companies to manipulate their formal tax residence and earn profits tax-free – without relocating real economic activity or changing real residence. They become free riders enjoying tax-financed public goods and services at their places of residence or production, without contributing sufficiently towards them.

In essence, tax arbitrage is possible because double tax avoidance rules leave governments' formal tax sovereignty untouched: they may design their tax systems so as to attract other countries' tax bases. So the regime of double taxation agreements (DTAs) not only succeeds in preventing double taxation; it also provides the institutional foundation for today's structure of harmful tax competition.

With increasing internationalisation of the economy, the negative effects of tax competition become more pronounced, and governments have failed to regulate it well, for several reasons. First, many low-tax countries and tax havens see themselves as 'winners' of tax competition, and oppose stricter regulation. Second, even, high-tax countries have ambivalent interests: they do not want to lose tax revenues to tax havens, but they also do not want to close all tax loopholes for 'their' own multinationals. Third, they do not want to endanger the tax treaty regime's coordinating function – the established solution to double tax avoidance – which rests on a non-binding standard. So they act cautiously: they try only incremental reforms, and selective deviations from the established principles.

Some reforms could be called rule-stretching. Governments take great care to reconstrue new rules to concur with the arm's length standard, rather than acknowledge their inherently unitary nature. They formally reinforce the 'separate entity' accounting principle, in order to continue to rely on the established DTA regime principles. Governments also pursue a strategy of layering: they layer additional regulations on top of existing ones so as to soften the negative consequences of the DTA regime and keep it operable.

What can be done?

Rule-stretching and layering do not explicitly challenge the sovereignty-preserving setup of double tax avoidance. Governments still remain largely free to devise national tax laws as they wish, and the unintended consequences – tax evasion, avoidance, or competition – are only addressed through administrative cooperation. The problem is – quite apart from the fact that there are gaping holes in the system – that it only provides an ex post remedy. Better information exchange and administrative cooperation are certainly necessary and worthwhile. But while national tax systems retain so many differences, they will present opportunities for international tax arbitrage, and the costs of ex post administrative enforcement will be high. What is needed in the medium to long term, is more ex ante cooperation, where governments are willing to harmonise at least parts of their national tax codes.

One solution would be unitary taxation with formula apportionment. The formula would ideally be based on factors like sales, payroll, or capital invested, to ensure that economic activity is taxed where it actually happens. A typical letterbox company in a tax haven would only be assigned a very small or no part of the enterprise's profit, because hardly any real economic activity, measured by these factors, happens there. This would make arm's length pricing superfluous, but it would require states to harmonise their tax bases and thus share some formal sovereignty with others. But they would remain free to apply the tax rate they wish to their share of the consolidated base.

However, a unitary taxation system, with a common consolidated tax base and formula apportionment, would face problems too. Tax competition would no longer be mostly about shifting 'paper profits.' Instead, companies and countries would structure tax competition on the factors that are part of the apportionment formula. How far this would be possible, or how harmful the effects would be, will depend on the formula. It may be necessary to agree on a binding minimum tax rate. Nevertheless, such a system would be better than the current state of affairs. Instead of relying on an opaque, hybrid system of arm's length pricing coupled with ad hoc formula apportionment through the administrative back door, effective formula apportionment would require elected governments consciously to decide on appropriate definitions of the common tax base and the formula. Democratic legitimacy would be increased.

Currently, the political prospects for this are poor. Even in the European Union – where the Commission planned to propose a directive on a common consolidated tax base this year –resistance is strong and the chances of real change in the near future are low. Governments seem not to have yet realised that globalisation means it is necessary to share formal tax sovereignty with others, in order to regulate international tax competition effectively and regain real tax sovereignty. Only collectively can they recapture what they have each lost.

September, 2008

Making the Link: Tax, Governance and Civil Society

Olivia McDonald

Drawing on our own experience and on analysis by experts in this field, and comparing different sources of government revenue, Christian Aid is now starting to explore the links between development finance and accountable governance. We have found evidence that tax, rather than aid and natural resources, is more closely linked to better governance. The way tax is raised, and who pays it, play an important role. For an organisation like Christian Aid, working with approximately 600 partners in 50 countries, this analysis has major implications for our lobbying and campaigning with the UK and Irish governments, and for our work with local civil society organisations.

While aid brings about much needed resources for development aid inflows often place heavy reporting burdens on governments with limited capacity and can actually weaken their abilities to budget effectively. Aid often bypasses not only institutions that scrutinise the government, like parliament, but government itself. Aid conditions mean recipients are more accountable to donors than to their citizens. Yet tax, and especially direct taxation like income taxes – can build healthy links of accountability and political representation between governments and their citizens. A government's imperative to collect taxes can also stimulate it to build better and stronger institutions so that it can do so.

Is aid like oil?

The 'curse' that accompanies the prevalence of natural resources like oil is well documented and broadly accepted. It is particularly evident with non-renewable resources like oil but a correlation has been identified between natural resource dependence (measured by the ratio of primary exports to GDP) and the probability of authoritarian government. Oil revenues do not come from citizens, so these revenues do not create the beneficial links of accountability that tax does. Aid can pose a similar problem.

Greater transparency can help, and this drives civil society campaigns such as Publish What You Pay and the Tax Justice Network's Country-by-County reporting initiative – which Christian Aid and its partners are closely involved with. Yet it is also important to generate a sense of ownership amongst citizens of natural resources. The Alaska Permanent Fund is a well-documented model of how the revenues from natural resources can be distributed to citizens, boosting people's incomes and increasing citizen interest in – and scrutiny of – the use of natural resources.

Donor commitments to improve aid effectiveness are important, and welcome. Yet even if donors displayed model behaviour – allowing recipients space to set policies in consultation with citizens – aid would still weaken accountability to citizens because it remains a revenue source independent of them. Full, proactive transparency of donors to citizens in recipient countries about what they are paying to governments and asking governments to do in return will mitigate this problem, but not overcome it.

The tax consensus has failed

Tax systems and tax reforms should clearly be designed with good governance as a core objective. Unfortunately, however, this does not happen at present. A widely-accepted international 'tax consensus' focuses strongly on revenue, at the expense of redistribution, re-pricing and perhaps most importantly representation.[17]

The groundwork is being laid for this to change. Research by Mick Moore[18], Michael Ross, James Mahon and others has shown a strong link between democracy, liberalism and tax. Tax reform has for long been the terrain of the technocrats, but the political implications are now coming into focus. At the OECD Development Assistance Committee, the governance network has now noted a potentially long-term dividend of improved governance to be gained from tax: a social fiscal contract.

What tax systems deliver better governance?

Technical quick fixes rarely work in development, but our analysis has identified four main areas to think about:

How are tax policies decided? Donors should focus more on the mechanisms by which tax policies are set, and who participates. Civil society needs to be able to offer its perspectives on tax policies. This occasionally happens, but not in a systematic way: attempts to introduce VAT in some countries, for example, have been met with protests.

Who pays tax and how? Indirect taxes like VAT may not be as effective as direct taxes in improving state-citizen relations. States are more likely to pursue tax policies that benefit favoured sectors of society. Broadening the tax base is important, yet in many developing countries very few people pay income tax, including the middle classes. This also means thinking about how to bring poor people into the formal tax system.

Is the taxation coerced or negotiated? Coercive taxation is arbitrary and forced, so those who are taxed are not in a strong position to demand accountability. This can damage state-society relations. By contrast, revenue-bargaining sees taxes being negotiated between state and society, with taxes being paid in exchange for services and security in ways more acceptable to citizens.

Where is tax paid? Decentralisation can make governments more responsive to citizens' preferences than centralised ones; and local taxation can bring opportunities to strengthen links between people and governments. But local tax systems are not without problems: they can be complicated, opaque, coercive and poorly coordinated with national government. More research at this level is essential.

What does this mean for Christian Aid and our partners?

For our policy and lobbying work, this analysis means promoting reforms that make revenue from natural resources and aid work 'more like tax'. But it also means calling for development of tax systems to be prioritised as the development finance source that delivers best for governance.

In developing countries we should, for example, support projects that mobilise citizens as taxpayers. We should support partners to analyse how people are taxed, to consider if it is done in a way that promotes accountability. And if it doesn't, we should support our partners to challenge that.

As we increase our work on corporate tax evasion, we need to ensure that our belief that tax forms a social contract remains central; that we ourselves do not reduce tax policy to a technical discussion about how to raise revenue.

September, 2008

The City of London Corporation:
The State Within a State

John Christensen

When people ask – as they often do these days – which is the biggest tax haven in the world, our answer is almost invariably the City of London. The City hosts Britain's largest offshore financial centre and is intimately linked to satellite tax havens across most time zones, ranging from Hong Kong and Singapore in the East, to the British Virgin Islands, the Turks & Caicos Islands, Bermuda, the Cayman Islands and the Bahamas in the West. All of these havens are in some respects the Frankenstein creations of the City, as are the Crown Dependency islands (Guernsey, Isle of Man and Jersey) which are easily accessible in less than one hour by jet from London.

Often called the Square Mile, the City is a geographically defined area of the London metropolis. The City is *not* a London borough, and unbeknownst to almost everybody outside the UK (and to most British people) it has its own distinctive political representative body, the City of London Corporation, which in addition to holding some rather unusual powers – such as the power to organise its own police force – is probably the most powerful and self-interested political lobby in the world.

Despite being at the heart of the London metropolitan area, the City has a tiny resident population, estimated at 7,800 in 2006. This is because real estate prices are so astronomical that the City is dominated by office blocks. By day the population swells to around 450,000, almost all directly or indirectly employed by the financial sector. This influx of day-time workers plays a crucial role in shaping the politics of the Corporation, since, unlike every other local authority in the UK, voting rights for the 100 elected members of the Corporation's Court of Common Council are given to both individual residents and businesses, with the latter outnumbering the former. Businesses are allocated votes according to a sliding scale determined by employee numbers, so businesses employing fewer than ten people are allocated one vote, whilst a business employing 3,500 staff can cast 79 votes.

Not surprisingly, this electoral system has attracted sharp criticisms. As far back as the 1890s a Royal Commission recommended that the Corporation should be amalgamated into the rest of London's machinery of government, but this was strongly resisted by vested interests, and subsequent reforms have been minimal. *The Rough Guide to England* is coruscating in its comments on how the Square Mile is governed:

> *Nowadays, with its Lord Mayor, its Beadles, Sheriffs and Aldermen, its separate police force and its select electorate of freemen and liverymen, the City of London is an anachronism of the worst kind. The Corporation, which runs the City like a one-party mini-state, is an unreconstructed old boys' network whose medievalist pageantry camouflages the very real power and wealth which it holds.*

John McDonnell MP, an economist who has warned for many years about the dangers inherent in Britain's *laissez faire* attitude towards banking regulation, describes the Corporation as 'a group of hangers-on, who create what is known as the best dining club in the City ... a rotten borough.'

Unsurprisingly, given the voting strength of banks, insurers, accounting firms and related financial intermediaries, the Common Council is dominated by their class interests. And come hell or high water this class doesn't miss a single opportunity to grab tax breaks and special treatment. In the midst of what may well prove to be the worst financial crash since the 19th Century, Alderman Ian Luder, the current Lord Mayor of London, made a speech to international bankers. An accountant by profession, Mr Luder is a tax specialist, and the real meat of his speech focused on tax policy: or more exactly on resisting any attempt by the UK government to tax the profits generated in London. Here is what he said on the subject:

> *There are some indications that the Government has learned not to kill the Golden Goose although it leers at it from time to time.*

(His timing is exquisite; given the massive cost to the general public of bailing out this particular golden goose, whose goose one might ask?)

Luder continues:

> *Tax exemption for foreign dividends is very good news, as is simplified asset management taxation and stamp duty land tax relief for alternative finance investment bonds.*
>
> *Most importantly, I would add to that the welcome review of the controversial taxation of Controlled Foreign Companies laws and the promise of a clear move towards a territorial approach to taxing foreign subsidiaries. This is very welcome as it hopefully marks the end of trying to tax companies' worldwide profits, a fact which has been the prime cause of the well publicised exodus of a number of headquarters of UK-based international groups.*
>
> *The Chancellor has the opportunity to create a streamlined, principles based tax regime for foreign profits and to turn the UK into a destination headquarters of choice. We will be encouraging him to do so.*

And indeed the Lord Mayor and his feudal entourage, plus the cheerleaders of the financial press, and all the king's horses and all the king's men, will never cease in their efforts to encourage the Chancellor to continue to give the City endless tax breaks, not to mention the 'light-touch' regulation which has contributed to the City's status as the big daddy of all tax havens and the largest offshore financial centre.

The City of London Corporation ranks as a political power without rival in Britain, possibly in the world. It has used its power to exert enormous political influence to resist regulation and extract tax exemption. It has fostered criminality by ensuring that the City ranks amongst the least accountable of financial centres on the face of the earth. Eva Joly, the indefatigable examining magistrate who investigated the Elf-Aquitaine scandal, singled out London as the tax haven she found particularly obstructive to investigators: 'The City of London, that state within a state which has never transmitted even the smallest piece of usable evidence to a foreign magistrate'.[19]

Prospects

Labour is to fight to break the grip of a bankers' elite controlling the City of London by putting up for the first time a slate of party candidates to run the Corporation of London.
Patrick Wintour, *Guardian*[20]

A new challenge for the City? Do turkeys vote for Christmas? The likelihood of bankers and financial intermediaries electing representatives capable of achieving even the mildest of reforms, let alone the wholesale changes required to make the City responsive to public interest, is close to zero.

And the chances of the UK government taking active steps to rein in the City's powers and privileges are also close to zero, since this government and its predecessors, have been almost wholly captive to the interests of financial capitalism. How right Michael Heseltine was when he quipped – in the context of John Smith's efforts to woo the City – that 'never have so many crustaceans died in vain.' The celebrated 'Prawn Cocktail Offensive' marked the end of the Labour Party and the birth of New Capital.

Given the high degree of political party dependence on funding from City interests; given the unhealthy revolving door between front-bench posts and City boardrooms; given the endless barrage of special interest pleadings from 'independent' think tanks and financial journalists with close links to City institutions; given the deep-rooted belief that what is good for the City is good for Britain, we can expect to see business as usual for the foreseeable future.

February, 2009

In Trusts We Trust

John Christensen

The Swiss tend to be outraged when they are criticised for their fabled bank secrecy. They correctly argue in response that Anglo-Saxon common law countries, which are so often the origin of the finger-pointing, routinely achieve even stronger and more devious forms of secrecy through trusts. TJN has always been extremely concerned about trusts, especially offshore trusts. Trillions of dollars' worth of assets are likely to be held through trusts worldwide – three to four hundred billion through Jersey-administered trusts alone – so this is an issue of global importance.

This long blog offers a simplified primer on trusts, to help foster better understanding of how trusts are used to create secrecy, to evade or avoid tax, and to get around rules, laws and regulations. It is illustrated mostly with reference to the United Kingdom, the original home of the trust concept, and to Jersey, a secrecy jurisdiction that has made it onto the OECD's 'white list'. It is simply descriptive: it is neither intended to be comprehensive and exhaustive, nor does it offer solutions for tackling abuse (something we intend to tackle in due course).

Introduction

Most people take it for granted that when they own an asset – a bank deposit, say, or a painting – it is a simple matter: they own it, and that is that. In fact, however, ownership is a more complex concept involving a bundle of different rights: these include the legal title to the asset; the right to an income stream from an asset; the right to control the asset and direct how it is used; and other things. Usually these rights are bundled together into one, and you don't notice the difference. Yet these rights can be, and frequently are, unbundled. For example, if you buy a house on a mortgage, you are the legal owner, but the bank or building society has rights to foreclose and take over the property if you default on the payments.

Trusts are ways to unbundle different the aspects of ownership into separate parts. This can be done for valid and legitimate reasons, or for abusive ones.

A trust typically involves three main parties. One party ('the settlor' or grantor or donor) – typically a wealthy person, hands over control of an asset to a trusted second party ('the trustee'), perhaps a lawyer, who in turn controls the property on behalf of a third party ('the beneficiary') who might be the settlor's child, for example. The trustees are the *legal* owners of the asset ('the trust property') but they are not the *beneficial* owners, and apart from fees the trustees should receive no benefits from the assets. Trustees are bound by a 'deed of settlement' (or trust deed) in which the settlor lays out instructions about how the assets of a trust can be used; the trustee is bound by law to follow these instructions. Trusts are generally meant to incorporate this split of roles, responsibilities and entitlements (although as described below there are trusts, sometimes known as purpose trusts, for which there is no intended beneficiary).[21]

The historical origins of the trust mechanism help illustrate what is happening. They were first used, the legend goes, in the early Medieval period in Europe when knights (in effect, the settlors) headed off to the Crusades and left their property and land in the hands of trusted stewards (trustees), who would look after them on behalf of third parties – typically their wives and families (the beneficiaries) – under a set of clear instructions (the deed of settlement).

In more recent times trusts were used typically for inheritance tax purposes: people with assets (settlors) created trusts to pass assets to their children (beneficiaries) and these assets were managed on the beneficiaries' behalf by trustees. For example: a settlor might say to a trustee: 'Here is a million dollars. You take it off my hands, and you are instructed to invest it; then when my oldest child is twenty-one you pay him a half of the current value; pay the remainder to my youngest when she is twenty-one.' The trustee should in theory be fully independent of the settlor. Again, although the trustee has *legal title* to an asset (so, for example, he or she can sell them – though the proceeds must go to the beneficiaries), the trustee is not the *beneficial owner* – so, for example, if a trustee becomes insolvent, creditors have no claim on it.

A body of law grew up around these arrangements so that they have become enforceable, and an industry has grown up around these laws, often to provide services to facilitate them, and trust facilities have become replicated in many jurisdictions around the world.

Why does the settlor have to give away assets as part of a tax avoidance or evasion strategy? Doesn't that drastic step more than defeat the original objective?

It can be hard to understand why a settlor would want to give away their assets. To lose the whole asset seems like an oversize price to pay if the aim is, say, to cut the tax bill on the income from that asset.

A first answer to this question is that the British upper classes, quite comfortable with sending their children away to be cared for by trusted strangers in boarding schools, also seem to be perfectly happy separating themselves from their money, to be managed by trusted strangers. This apparently light-hearted answer conveys an important point, however, that there is a significant cultural element here: people in Anglo-Saxon traditions have tended to be more comfortable with trusts than are people from other jurisdictions.

A second, more serious answer is that while the settlor has, in theory, given the assets away to a trustee, who has legal title to them, the settlor can still exert a measure of control over the assets. Offshore jurisdictions in particular allow very wide powers to settlors – which mean they can still pretend to have been separated from the assets, while in reality they exert a large measure of ongoing control and can, to all intents or purposes, be considered to be the real beneficiary. This can become a game of smoke and mirrors. Several examples of how this is done are given below.

How is secrecy obtained through trusts?

This happens in several layers. The first two described below are specific to trusts; the others are techniques commonly used with trusts but which are common with other structures, such as companies, too.

In a first layer, trusts create a legal barrier between the trustee, on the one hand, and the settlors or beneficiaries, on the other – and in the process this creates the potential for an information barrier in the same place as the legal barrier. Even if you can find out who a trustee is, the trustee may be bound by a confidentiality arrangement not to reveal who the settlors or beneficiaries are. Often, and especially in a secrecy jurisdiction, the trustee will be an anonymous trust company that specialises in being a trustee for many thousands of trusts, and there will be no obvious clue to suggest who the settlors or beneficiaries might be.

A second layer of secrecy is typically provided for in onshore and offshore legislation, which may stipulate – as in the case of the Cayman Islands or Jersey – that trusts do not need to be registered. (A trust is just a legal instrument; it does not have its own legal identity which might require registration.) If there is no register of trusts, you may not know what you are looking for. For example, a Jersey trust provider, Appleby, said this:

A trust is not a public document and does not need to be registered with the Jersey authorities. Furthermore, neither the settlor nor the beneficiaries will be the registered owner of any trust assets. As a result, a trust arrangement can be regarded as highly confidential.

A third layer of secrecy may involve several layers. This might split the trustee, the settlor and the beneficiary between three different jurisdictions, with the assets themselves parked in a fourth jurisdiction (or many jurisdictions.) Not only that, but a trust might be layered upon another trust or another structure, itself split between two or three further jurisdictions. For example a trust's assets may be shares in a company controlled by nominee directors in a jurisdiction where it is impossible to find out who the company directors are or what the company does. That company's assets may also turn out to be deposits held in a bank account in a country with strong bank secrecy laws. This layering process can, and frequently does, go on for several more steps, making it fiendishly hard for the forces of law and order to work out what the trust is really about – if they can identify it in the first place.

A fourth layer of secrecy, which does not only apply to trusts, involves the international protocols by which information is exchanged. Some countries simply refuse to exchange meaningful information with others, although this is becoming less common as a result of international pressure. Nevertheless, many generally agreed protocols such as the OECD's standards of 'exchange of information only on request' (as opposed to automatic, multilateral exchange of information) are pitifully weak, making it exceedingly hard to find out information even if you know what you are looking for (and frequently it is hard to know where to start looking in any case.) One such protocol is the Tax Information Exchange Agreements (TIEAs). An official Jersey website says, for example:

> *A high threshold therefore exists before the Jersey authorities will accede to a request under a TIEA. For example in the past year, there have been just four requests from the US under the terms of the TIEA. There is no automatic exchange of information under any circumstances and no 'fishing expeditions' for information. Strict confidentiality provisions in the agreement preclude any information being passed to third parties without the express written consent of the requested country.*

Not only that, but trusts constitute major loopholes in international treaties and arrangements. A good example is the European Savings Tax Directive, which applies to income on bank deposits, but not to income from trusts.[22] This may be amended.

A fifth layer of secrecy involves the many other offshore tricks that assist secrecy, though these are generally not exclusive to trusts and will not be discussed in detail here. These might include, for example, 'flight clauses' that require trustees and company administrators to transfer assets to a different jurisdiction at the first hint of investigation.

In a slightly different context, when somebody dies trusts are often used in place of wills, as a way of keeping financial affairs secret; wills must be filed in a probate court to be executed, meaning that they become public documents. Trusts can stay secret.

Where are trust assets actually located

This is important. If a trust is administered in one jurisdiction, the underlying assets may be located anywhere. If a newspaper somehow finds out about this trust, it may say 'a trust in Jersey' – but in fact although the trustees are in Jersey, the underlying asset will typically be held in London. In fact, Jersey serves as a conduit and a satellite of the City of London, sweeping up assets from around the world and parking them in London – even if the trust is supposedly located in Jersey.

How are trusts taxed?

Trust tax law is a complex area, and the principles vary according to the jurisdiction, so this blog only gives some basic notions.

In the UK, for example, trust tax is paid by the trustees (the legal owners of the trust property) out of trust funds. However, a trust beneficiary may also have to pay tax separately on the income they receive from a trust. (Sometimes inheritance or other taxes may also be paid upon the transfer of some property into trusts.) Yet trustees in Jersey, by contrast, do not pay Jersey income tax on certain common types of income, at least if the settlor and beneficiaries are resident elsewhere.

Adding to the complexity, trusts may or may not produce income. For example, an antique painting held in trust constitutes capital, but it will not produce any direct income, whereas $100,000 sitting in a bank will produce bank interest. The income, and the capital, may go to different beneficiaries, and different taxes may apply on the different elements: income tax, capital gains tax and so on – each of which may be taxed at different rates. The UK, for example, currently has an income tax rate and an inheritance tax rate of up to 40%, and 18% on capital gains. Jersey, by contrast, does not have capital gains tax or inheritance tax, and it has zero tax on certain common types of income. UK Revenue and Customs give some basic principles on its website.

How are trusts used to avoid and evade tax, in theory?

In summary, two main themes are involved.

First, because a trust creates a distinction between the legal owner, the trustee, and the beneficiary, this complicates the issue of how to tax the trust. This creates many avenues for both avoidance and evasion.

Second, because trusts create the potential for great secrecy, tax authorities cannot easily find the assets to tax them. This typically creates possibilities for tax evasion. Often the two themes: the legal distinction, and the secrecy, apply simultaneously.

In theory, once a settlor passes the assets into a trust, he or she no longer owns it, so cannot be taxed on its income. So a settlor should not be a beneficiary too. If a settlor could say in the deed of settlement: 'make all the assets available to me whenever I want them' then the tax authorities could judge them still to be the real owner of the asset – and tax them on the income. If the ownership were not really split, what would the point of a trust be? The property would be owned absolutely by one person, for own benefit.

However, as explained above, if the settlor is able to *pretend* to let go of the assets in order to escape a tax bill, while not having let go of them *in reality*, then he or she may be able to enjoy the income or other benefits of the asset without paying tax. The question of whether or not the settlor has really become separated from the assets can be a legal grey area, raising difficult questions over whether this is avoidance or evasion.

The U.S. IRS notes this, in a primer on trusts:

> *Abusive trust arrangements often use trusts to hide the true ownership of assets and income or to disguise the substance of transactions. Although these schemes give the appearance of separating responsibility and control from the benefits of ownership, as would be the case with legitimate trusts, the taxpayer in fact controls them.*

Games of smoke and mirrors can also be played between the trustee and the beneficiary. The discretionary trust is an example, below.

How are trusts used for tax avoidance and evasion, in practice?

A wide variety of other mechanisms are used to cut tax bills. Just a few examples are given below; new ones are being invented or modified all the time. One of the central mechanisms, as explained above, is for the settlor to enjoy benefits from an asset while pretending to have become entirely separated from them. (One might call this the 'settlor's pretence'.) Secrecy is often a counterpart of such schemes. Some of the world's finest legal minds spend their time dreaming up schemes using these kinds of principles – generally, the more complex ('sophisticated') they are, the harder it is for tax authorities or crime-fighters to penetrate.

Permissive or 'flexible' laws giving special powers to the settlor

Laws in secrecy jurisdictions in particular are set up with the intention of helping create the 'settlor's pretence'. As one Jersey commercial website puts it:

> *Jersey trusts are created and governed pursuant to the Trusts (Jersey) Law 1984, as amended. The 1984 Law is essentially a permissive law which provides, in effect, that the terms of the particular trust determine the duties and obligations of the trustee thereof.*

Note the word 'permissive' and the suggestion of how the flexibility of offshore arrangements can create trust products tailor-made for tax evasion. The U.S. Congressional Research Service describes another way of achieving the settlor's pretence:

> *Trusts may involve a trust protector who is an intermediary between the grantor (settlor) and the trustees, but whose purpose may actually be to carry out the desires of the grantor.*[23]

The Cayman Islands' Star trusts are even more stark versions of the settlor's pretence While Star trusts are used for many purposes, another commercial operator describes this possibility:

> *The settlor has the power to make the trust's investment decisions and the trustee is under no obligation to ensure the investments are in the interests of the beneficiaries.*

Other examples include:

Replacing the trustees

A trustee might, for example, appear to be independent from the settlor when the trust is set up, but then be replaced later by a more pliable trustee, or even by the settlor himself, in disguise, perhaps through another complex offshore secrecy arrangement involving trusts elsewhere.

Sham trusts

Jersey's sham trust is another example of the 'settlor's pretence'. Jersey Finance says this of its new laws introduced in 2006

> *Among the amendments is the introduction of settlor-reserved powers. . . the powers that may be reserved by the settlor will include the power to appoint and remove trustees, to amend or revoke the terms of the trust and to appoint or remove an investment manager or investment adviser*

Richard Murphy analyses what this means:

> *Jersey will now allow the creation of what can only be called 'sham trusts', although they're calling them trusts with 'reserved powers for the settlor'. What are those reserved powers? Well, the settlor can tell the trustee what to do, which means the trustee only has a nominee role. And the settlor can claim the property back . . . In other words, the settlor continues to have complete beneficial ownership of the asset and there is in fact no trust in existence at all, just a sham that suggests that there is. . . . This is a completely bogus transaction. I have no doubt that Jersey knew the new laws would facilitate tax evasion. Indeed, it is hard to see what other purpose they could have.*[24]

Belize, a 2008 US Senate report notes, offers something even more blatant:

> *In Belize you can be the grantor, the trustee, and the beneficiary, and have the trust considered valid.*

Revocable trusts

A more specific way to achieve the settlor's pretence is through a revocable trust (that is, the settlor could decide to revoke the trust and get their property back whenever they wanted.) In such a case, it is hard to see how the settlor has really let go of the asset if they can always get it back: trusts should in theory be irrevocable for the settlor to get the tax benefit. However, it can be hard for tax authorities to find this out or fight legal battles in support of a tax claim. Laws passed by Jersey in April 2006, for example, said that every single Jersey trust can now be revoked.[25]

Private Trust Companies

Another way to give the settlor more control is to appoint a Private Trust Company (PTC) as the trustee, then have the settlor (or perhaps a family member) be a director of the PTC, giving the settlor a significant degree of control. As one offshore promoter puts it:

> If you're familiar with the concept of an offshore trust but always had issue with handing over control of your assets to a third party you are not alone. Many people fear that the establishment of a trust really leaves them in too tenuous a position regarding the protection and management of their own assets ... which is why private offshore trust companies came into being. They give the settlor far greater asset control.

In the Cayman Islands, for example, it is extremely hard to find out who a company's directors are, so it can be hard to work out that the settlor has this measure of control.

Similarly, Jersey Finance says this:

> A PTC (Private Trust Company) can be established in Jersey on a fast track basis within 24 hours and other than providing the name of the PTC to the JFSC, there are no other regulatory hurdles to surmount. For the reasons set out above, PTCs have become increasingly popular with high net worth individuals . . . . PTCs

are also typically used to act as the trustee of family charitable or philanthropic trusts or where the assets to be held in trust are regarded as being of the sort which carry greater risk for a trustee than usual.

In other words, you only need to provide the name of the PTC to the authorities, but not the underlying information. Note the remark about risk, and ask what this means. Is it most likely to mean the risk of getting caught engaging in malfeasance?

Discretionary Trusts

A discretionary trust is one where the trustees can pay out income or capital to one or more of a group of beneficiaries, entirely at the trustees' discretion. This is not about the settlor's pretence. The beneficiaries have no right to demand income from a discretionary trust. Discretionary trusts can, for example, protect trust assets against the bankruptcy of a beneficiary: since a beneficiary has no claim to any specific part of the trust fund, none of it can be claimed by creditors in the event of the beneficiary's bankruptcy.

Yet from tax authorities' points of view these kinds of trusts have another crucial feature: because no single beneficiary can be said to have title to any trust assets prior to a distribution, there is no obvious taxable asset for tax authorities to be able to get a handle on. This makes it a powerful weapon in the tax-dodgers' arsenal.

Illustrating how difficult it is for tax authorities to tackle these trusts, the Society of Trust and Estate Planners (STEP) has said of efforts by the European Union to update its EU Savings Tax Directive to include discretionary trusts:

It would appear difficult to draft practicable trust-related amendments to the Savings Directive of the kind referred to in the Working Document which would be 'litigation-Proof'

The EU is likely to take a contrary view.

Other mechanisms for promoting tax evasion

Secrecy

The simplest is tax evasion through subterfuge: assets generating income and capital gains are parked in a secrecy jurisdiction where the owner's tax authorities are simply unaware of what is going on. This may be the commonest form of tax loss, though it is impossible to measure with any precision, and it is of course not only a problem for trusts.

Bogus expenses

Bogus expenses might be charged against income at one layer. After these expenses are deducted, the remaining income is distributed to another trust, and the process is repeated until, in many cases, the income falls to zero. Tax is eliminated from the trust income by distributing all that income to the beneficiary; and tax on the beneficiary is eliminated through the claiming of bogus expenses to set off against tax. This scenario is a criminal matter.

Complexity and jurisdiction shopping

If the trustee, the beneficiary, and the trust assets are located in the right combination of jurisdictions, tax can often be avoided altogether without technically breaking the law. This is not always a simple matter: a German resident, for example, should generally expect to pay tax on their income and capital gains, wherever in the world they are realised. But some countries create categories such as the non-domiciled residents: usually wealthy individuals who are absolved of the need to pay tax on their worldwide income. This creates opportunities to cut the tax bills through jurisdiction shopping, again without technically breaking the law, though this end need not be achieved through trusts.

A tax bill on a trustee can be made to fall upon a beneficiary, if so intended, perhaps because of where the trustee and beneficiary are located. So a trustee may distribute all the trust income to beneficiaries, then legally deduct these distributions from its taxable income, reducing its taxable income, and its taxes, to zero. If the trust is offshore, the tax rate on trust income may well be zero in any case. For example, the trustees of a Jersey trust are not liable to income tax on the income from trust assets where none of the beneficiaries is Jersey resident.

Complexity is a classic support for secrecy. For example, you might have a trust whose trustees are a Jersey law firm (but which is not registered), whose trust assets consist of shares in a company in Luxembourg which has nominee directors. The company might have a bank account in Liechtenstein, but the bank account might be managed by a Geneva private banker, which invests the funds in Hong Kong. Many structures are more complex than this – and a secrecy wall must be penetrated at every step.

As one former trustee put it:

You will not get any disclosure of who's behind them. There will be no register anywhere of who is the real owner, or who is the beneficiary. You will never find them for tax purposes – these are far more secretive than bank accounts under bank secrecy.

In the promotional literature, the euphemisms for 'complex' or 'complexity' being used to create secrecy are words like 'sophisticated' and 'sophistication.' These words should generally be taken as a red flag.

What else can trusts be used for, apart from tax evasion?

Trusts can be used in a number of legitimate ways. For example, they can be used for the genuine charitable transfer of assets; or to hold assets for minors and those unable to handle their financial affairs.

However, take a look at this list of other possible uses of a trust, from the Jersey Association of Trust Companies (JATCO): preservation of family property and protection against political risk; tax planning; avoidance of inheritance laws or probate formalities; employee benefit trusts and employee share option schemes; charitable trusts; purpose trusts; trading trusts; unit trusts; avoidance of exchange controls; ownership of special purpose vehicles.[26]

It is useful to unpack this list to understand its meaning. Note how many of these items refer to undermining the laws of other jurisdictions – that is, helping the wealthy (who can afford the fees) escape their responsibilities to the societies upon which they and their wealth depend.

Note 'avoidance of inheritance laws'. Is it right that a tax haven should get to decide whether wealthy individuals should be provided with facilities that enable them to escape the laws that normally affect the rest of us? Exactly the same could be said of 'avoidance of exchange controls'. Whatever one thinks of exchange controls, if, say, a democratic developing country's government decides it wants to impose certain types of controls to try and counteract massive capital flight by the wealthiest sections of society– is it right that tax havens should provide trust facilities to undermine that?

'Preservation of family property and protection against political risk.' This is a complex area. 'Preservation of family property' may well mean, in practice, 'protection from the tax authorities' or 'protection from creditors'. The latter often protects the proceeds of 'take the money and run' illegal activity that is a common feature of the international criminal underworld. 'Protection against political risk' is typically a euphemistic term for 'protection' against one's own government and particularly its tax authorities and/or other law enforcement bodies.

A trust provider in Jersey is more explicit:

A trust can provide for the transmission of wealth in a manner which may not be allowed, and to persons who may not be entitled, in some countries.

In a similar light, another company boasts of 'enhanced protection of Jersey trusts from adverse foreign court judgments.'

Jersey Finance adds this:

The validity of a trust governed by Jersey law will not be affected by any rights conferred on anyone under a foreign law.

In other words, 'we will help you get around the laws of the place where you live.'

What other mechanisms are used, apart from trusts?

Other common mechanisms are anstalts (establishments, used in Liechtenstein) and stiftungs (foundations) and various other types of corporate entity. These are outside the scope of this primer.

What countermeasures are taken?

Tax authorities in foreign countries routinely seek out, and take countermeasures against, abusive trust arrangements. Tax authorities try to determine the economic substance of a transaction, rather than take a purely legalistic view, and they can and do overrule what a taxpayer thought was a bullet-proof asset 'protection' mechanism.

The U.S. IRS, for example, would take a very dim view of a US taxpayer using a Jersey sham trust, and would not let the settlor get away with it, if discovered. Yet to do this the IRS must first find out that this is going on – the secrecy involved makes this hard, and Jersey will not volunteer this information.

If the well-resourced IRS has enough trouble keeping track of these criminal or questionable arrangements, how much hope is there for countries with less well resourced or skilled tax authorities?

Postscript 1: Confusingly, there are companies out there that call themselves 'trust companies' or 'trust services companies' which in reality are not directly related to the concept of the trust.[27]

Postscript 2: As the JATCO list above notes: one purpose of trusts can be 'ownership of special purpose vehicles (SPV)'. These kinds of bodies have been a central feature of the latest global economic crisis. Why are trusts often used for these arrangements?

Trusts split ownership. If a company puts its assets into a trust, for example, it can be treated as if it is so that it is no longer the beneficial owner of the assets, then it can be arranged so that the assets are no longer bound by the regulatory or tax requirements of the jurisdiction where it is incorporated. A trust arrangement might help a bank, say, shift assets off its balance sheet. As one analysis put it, 'the company (then) belongs to no-one'.

SPVs are not only set up for tax reasons but for other specific purposes (which is why they are called 'special purpose' vehicles – they may be used to ring-fence one part of a business, perhaps to prevent it from 'contaminating' (through, say, uncontrolled losses) another part of the business, or vice versa. A company may want to, say, invite investors into a particular project, but protect them from risks inherent in the parent company itself. The trusts involved are often known as 'purpose trusts' – which are neither charitable nor for obvious beneficiaries, but for a special purpose.

Quite often, charitable trusts are involved. A famous example was in the case of the failed British bank Northern Rock, which was discovered to have a charity for children with Down's Syndrome – with the charity unlikely ever to receive a penny from the arrangement, and even unaware that it was the beneficiary. The charity said:

> *We are investigating why our charity appears to have been named as a beneficiary of a Trust without our consent.*

Why did Northern Rock do this? Because trusts need beneficiaries – although because of the way it was set up there was no real need to pay any money to beneficiaries: all the important business was between settlors and trustees. As one commercial analysis put it:

> *A trust must have an identifiable beneficiary to exist and, for that reason, nearly all trusts include a long stop charity as a beneficiary in case all of the named beneficiaries should die. To use a trust for commercial purposes it is therefore necessary to employ a charitable trust whose real purpose is commercial.*

While trusts have sometimes been used as special purpose vehicles themselves, often the SPV is an 'orphan' company whose equity share capital is held by the trustees of a general charitable or purpose trust.

July, 2009

The Social Injustice of Corporate Tax Avoidance

Martin O'Neill[28]

Corporate tax avoidance is one of the most pressing manifestations of social injustice seen in contemporary liberal democracies: it undermines the democratic character of our societies, while unfairly transferring resources from the needy to the wealthy. Appreciating the conventional nature of the corporate form should lead us to insist that corporations really earn their 'social license to operate', and one of the most significant ways in which they can do so is by paying their fair share of tax.

When thinking about the injustice of corporate tax avoidance, the most important single thought to keep in mind is that there is nothing 'natural' or unavoidable about the particular structure of that now-ubiquitous economic institution, the limited-liability corporation. These institutions, with their particular legal structure and privileges, are a product of a particular set of historical circumstances, and their ongoing existence and regulation should be a matter for collective democratic deliberation. In the past corporations, such as the East India Company or the South Sea Company, were chartered for a limited time, and for the performance of some particular public good. Initially there was much suspicion about the idea of a limited liability company. After the 'South Sea Bubble', which saw the collapse of the British South Sea Company's share price in 1720, joint stock companies were banned in the UK by the 1720 South Sea Bubble Act. General purpose joint-stock limited-liability companies are a surprisingly recent invention, dating in the UK from the 1862 Companies Act (as commemorated in Gilbert & Sullivan's *Utopia Limited* of 1863).

It is significant to note that the corporation, in its modern form, is granted certain significant privileges: firstly, the privilege of limited liability, whereby corporate investors are not held liable for losses beyond the value of their investments; and, secondly, the privilege of corporate legal 'personality', whereby the corporation is treated as an 'artificial person', legally distinct from its owners and managers, and with its own legal rights and entitlements. As a society, we collectively have no reason to grant these kinds of privileges if it is not for a concomitant public benefit. A straightforward conception of reciprocity suggests that, as we have granted these organizations the benefit of being treated as self-contained legal entities, so we can demand some social good back from them in return. Moreover, the benefit provided by corporations needs to be sufficiently substantial, such that we are able to justify these arrangements to the members of society who are affected by them.

There is a conventionality to the corporate form, just as there is a conventionality to the distribution of property under any particular system of taxation and property rights. There is, indeed, an analogy between these two kinds of convention, and between the ways in which each convention has become so deeply entrenched that it can create certain kinds of distortions in our political thinking. As political philosophers Thomas Nagel and Liam Murphy put it, in the case of the strength of people's intuition that they have some right of ownership of their pre-tax income: 'Most conventions, if they are sufficiently entrenched, acquire the appearance of natural norms; their conventionality becomes invisible. That is part of what gives them their strength, a strength they would lack if they were not internalized in that way.'[29] Thus, argue Murphy and Nagel, it may seem natural to appeal to property rights when arguing about rules of taxation *even though* property rights are the result of a general system of legal and political rules, which include the rules of taxation. But, even though it may seem *natural* to argue in this way, it involves a deep confusion. For, if actually-existing property rights are constructed by the legal rules of property, including the rules of taxation, then one is making an error of reasoning in appealing to property rights in order to justify specific kinds of changes in, say, taxation rules. As Nagel and Murphy, put it: 'To appeal to the consequences of a convention or social institution as a fact of nature which provides the justification for that convention of justification is always to argue in a circle. One can neither criticize nor justify an economic regime by taking as an independent norm something that is, in fact, one of its consequences.'[30] So, similarly, an error of circular reasoning is made whenever one hears an appeal to corporate rights, or to the entitlements of corporations considered as legal persons, with regard to questions of how we should regulate or tax those corporations.

Murphy and Nagel's treatment of the power of convention is with regard to the conventionality of property entitlements in general: "Private property is a legal convention, defined in part by the tax system; therefore, the tax system cannot be evaluated by looking at its impact on private property, conceived as something that has independent existence and validity."[31] If one believes in the conventionality of both the distribution of property within a society, and of the corporate form itself, then there is a kind of *double conventionality* with regard to corporate property rights. Corporations, rather than being holder of *ex ante* entitlements, therefore instead need to earn their 'social license to operate'. One important way in which they can do this is if they can be placed in a regulatory framework, and taxed in such a way, that they are conducive towards the pursuit of social justice, rather than inimical to such goals. If particular corporations cannot demonstrate that they meet such a standard, then we have no reason to grant them their 'social license to operate'; and we would be infringing no *ex ante* rights or entitlements if we outlawed any forms of corporate activity that created substantial barriers to the attainment of social justice, or other shared democratic goals.

With this general framework for thinking about corporations, property rights and taxation now in place, we can now turn to deal directly with the injustice of corporate tax avoidance itself.

Across the world, governments have found it more and more difficult to tax corporations, and so the tax burden has instead fallen squarely and heavily onto the shoulders of individuals. Making sense of how and why this has happened is fairly straightforward. With the emergence of industrial capitalism in the late 19th and early 20th centuries, governments in the developed world realized a balance had to be struck between the demands of the market and the demands of the broader society in which markets were located. This realization came sooner in some places – as with Bismarck's development of the welfare state in Germany in the 1880s. In Britain, the process of taming the market started perhaps a little later, beginning with Lloyd George's radical reforms as Chancellor in the early years of the previous century, and reaching its zenith in the post-war settlement created by the Attlee Government of 1945-51.

What marked out this earlier stage of the relationship between markets and societies was that it all happened under the roof of one particular state. A balance could be struck, therefore, between the demands of economic growth and of social protection, because the nation state was in a powerful position to impose whatever regulation it saw as necessary on corporations. Now globalisation has shattered that balance. Capital can move jurisdiction at will. The mechanisms of taxation and regulation that can be used by the state have grown useless and atrophied. States cannot set the terms of operation for corporations that are free to relocate to more benign host countries. The balance of power has slipped from democratic governments to globally mobile corporations, with states reduced to adopting beggar-my-neighbour policies of tax competition.

It is unsurprising, given this reallocation of political power, that the benefits of the world economy accrue increasingly to the owners of capital rather than to the providers of labour, and that the tax burden in countries like the UK falls disproportionately on individuals rather than corporations.

How do these companies manage to pay so little tax? Well, primarily, through the operation of mechanisms of 'transfer pricing', whereby semi-imaginary deals between different subsidiaries of the same company are used to move profits from one jurisdiction to another. Corporations are also able to use tax haven jurisdictions, so that, for example, UK banana sellers are able to make use of webs of transactions of such byzantine complexity that, on its way from Latin America to our supermarket shelves, a bunch of bananas will have passed through virtual balance sheets in the Isle of Man, Ireland, Bermuda, Jersey and the Cayman Islands. The combination of tax havens and transfer pricing allows large multinational corporations to set their tax rates more or less at will.

As things stand, of course, none of this is actually illegal. Traditionally, the distinction has been drawn between tax evasion, which is the illegal activity of evading one's full tax liabilities, and tax avoidance, which is the legal activity of arranging one's affairs, within the letter of the law, so as to minimize one's tax exposure. Unsurprisingly, it is hard to hold a clear line between the two, and many schemes of tax avoidance shade over towards the borders of tax evasion. Indeed, some writers on tax have coined the term 'avoision' to refer to those schemes which fall somewhere in the disputed borderlands between tax avoidance and tax evasion. Clearly, large corporations are concerned to avoid downright illegality, and so tend not to practice tax evasion. But they are very concerned to minimize their tax exposure, and so practices of tax avoidance are extremely widespread.

Despite its technical legality, tax avoidance is an extremely troubling business, especially when practiced on the scale that it is practiced by large corporations. Insofar as we are concerned to create just, democratic societies, the question of how tax avoidance might be addressed and curtailed is an extremely important one. Some of the problems with practices of tax avoidance are these:

(a) Tax avoidance is deeply anti-democratic. It frustrates the legislative intentions embodied in tax legislation, in favour of allowing the distribution of ownership in the economy to be determined by the machinations of tax avoiders themselves.

(b) Tax avoidance ignores the principle of reciprocity discussed above. If the privileges of limited liability incorporation are to be balanced by corporate responsibilities to society, then the very minimum of meeting those responsibilities should be meeting the full expectation of a corporation's tax contribution. Tax avoidance thereby oversteps the legitimate freedom of movement of corporations in a democratic society. It makes corporate tax avoiders fail in living up to their side of the social contract.

(c) Tax avoidance destabilizes the fair division of responsibility between the state and the corporation. Corporations earn their "social license to operate" insofar as they contribute to the general good of the societies in which they exist, and facilitate rather than frustrating the achievement of social justice. They do this when, as well as contributing broadly to a society's economic prosperity, they also contribute directly towards the achievement of social justice through providing revenue to the state that can be used to pursue valuable social policies. A corporation that shirks its minimal commitment to uphold "the basic rules of society", including its taxation rules, frustrates the agencies of the state in performing the functions which hold up the state's side of the division of moral labour. It thereby undermines the conditions of background justice which would otherwise legitimize the corporation as existing as a purely profit-seeking entity within a regulated market.

So, it is clear how corporations get away with tax avoidance, and it is straightforward to explain what is wrong with their doing so, especially when one considers the fundamental nature of the relationship between corporations and states. What is much more difficult is to understand how this situation can be changed. Once markets are global, the individual state has little room for manoeuvre in its efforts to grab social value from internationally mobile capital, Indeed, it would seem that tax avoidance is the inevitable result of a co-ordination problem among competing firms. If your competitor is avoiding tax, then you will have to do so as well, if you are not to suffer a sizeable commercial disadvantage by comparison. Moreover, tax avoidance is incredibly wasteful: it consumes the efforts of thousands of high-energy, talented, imaginative people; and it does so for a destructive social end.

If tax avoidance could be structurally outlawed, then the enormous energy and imagination that goes into pursuing it could be redeployed to more genuinely productive occupations, and directed towards technical and managerial innovation, instead of just 'cooking the books'. There is, then, something of a Prisoner's Dilemma in operation. We would all be better off if this practice of tax avoidance could be eliminated, but it is individually rational for each corporation to engage in such practices. The questions to be faced, therefore, are why it might be that such practices are currently legally permissible, and how we might bring it about that such practices could be stopped.

This is one of the most pressing political issues of our day. How can we re-empower our collective institutions, given their powerlessness in the face of globally mobile capital?

When society and the market are no longer 'under one roof' these sorts of problems emerge. There are two broad ways in which they could be brought back under the same roof. One is a retrograde policy of closed-borders and protectionism, which would attempt to re-localize markets. This approach is likely to throw away the material gains of globalization while trying to solve problems of capital mobility.

The forward-looking approach is instead to look for transnational regulatory mechanisms, operating at the EU level (in the first instance) or eventually perhaps even at a global level. Through this approach, we might hope to keep the material benefits of globalization, whilst rebalancing the relationship between corporate power and the power of democratic governments and our collective institutions. Politicians of all parties should be addressing this agenda with much more energy than we have seen.

Moreover, shifting the tax burden away from individual income from work, and towards the owners of capital, is a policy that could be highly popular, and surprisingly easy to sell. People could be brought around to an agenda of clamping down on corporate tax avoidance if they were told that it meant that they could pay less personal tax, if only corporate scroungers and tax-cheats paid their fair share.

In the long run, we need a better global fiscal architecture. In the shorter term, a raft of specific policies could be pursued, hopefully in co-operation with other states. Firstly, we need better public information. Companies should be required by law to publish in full their tax payments in every jurisdiction in which they operate, so that individual citizens and voters can see whether those companies are good corporate citizens or scrounging cheats. Secondly, we need to clamp down on tax havens, especially those in our own back yard, like Jersey and the Isle of Man. If need be, consideration should be given to refusing legal recognition to corporate entities based in tax havens. Thirdly, we need to move towards international accounting practices that rule out the most shameless examples of financial hocus-pocus, such as the worst abuses of transfer pricing.

Moreover, we need to clamp down very hard indeed on accounting firms that market the more exotic forms of tax avoidance schemes, by subjecting them to much tougher regulatory legislation. (If a softer approach does not work, then perhaps we should consider legislative measures that could lead to a few senior accounting partners being banged-up for a few years, *pour encourager les autres*.)

Most of all, democratic states need to take the power back before it's too late. What this will involve is the reorientation of tax laws so that they take more account of where real economic activity takes place, rather than being too bamboozled by the formal paper structures of imaginary subsidiaries and dubious holding companies.

More aggressive regulation, pursued at a European level, could provide more government income whilst reducing individual income tax burdens. Best of all, perhaps, all those clever and ingenious corporate accountants who spend their working days devising ever more complex ways of defrauding their fellow citizens could instead expend all that ingenuity and intelligence on doing something more productive instead.

January, 2010

The Eye of the Needle

John Pugh

'Render unto Caesar that which is Caesar's' is one of the better known New Testament sayings. I take it as tacit support from Jesus for the Inland Revenue and prompt tax payment. The follow on – 'render to God what is God's' – cements the division between the sacred and the secular.

The message? That bothering unduly about the legitimacy of tax is a distraction from higher purposes. It does not, however, imply that paying tax itself could be a contribution to a higher purpose. Nor does it recognise that withholding tax could frustrate plans for morally questionable expenditure (government spending on armaments, say). Thus Jesus' side-stepping of the issue leaves the crux of the Pharisee's question about whether to pay Roman taxes largely unaddressed.

Thereafter, however, the churches have tended to regard taxes for godly purposes – such as supporting the church – as thoroughly justified, whilst taking a fairly agnostic position on the obligatoriness of secular state tax. Even if the level of tax was democratically fixed it was not axiomatic that it should never be evaded or avoided. After all, even the democratic majority can potentially have a sinful, or at any rate a mere worldly, purpose. Thus in Italy – where elements of the Catholic hierarchy have long voiced misgivings about liberal democracy – it has not been unknown for clerics to take a 'relaxed' view of their tax affairs.

Yet moral outrage at tax avoidance and tax evasion stems, in essence, from a feeling that its motives are venial, selfish, acquisitive and stimulated by the desire of an individual or institution to dodge their fair share of a social burden. Or still worse, to profit from social benefits that others in society – often themselves less well resourced – have to fund, whilst free-riding on that contribution. And a greedy free-rider is not a figure Christian ethics supports.

However, someone who questions the legitimacy, purposes

or efficacy of tax, and acts accordingly, is not always so easily or appropriately demonised. Those who overtly resisted paying Charles I's taxes, or later in America those imposed by George III, for many still hold an honoured place in history, and it is not simply due to their resistance taking a very overt fashion, with spectacular consequences. Neither *vox regis* nor *vox populi* counts as *vox dei*. Refusing to pay tax is not always regarded with moral disdain by those with a Christian ethic.

A faith perspective, however, does not resultantly license a judicious moral agnosticism on the issue – if only because it in essence requires a sincere and continuous self evaluation of one's mortal journey. Although there are differing intellectual and moral takes on tax, one is not spared the task of explaining what, as an individual, one thinks one is up to when one nails the brass plate to the door of an accommodation address in the Cayman Islands. If the answer is that one is seeking venial advantage and to escape social responsibility – and let's be honest, it usually is – clever defences are mere masking rhetoric. Hypocrisy and the avoidance of moral insight compound the evil, they do not dispel it.

The vast bulk of those who busy themselves, either in a corporate or an individual capacity, with the construction and utilisation of schemes to avoid or evade tax fail to provide an account of their activities which is both coherent and commendable within a faith perspective. Oddly enough it is only by illogically keeping at arm's-length the sacred and the secular in one's personal life that the veniality and deception that characterises tax avoidance and evasion can co-exist with a faith perspective. One cannot serve God and Mammon – but many try.

January, 2010

Land Value Tax: A Tool for Economic Development

Nicolaus Tideman

A land value tax is a periodic tax (monthly or yearly) on those who have title to land, levied in proportion to the value that the land would have if it were not improved. A land value tax reflects the value that is added to land by public improvements such as streets, water service, sewers, parks, etc., but not the value of structures, fences, grading, draining or other improvements to an individual parcel of land.

Land value taxation promotes economic development in at least six different ways. First, land value taxation serves as a regular reminder to those who have title to land that they are not using, that they have something of value that could be put to use. Land is often in the hands of people who have other concerns and prefer not to think about what might be done with their land. A regularly recurring tax bill reminds people that they have something of this and if they have no use for their land themselves, they could save on their taxes by transferring the land to someone else. By putting land in the hands of people who will use it, such transfers of land promote economic development.

Second, land value taxation provides revenue for governments, permitting them to reduce taxes that have harmful effects on economic development. Taxes on wages discourage people from working. Taxes on saving or investments discourage people from saving and investing. Sales taxes and value added taxes discourage productive activity generally. But a tax on land values does not discourage any productive activity. Thus any substitution of a tax on land value for a tax on wages, incomes, savings, sales or value added will increase the efficiency of an economy and promote economic development.

Third, land value taxation reduces the profit from land speculation. Land speculators leave land unused because they think its value will rise rapidly, so it should not be improved now. These expectations of speculators are often disappointed. Valuable land in the centres of cities is often left unused or very poorly used for generations. The inefficient decisions of land speculators to not develop land mean that economies must contend with artificial scarcities of land. When a tax on land value is implemented or increased, the potential profit from land speculation falls. Regular tax bills limit the capacity of speculators to speculate. As a result, less land remains in the hand of speculators and more land goes into the hands of those who wish to use it. With more land in the hands of those who wish to use it, economic development improves.

Fourth, land value taxation provides a special benefit to those who have limited access to capital, and in the process it promotes economic development. Other things being equal, when the tax rate applied to land value is increased, people who might want to buy land will reduce their offers according to the present discounted value of the increase in taxes. But every potential investor will use his own interest rate in determining the amount by which to lower his or her offering price in response to an increase in the rate of a land value tax. Those who have high discount rates will have lower present discounted values for future taxes, and will therefore have smaller reductions in the prices that they will offer for land, compared to those who face low interest rates and therefore have high present discounted values for future taxes. Thus a tax on land value will tend to move land from those who have low discount rates to those who have high discount rates. And those who have high discount rates (those with limited access to capital) tend to get returns on their assets that reflect those discount rates. Thus land value taxation puts land in the hands of those who do more with it, thereby promoting economic development.

Fifth, land value taxation has a particular capacity to finance infrastructure improvements such as road paving, bridges, water lines, and sewers. An infrastructure improvement is worthwhile if its benefits are greater than its costs. Because of the mobility of labour and capital and the fact that benefits of infrastructure tend to be limited to the vicinity of the infrastructure, the benefits of infrastructure tend to be reflected in increases in the rental value of the land in the vicinity of the infrastructure. This means that financing infrastructure by a tax on the land in the vicinity of the infrastructure has three important benefits.

1. When infrastructure is financed by taxes on land there is no dead-

weight loss from the taxes as there would be with most other sources of financing.

2. When infrastructure is financed by a tax on land in the vicinity of the infrastructure, assessed so as to reflect the increase in the value of the land that is caused by the infrastructure, no one is harmed by the decision to produce the infrastructure. Everyone is a net beneficiary. Even if the tax cannot be assessed so perfectly that no one is harmed, the effort to assess the costs according to the benefits to owners of land greatly reduces the extent to which net harm to individuals is caused by the taxes that finance infrastructure.

3. By financing infrastructure through taxes on those who will benefit from the infrastructure, land taxes avoid the problem of efforts by beneficiaries to persuade governments to provide infrastructure that is not actually worthwhile. When the beneficiaries are the ones who will pay for infrastructure, they have an incentive to push the government to provide the infrastructure only when it actually is worthwhile.

The sixth way that land value taxation promotes economic development is by generating confidence in governments. Economic development is often financed by foreign investment, and foreign investors ask themselves, before investing, how confident they can be that they will not lose their investments as a result of confiscatory taxes or regulations. Potential domestic investors will also ask themselves whether, considering the risk of confiscatory government action, they would achieve higher expected returns with investments abroad than with domestic investments.

There may be no way that a government can provide an absolute assurance that no future government will confiscate investments, but a government can provide evidence of responsible planning for a future that does not require confiscating investments. By collecting the rent of land and using it for public purposes, a government can provide a signal that it plans to provide for its future revenue needs without having to confiscate the capital that investors bring to the country. Thus in this way too, a tax on land value promotes economic development.

June, 2010

Harnessing Land Value as a Green Tax

Molly Scott Cato

The sense of vertigo you experience when trying to understand how financial alchemists have created so much meaningless monetary value out of thin air is an indication of the dislocation that financialisation has brought to the world economy. One reason why the regulators did not do their job was that the process of debt creation was alienating: it was technical and abstract and human minds are repelled by such stuff.

Ever since value slipped its attachment to the natural world – around the time the technique of fractional reserve banking was invented in the 17th century – money has become increasingly important and the planet and its resources less so. The early economic theorists – who called themselves Physiocrats – stated in their name their view that the land was the source of all value. But they were defeated by the mercantilists and then by classical economists, who argued that trade was what really mattered: it was trade that enabled the accumulation of money. Since that time economists have not been able to distinguish between money, wealth and value.

To find solutions to the financial crisis, as well as the environmental crisis, we need to get our feet back on the ground.

Whose Land is it Anyway?

From the perspective of a green economist, land is the primary source of all value; the nature of its allocation is therefore an issue of great political salience. This raises critical questions concerning the legal origin of a right to own land. In indigenous societies it would be considered blasphemous to make such a claim and even the notoriously legalistic Roman Empire had a law of usufruct that established the right of local people to make use of land if the landowner was not doing so. How many farmers who live from grants

159

and subsidies would be able to justify their right to continued use of their land under such a legal stricture?

Behind these laws and customs lies the fundamental understanding within human communities of the inevitability of land as a common resource – how could something so fundamental to survival pass in perpetuity into the hands of a minority? The history of the alienation of peasants from their land during the Enclosures in England is well known although, unlike the Highland Clearances, it is not burnished with the same continuing sense of injustice. It should be. Because the lowland clearances that removed subsistence farmers from their livelihood opened the way for over-exploitation and species holocaust. Neeson (1989) even argues that the disruption of this ancient way of life led to the population explosion that caused such distress to Malthus and the economists who followed his path.

It is interesting that this year's Swedish Bank Prize (in spite of attempts by the economics profession to delude us to the contrary it is not a Nobel Prize) was given to a woman who is not an economist and has spent her life studying systems of allocation by commons. Elinor Ostrom's citation – 'for her analysis of economic governance, especially the commons' – might be a hint that even in the higher realms of what Hazel Henderson called the snake-oil priesthood there are uneasy feelings that the private-property free-for-all may have gone a little too far.

The horrifying levels of inequality that have resulted from 30 years of neoliberalism have pushed the issue of redistribution up the political agenda. But the failure of the redistributive measures, despite their vast expense, to solve the problem of persistent poverty makes clear the inefficiency of solutions that rely on redistribution rather than the predistribution that green economists have long been arguing for. Land redistribution is one such means of predistribution, but introducing a tax on those who currently own land so that the value they derive from it could be fairly shared is another. From a radical perspective, land is a common source of wealth for the inhabitants of a nation, and should therefore be shared fairly between them. Taxing owners of land and distributing the receipts to those who do not own would be a crucial aspect of predistribution.

Land in a Sustainable Economy

These are not new arguments but what gives them added salience is the limit and pressure for change exerted by climate change. No longer can we rely on the production of food and its transport across the globe to feed our families. Climate change brings irregular harvests and rising food prices; it limits the amount of carbon we can waste in pointless food swaps; and it undermines the security of the infrastructure that a global food market relies on. No wonder that food security is the political issue of the moment.

As food becomes scarcer and more expensive the exclusive ownership of land becomes an increasingly indefensible privilege. Unless we find a way of treating the world's productive land as a common good the 21st century is going to degenerate into an era of food and other resource wars. This is why the virtual money that was created in the casino economy during the bubble was invested in land before it burst. The buying up of huge tracts of land in the poorer countries of the world that has become known as 'the great land grab' illustrates how, although the money was created by a computer, its power in the world is real.

Green economists argue for an economy that is just and sustainable, but such a world is not attainable without a reallocation, occupation or requisitioning of land. At the policy level we might suggest the immediate introduction of a Land Value Tax, which would require those currently in ownership of land to pay for this privilege. The value of land ownership could then be shared between the people of each nation or region – a policy response to Gerard Winstanley's definition of land as 'a common treasury'. Far from Hardin's empirically ungrounded critique of commons (1968), Neeson's account demonstrates how the best means of protecting a resource is to reconnect use-rights with shared ownership rights, backed up by a system of local social control. Being dependent on a resource emerges as a better protection than legalistic property rights.

It is money that has got us into this mess. The abstract nature of money has facilitated our dislocation and disembedding from the planet so that we can get more excited about an iPad than a squirrel or our own best friend. And it is the growth logic that is inherent in the way money is created under capitalism that is driving the planet to destruction.

So three steps to Green heaven? First, replace money with land as the source of true value. Second, challenge the right of those currently in ownership to enjoy that privilege when it is so socially and environmentally destructive. And third, argue with renewed vigour for the immediate introduction of the taxation of land value as the central source of national revenue.

June, 2010

A Tale of Two Cities

Josh Vincent

LVT is used most extensively in the state of Pennsylvania. Indeed, the first tax in Pennsylvania in 1693 was a land tax.

Harrisburg

Harrisburg first employed LVT in 1975 to battle the twin disasters of nature (Hurricane Agnes) and humanity (land speculators). After the storm had wiped out much of the downtown and industrial sector, speculators quickly snatched up land and held it for future gain. At the time Mayor Arthur Swenson reasoned that LVT would both promote construction through the tax relief afforded buildings and provide an incentive to use vacant land.

Recent long-time Mayor Stephen R. Reed and other City administrators credit Harrisburg's use of LVT as a key initiative in promoting the revitalisation of their City. LVT encourages the highest and best use of land and rewards those who properly maintain or invest in buildings.

One of the effects of LVT is to benefit the lower-income homeowner and small business owner to keep and maintain their homes and businesses. It also has the residual effect of keeping rents lower than they would otherwise be. It rewards productivity and investment, in contrast to a flat rating tax rate system that penalises both.

Once considered the second most distressed cities in the nation, Harrisburg, since 1982, has sustained economic resurgence that has garnered national acclaim. Mayor Reed was voted 'US Mayor of the Year' in 2006.

In 2002 the City issued 1,567 building permits. They represent a total of \$269.7 million in new investment, the highest total for any year in the City's history. Even in the face of the recession, in 2008, 1,623 building permits were issued with a value of \$90.2 Million.

Since 1982 Harrisburg has issued a total of about 30,000 building permits reflective of $3.2 billion in new investment. In 1982 the total assessed value of taxable real estate in Harrisburg was $212 million. In 2007, it was over $1.8 billion, which is reflective of the additions to the tax rolls from new investment.

By the end of 2007, the number of businesses on the City's tax rolls had risen to 5,278 – the highest number ever recorded. This is in sharp contrast to the number that existed in 1985: 1,908.

Harrisburg is the only municipality in Central Pennsylvania to subsidise the area's transit system. Harrisburg received the "Distinguished Budget Presentation Award" from the Government Finance Officers' Association, and was awarded the "Certificate of Achievement for Excellence in Financial Reporting" by GFOA.

These results are impressive when one considers the fact that 45 percent of the land in Harrisburg cannot be taxed because it is state, county, or non-profit real estate.

Administrative costs to implement the two-tiered tax system were minimal. The appearance of the bills and an explanation of the change to a two-tiered tax system were the only administrative changes that took place. The current ratio of land to buildings is 6:1.

A current city fiscal crisis brought on by the failure of an independent authority has brought Harrisburg back into the news recently. Current Mayor Linda Thompson will resort to land value taxation to close a huge hole caused by the default of this authority's debt, which can't be paid; legally the city and county then must step in to pay off the bonds. LVT may again be called upon to provide revenue stability and a modicum of local control over its economic destiny.

Pittsburgh

The story of Pittsburgh and LVT goes back a long way. Implemented in 1911 by an act of the state legislature, the growth and low tax atmosphere of Pittsburgh during those early years and especially during the expansion of LVT in the late 1970s was remarkable. Research in the mid-1990s concluded:

> *The basic data are clear on certain things. Following the change in regimes at the end of the 1970s, Pittsburgh experienced a striking*

building boom, far in excess of anything that took place in the other major cities in the region. The building boom was basically a city phenomenon; it did not extend to the rest of the metropolitan area. It was, moreover, a boom primarily in commercial building activity.

The residential sector experienced only a modest increase in new construction (although even this is noteworthy in the context of the nationally depressed housing markets of the early 1980s). The central thrust took the form of several major new office buildings in the Central Business District in response to a marked shortage in office space that characterised the transformation of the Pittsburgh economic base from its earlier heavy manufacturing orientation to a more diversified, service-oriented economy."[32]

How to measure the success of LVT in Pittsburgh? It is accepted by most urban development experts that tracking the dollar value of building permits is the place to start. The Oates and Schwab numbers are impressive: Splitting 15 "Rust Belt" cities into two time frames (1960-1979 and 1980- 1989), the rapid decline in construction was notable in its severity. These time frames are important since they mirror the period from relative industrial health to a near total collapse of traditional heavy industry in the region. Yet, Pittsburgh surged against its analogs: only Columbus, Ohio registered a gain, and that was due to annexation of land outside the city.

Pittsburgh rescinded LVT in 2001. Why? In the midst of a botched property valuation, there was a bitter mayoral primary campaign. Wealthy areas were struck by inaccurate assessments. Rather than strike at the root problem, the challenger called LVT the enemy, not acknowledging that largely working-class communities would pay higher tax if LVT were lost. He claimed that the downtown buildings crowded into Pittsburgh in the last 30 years would pay more without LVT (true), although Pittsburgh's traditionally business-friendly LVT kept rents low for tenants and productive businesses. "Economic development" is reserved for deep-pocket speculators who refuse to do anything without tax abatements and givebacks shouldered by the poor and middle class homeowners.

What happened to Pittsburgh after it lost LVT?

The Center for the Study of Economics and Dr. Steven Cord looked at building permit issuance after rescission. Pittsburgh's private new construction (now more taxed) declined 19.57% (inflation-adjusted) in the three years after rescission as compared to the three years before, while the value of construction nationwide increased 7.7% (also inflation-adjusted).

An analysis of the Pittsburgh assessment data found that rescission caused 54% of all homeowners to pay more property tax and 70% of poorer homeowners. As for non-landowning tenants (office tenants also), eventually they all paid more space-rent because more building tax was passed on to them but the land value tax never can be.

Since that time, vacancy rates in Pittsburgh have been higher than the suburbs and the city has flirted with insolvency with no end in sight.

June, 2010

PUBLICATIONS, 2011-2012

Didn't They Notice?

David Runciman[33]

How to sum up Saif al-Islam Gaddafi, that emblematic figure of our times, with his doctorate from the LSE ('The Role of Civil Society in the Democratisation of Global Governance Institutions'), his charitable foundations, his extensive property portfolio, his playboy lifestyle, his motley collection of friends (Peter Mandelson, Nat Rothschild, Prince Andrew), his ready access to Libya's sovereign wealth fund, and his recently professed willingness to eliminate the enemies of his father's regime one bullet at a time? He's a hypocrite, of course, but that hardly does him justice (who isn't?). He is also, on some accounts, a victim: his unfortunate mentor at the LSE, David Held, has described the predicament the ostensibly reform-minded Saif found himself in after his father's people had revolted as 'the stuff of Shakespeare', but that surely is letting everyone concerned off far too lightly. He may just be a smooth-talking thug, and many online observers have noted that he seems to model himself on the smooth-talking thug and would-be businessman Stringer Bell from *The Wire*. But the word that best captures Saif Gaddafi comes from Nicholas Shaxson's blistering account of the role that tax havens play in international finance. Shaxson doesn't discuss the Gaddafis themselves, but he does paint a picture of the world in which the young Gaddafi, until very recently, felt right at home. This is the world of 'offshore'. Shaxson doesn't limit the term to its technical meaning, as a simple description of the particular jurisdictions that enable people to eliminate their tax bills. He applies it to people as well as places, and to a way of life along with a state of mind. Seen like this, it turns out to be a very useful word. Saif Gaddafi is just an offshore guy, living in an offshore world.

The essence of offshore is the need to keep up a solid appearance of respectability, while allowing money in and out with as little fuss as possible. Tax avoidance (unlike tax evasion) is not a clandestine activity, and tax havens don't exist just to enable people to squirrel their money away from the authorities. The money needs to be accessible, and it needs to be liquid. For that reason, people prefer tax havens where they can conduct their business relatively openly, and the most successful offshore jurisdictions are the ones that ask no questions but also tell no lies. Shaxson's memorable phrase for this is 'theatre of probity'. The Swiss have always been the masters, with their formal manners and careful paperwork. But it turns out that the other champions of this way of doing business are the British. Shaxson's book explains how and why London became the centre of what he calls a 'spider's web' of offshore activities (and in the process such a comfortable home for the likes of Saif Gaddafi). It is because offshore is the offshoot of an empire in decline. It perfectly suited a country with the appearance of grandeur and traditionally high standards, but underneath it all a reek of desperation and the pressing need for more cash.

As Shaxson shows, many of the world's most successful tax havens are former or current British imperial outposts. These include Hong Kong, the Channel Islands and remaining overseas territories like the Cayman Islands. What such places offer are limited or non-existent tax regimes, extremely lax regulation, weak local politics, but plenty of the trappings of respectability and democratic accountability. Depositors are happiest putting their money in locations that have the feel of a major jurisdiction like Britain without actually being subject to British rules and regulations (or British tax rates). The Caymans, or Jersey, make full use of their British connections to reassure people that their money is safe (the Cayman national anthem is still 'God Save the Queen'), but when anyone complains to the authorities back in London that these places are being used by criminals and dictators to launder their assets, they are told that it is no longer Britain's role to tell its dependencies how to run their own affairs. It was a function Hong Kong fulfilled before its handover to China in 1997: it could be presented to the outside world as somewhere with British values but without its unfortunate tendency to raise either taxes or regulatory standards in response to political pressure. Strikingly, it plays the same role for China today. After 1997 China preserved Hong Kong as a 'special administrative zone' autonomous of the mainland in all matters except foreign relations and defence. As Shaxson puts it, 'The resemblance with the ambiguous Britain-Jersey link, or the Britain-Cayman arrangement, is no coincidence. Chinese elites want their own offshore centre, complete with political control and judicial separation.' So offshore suits empires on the rise as well.

The other thing most of these places have in common is that they are islands. Islands make good tax havens, and not simply because they can cut themselves off from the demands of mainland politics. It is also because they are often tight-knit communities, in which everyone knows what's going on but no one wants to speak out for fear of ostracism. These 'goldfish bowls', as Shaxson calls them, suit the offshore mindset, because they are seemingly transparent: you can see all the way through – it's just that when you look there's nothing there. Jersey is the template: a nice, genteel place, with a strong sense of civic responsibility and plenty of opportunities for public participation, including elections to all manner of public offices (senators, deputies, parish constables), but weak political parties, staggered 'general' elections, and never a meaningful change of government. 'If you don't like it, you can leave' is the basic refrain of Jersey politics. Dissent is not obviously suppressed, as it might be under a dictatorship (which is why dictatorships make bad tax havens: you never know when the whole thing is going to blow up). Instead, dissent is simply allowed to wither away. The same thing happens on the Cayman Islands, with its tiny population (around 55,000), its elected legislature and its governor-general appointed from London, who takes all the difficult decisions but allows the locals to have their say. As one former governor-general put it, 'I think we are in the world of semantics here. The more Caymanians we can put in positions of power, the better; they will act as lightning conductors for political dissent.'

This is the web, but where is the spider? At the heart of Shaxson's story lies the City of London, itself a kind of island within the British state. Again, the rise of the City as the favourite place for foreigners to park their money, no matter who they were or where it came from, is related to imperial decline. After the Second World War, sterling still financed much of global trade, but the British economy was no longer able to sustain the value of the pound against the dollar. In the aftermath of Suez, which caused a run on the pound, the government attempted to impose curbs on the overseas lending of London's merchant banks. The response of the banks, with the connivance of the Bank of England, was to shift their international lending into dollars. The result was the creation of the so-called 'Eurodollar market' – which was effectively an offshore haven. Because the trade was happening in dollars, the British saw no need to tax or regulate it; because it was happening in London, the Americans had no means to tax or regulate it. Among the first people to spot the advantages of this new system were the Soviets, who wanted a secure place outside the US to hold their dollars so that the Americans could not seize them if relations between the countries deteriorated. They were soon followed by the Americans themselves – that is, American banks and wealthy individuals – who saw the London market as somewhere to do business free from the grasping hand of the US authorities. The money started to pile in.

The Bank of England was happy: London was once again a lynchpin of international finance. The American authorities, unsurprisingly, were not so happy: they feared a balance of payments crisis. But when in 1963 President Kennedy tried to stem currency outflows by taxing the interest on foreign securities, in an effort to reduce the incentive to export dollars to more lucrative overseas markets, it had the opposite effect, and produced what Shaxson calls 'a stampede for the unregulated London offshore market, free of tax and regulations'. US policy-makers were now in a dilemma. They could try to face down the threat of offshore, either with higher domestic interest rates, or with tighter controls on currency outflows and a tougher regulatory regime requiring US banks to share information about their overseas activities. Or they could copy London by creating an offshore world of their own closer to home: in other words, if you can't beat them, join them. The second was the path of least resistance – among other things it was a useful way of reinforcing the dollar's position as the global reserve currency – and over time it was the one they took. Slowly in the later 1960s and 1970s, and then much more rapidly in the 1980s and 1990s, America deregulated its financial controls and allowed money to move in and out with fewer if any questions asked, in the hope that more of it would stick to the sides.

Once this process began, it also unleashed a new wave of competition between individual American states to offer the most hospitable, least intrusive regulatory environment for outside companies to work in. Leading the way was little Delaware, which had always tried to compensate for its lack of size by being open for any business. Since the 1980s more and more corporations have moved to Delaware to take advantage of the state's extreme laissez-faire attitude to the rights of shareholders and employees against company managements. If you took your business to Delaware (and this was often just a question of establishing a shell office and filling in some forms), it would be much harder for anyone to prove anything against you, because the Delaware courts did not think that much of what you did was any of their concern. Again, other states faced a choice: they could try to isolate Delaware by tightening up their own standards or they could try to compete for a share of the spoils. Enough of them decided to compete to start a race to the bottom. Offshore had moved onshore.

When officials from Delaware toured the globe in the late 1980s advertising their services (and hoping, among other things, to provide a haven for all the hot money that was expected to flow out of Hong Kong in the run-up to the handover to China), they did so under the slogan 'Delaware can protect you from politics.' Shaxson defines a tax haven as 'a place that seeks to attract business by offering politically stable facilities to help people or entities get around the rules, laws and regulations of jurisdictions elsewhere'. But this is the crux: where is the politics? Why aren't these moves more politically unstable, or at least politically contentious? In the case of Delaware, as with other goldfish bowl communities, size probably tells (for a long time Delaware politics was shaped by the influence of the Du Pont family, whose vast chemical operations dominated the local economy). What, though, about Washington, where the shift to an offshore mindset at the national level might be expected to run up against some serious political opposition? What happened to the representatives of all those people who don't have lots of money to move around, who can't relocate even if they wanted to, and who have an interest in a fair, open and broadly progressive tax system? Didn't they notice what was going on?

This is the question that Jacob Hacker and Paul Pierson tackle in *Winner-Take-All Politics*. They don't spend much time talking about offshore, but the story they tell has striking parallels with the one laid out by Shaxson. One of the ways you can identify an offshore environment, according to Shaxson, is that local politics gets captured by financial services. In that sense, Washington has gone offshore: its politics has been captured by the interests of a narrow group of very wealthy individuals, many of whom work in finance. For Hacker and Pierson this, more than anything else, explains why the rich have got so much richer over the last 30 years or so. And by the rich they don't mean simply the generally wealthy; they mean the super-rich. The real beneficiaries of the explosion in income for top earners since the 1970s has been not the top 1 per cent but the top 0.1 per cent of the general population. Since 1974, the share of national income of the top 0.1 per cent of Americans has grown from 2.7 to 12.3 per cent of the total, a truly mind-boggling level of redistribution from the have-nots to the haves. Who are these people? As Hacker and Pierson note, they are 'not, for the most part, superstars and celebrities in the arts, entertainment and sports. Nor are they rentiers, living off their accumulated wealth, as was true in the early part of the last century. A substantial majority are company executives and managers, and a growing share of these are financial company executives and managers.'

Hacker and Pierson believe that politics is responsible for this. It happened because law-makers and public officials allowed it to happen, not because international markets, or globalisation, or differentials in education or life-chances made it inevitable. It was a choice, driven by the pressure of lobbyists and other organisations to create an environment much more hospitable to the needs of the very rich. It was even so a particular kind of politics and a particular kind of choice. It wasn't a conspiracy, because it happened in the open. But nor was it an explicit political movement, characterised by rallies, speeches and electoral triumphs. It relied in large part on what Hacker and Pierson call a process of drift: 'systematic, prolonged failures of government to respond to the shifting realities of a dynamic economy'. More often than not the politicians were persuaded to do nothing, to let up on enforcement, to look the other way, as money moved around the globe and up to the very top of the financial chain. This chimes with what Shaxson says about the way the offshore system was allowed to develop over the last four decades. Here too there was no real conspiracy, because there was no real need. Instead, it happened because 'nobody was paying attention.'

One of Hacker and Pierson's complaints about the way we usually regard politics is that we miss what's really going on by focusing on the show of elections and the competition between parties. This is the theatre of electoral politics, to set alongside the theatre of probity. Too often, they say, we reduce politics to the level of sport: 'This is no doubt why politics as electoral spectacle is so appealing to the media: it's exciting and it's simple. Aficionados can memorise the stats of their favourite players or become experts on the great games of the past. Everyone, however, can enjoy the gripping spectacle of two highly motivated teams slugging it out.'

I have to plead guilty here. I have often wondered whether I am interested in politics because I am interested in sport, and sometimes I have felt vaguely guilty about this, suspecting it means I don't actually understand what's happening. Elections are seductive, and these days the build-up is so protracted that they can drown out the real business of politics: the way organised groups use pressure – money, lobbying, threats – to squeeze whichever politicians happen to be in power, in order to influence the shaping of policy. Elections also suggest false historical turning points. It is easy to assume that if the rich have been winning in recent decades, the process must have started with the election of the pro-big business, anti-big government Ronald Reagan in 1980 (and concomitantly, Margaret Thatcher in Britain in 1979). But Hacker and Pierson argue that the real turning point came in 1978, during the presidency of Jimmy Carter. This was the year the lobbyists and other organised groups who were pushing hard to relax the burden of tax and regulation on wealthy individuals and corporate interests discovered that no one was pushing back all that hard. Despite Democratic control of the White House and both Houses of Congress, 1978 saw the defeat of attempts to introduce progressive tax reform and to improve the legal position of trade unions. Instead, legislation was passed that reduced the tax burden on corporations and increased the burden on their employees (through a hike in the payroll tax, a regressive measure). All this happened because the politicians followed the path of least resistance – as elected politicians invariably do – and the better organised and better-funded resistance came from the representatives of big business, not organised labour.

What took place in the 1980s was therefore an extension of the Carter years, not a reversal of them. The process of deregulation and redistribution up the chain accelerated under Reagan, who was broadly sympathetic to these goals. Yet it happened not because he was sympathetic to them, but because his sympathies were allowed free rein in a political environment where the opposition was muted and the expected coalition of interests opposed to the changes never materialised. After all, as Hacker and Pierson point out, Richard Nixon, who might have been expected to share some of Reagan's sympathies, had gone the other way in his actual policies a decade earlier, shoring up the legislative framework of the welfare state and maintaining a broadly progressive tax system. (Something similar happened in Britain under Edward Heath.) He acted like this because he felt he had little choice: the organised pressure ready to resist change appeared much too strong. It was only during the Carter years – and to some extent the Callaghan years in Britain – that this pressure turned out to be weaker than anyone thought. The politicians of the Reagan/ Thatcher revolution did what they did not because they were committed ideologues, determined to stick to their principles. They did it because they found they could get away with it.

So where did the resistance go? This is the real puzzle, and Hacker and Pierson take it seriously because they take democracy seriously, despite its unhealthy fixation on elections. Democracies are meant to favour the interests of the many over those of the few. As Hacker and Pierson put it, 'Democracy may not be good at a lot of things. But one thing it is supposed to be good at is responding to problems that affect broad majorities.' Did the majority not actually mind that they were losing out for the sake of the super-rich elite? In the American case, one common view is that the voters allowed it to happen because they minded more about other things: religion, culture, abortion, guns etc. The assumption is that many ordinary Americans have signed a kind of Faustian pact with the Republican Party, in which the rich get the money and the poor get support for the cultural values they care about. Hacker and Pierson reject this view, and not just because they don't think the process they describe depends on there being a Republican in the White House: they see strong evidence that the American public do still want a fairer tax system and do still see it as the job of politicians to protect their interests against the interests of high finance. The problem is that the public simply don't know what the politicians are up to. They are not properly informed about how the rules have been steadily changed to their disadvantage. 'Americans are no less egalitarian when it comes to their vision of an ideal world,' Hacker and Pierson write. 'But they are much less accurate when it comes to their vision of the real world.'

Why is no one paying attention? Perhaps it's the fault of the internet, which is making it increasingly hard for anyone to focus on anything for long. Yet it is striking that Hacker and Pierson's argument is really a return to a much longer-standing critique of democracy, one that flourished during the 1920s and 1930s but was supplanted in the postwar period by expectations of rational behaviour on the part of voters. This traditional critique does not see the weakness of democracy as a matter of the voters wanting the wrong things, or not really knowing what they want. They know what they want but they don't know how to get it. It's because they don't understand the world they live in that democracy isn't working. People aren't stupid, but when it comes to politics they are ignorant, lazy and easily satisfied with pat answers to difficult questions. Hacker and Pierson recognise that it has become bad manners to point this out even in serious political discourse. But it remains the truth. 'Most citizens pay very little attention to politics, and it shows. To call their knowledge of even the most elementary facts about the political system shaky would be generous.' The traditional solution to this problem was to supplement the ignorance of the voters with guidance from experts, who would reform the system in the voters' best interests. The difficulty is that the more the experts take charge, the less incentive there is for the voters to inform themselves about what's going on. This is what Hacker and Pierson call the catch-22 of democratic politics: in order to combat what's taking place under the voters' radar it's necessary to continue the fight under the voters' radar. The best hope is that eventually the public might wake up to what is going on and join in. But that will take time. As Hacker and Pierson admit, 'Political reformers will need to mobilise for the long haul.'

Yet time may be one of the things that the reformers do not have on their side. As Shaxson points out in his account of the rise of the tax havens, one of the reasons for the drift towards deregulation is that politics has been too slow to resist it. This, again, is one of the traditional critiques of democracy: while decent-minded democrats are organising themselves to make the world a better place, the world has moved on. In a fast-moving financial environment, it is usually easier to assemble a coalition of interests in favour of relaxing the rules than one in favour of tightening them. Similarly, it's easier not to enforce the rules you have than to enforce them: non-enforcement is the work of a moment – all you have to do is turn a blind eye – whereas enforcement is a slow and laborious process. Shaxson, like everyone else, is torn. On the one hand, he thinks the key to resisting the rise of offshore is a more transparent system, based on what he calls 'automatic information exchange on a multilateral basis'. This is the equivalent of putting the experts in charge. On the other hand, he wants national governments to be more active, dynamic, responsive to the interests of their citizens. But a speeded-up national politics may go against the international co-ordination needed for a fully transparent system. If you reawaken democratic politics at the national level, it will by definition be harder to co-ordinate it at the international level. This is the catch-22 of globalisation.

Shaxson illustrates the problem at the end of his book, where he lists his proposals for changing the culture of offshore. One example he gives of how it can be done comes from the United States, where in 2001 Congress finally passed stronger anti-money laundering legislation and clamped down on the spread of offshore shell banks, which hide behind nominees and trustees so no one knows who their real owners are. But the date is important: these measures were included in the Patriot Act, and the reason they were passed was that national politics had been woken up by 9/11. Yet no one could argue that the ultimate consequences either of that act or the vitality of American politics in the aftermath of 9/11 was a better integrated, more transparent world. Another of Shaxson's demands is that governments do more to keep money onshore. One of the drivers of the offshore world is what he calls the 'tides of looted or tainted oil money [that] sluice into the offshore system, distorting the global economy in the process'. One radical solution is to get a country's mineral windfalls out of the hands of a few super-wealthy individuals and into the hands of ordinary citizens, by redistributing the money directly to every inhabitant. This may sound unrealistic but such schemes have been implemented in a few places, including Alaska. However, Shaxson doesn't see fit to tell us the name of the politician who spread the wealth there: it was Sarah Palin. So yes, dynamic, quick-thinking democratic politicians can make a difference, but no, it doesn't follow that greater understanding between nations will be the result. These two brilliant books are right to suggest that politics is the answer. Still, politics is also, as always, part of the problem.

April, 2011

The Price of Offshore Revisited: Key Findings

James S. Henry

Overall size

A significant fraction of global private financial wealth – by our estimates, at least $21 to $32 trillion as of 2010 – has been invested virtually tax free through the world's still expanding black hole of more than 80 'offshore' secrecy jurisdictions. We believe this range to be conservative, for reasons discussed below.

Remember: this is just financial wealth. A big share of the real estate, yachts, racehorses, gold bricks – and many other things that count as non-financial wealth – are also owned via offshore structures where it is impossible to identify the owners. These are outside the scope of this report.

On this scale, this 'offshore economy' is large enough to have a major impact on estimates of inequality of wealth and income; on estimates of national income and debt ratios; and – most importantly – to have very significant negative impacts on the domestic tax bases of key 'source' countries (that is, countries that have seen net unrecorded private capital outflows over time).[34]

Our 139-country focus group: who are the real debtors?

We have focused on a subgroup of 139 mainly low-middle income 'source' countries[35] for which the World Bank and IMF have sufficient external debt data.

Our estimates for this group underscore how misleading it is to regard countries as 'debtors' only by looking at one side of their balance sheets. Since the 1970s, with eager (and often aggressive and illegal) assistance from the international private banking industry, it appears that private elites in this sub-group of 139 countries had accumulated $7.3 to $9.3 trillion of unrecorded offshore wealth in 2010, conservatively estimated, even while many of their public sectors were borrowing themselves into bankruptcy, enduring agonizing 'structural adjustment' and low growth, and holding fire sales of public assets.

These same source countries had aggregate gross external debt of $4.08 trillion in 2010. However, once we subtract these countries' foreign reserves, most of which are invested in First World securities, their aggregate net external debts were minus $2.8 trillion in 2010. (This dramatic picture has been increasing steadily since 1998, the year when the external debts minus foreign reserves was at its peak for these 139 countries, at +$1.43 trillion.[36])

So in total, by way of the offshore system, these supposedly indebted 'source countries' – including all key developing countries – are not debtors at all: they are net lenders, to the tune of $10.1 to $13.1 trillion at end-2010. The problem here is that the assets of these countries are held by a small number of wealthy individuals while the debts are shouldered by the ordinary people of these countries through their governments.

As a U.S. Federal Reserve official observed back in the 1980s: 'The real problem is not that these countries don't have any assets. The problem is, they're all in Miami' (and, he might have added, New York, London, Geneva, Zurich, Luxembourg, Singapore, and Hong Kong.)

These private unrecorded offshore assets and the public debts are intimately linked, historically speaking: the dramatic increase in unrecorded capital outflows (and the private demand for First World currency and other assets) in the 1970s and 1980s was positively correlated with a surge in First World loans to developing countries: much of this borrowing left these countries under the table within months, and even weeks, of being disbursed.[37]

Today, local elites continue to 'vote with their financial feet' while their public sectors borrow heavily abroad – but it is First World countries that are doing most of the borrowing. It is these frequently heavily indebted source countries and their elites that have become their financiers.

In terms of tackling poverty, it is hard to imagine a more pressing global issue to address.

How this wealth is concentrated

Much of this wealth appears to be concentrated in the hands of private elites that reside in a handful of source countries – many of which are still regarded officially as 'debtors'. By our estimates, of the $7.3-$9.3 trillion of offshore wealth belonging to residents of these 139 countries, the top 10 countries account for 61 percent and the top 20 for 81 percent.[38]

Untaxed offshore earnings start to swamp outflows.

Our estimates also correct the sanguine view that since new outflows of capital appear to have recently declined from countries like Mexico and Brazil, capital flight is no longer a problem for these countries.

Once we take into account the growth of large untaxed earnings on accumulated offshore wealth, it turns out that from 1970 to 2010 the real value (in $2000) of these earnings alone may be as much as $3.7 trillion – equivalent to about 60 percent of the global total unrecorded capital outflows during this period.[39]

For Latin America, Sub-Saharan Africa and the Middle East that have long histories of accumulating offshore wealth and unreported earnings abroad, the ratio is close to 100 percent or more.

By shifting attention from flows to accumulated stocks of foreign wealth, this paper calls attention to the fact that retention of investment earnings abroad can easily become so significant that initial outflows are eventually replaced by 'hidden flight', with the hidden stock of unrecorded private wealth generating enough unreported income to keep it growing long after the initial outflows have dried up.

Offshore earnings swamp foreign investment

Another key finding is that once we fully account for capital outflows and the lost stream of future earnings on the associated offshore investments, foreign direct and equity investment flows are almost entirely offset – even for some of the world's largest recipients of foreign investment.

Wide open and 'efficient' capital markets: how traditional theories failed

Standard development economics assumes that financial capital will flow predominantly from 'capital-rich' high-saving rich countries to 'capital-scarce' countries where returns on investment are higher.

But for many countries the global financial system seems to have enabled private investor motives – understandable ones like asset diversification along with less admirable ones like tax evasion – to swamp the conventional theory. Reducing frictions in global finance, which was supposed to help capital flow *in* to capital-starved developing countries more easily and efficiently, seems to have encouraged capital to flow out. This raises new questions about how 'efficient' frictionless global capital markets are.

The active role of private banks

Our analysis refocuses attention on the critical, often unsavory role that global private banks play. A detailed analysis of the top 50 international private banks reveals that at the end of 2010 these 50 collectively managed more than \$12.1 trillion in cross-border invested assets from private clients, including via trusts and foundations. Consider the role of smaller banks, investment houses, insurance companies, and non-bank intermediaries like hedge funds and independent money managers in the offshore cross-border market, plus self-managed funds, and this figure seems consistent with our overall offshore asset estimates of US\$21-\$32 trillion.

A disproportionate share of these assets were managed by major global banks that are well known for their role in the 2008 financial crisis, their generous government bailouts and bountiful executive compensation packages. We can now add this to their list of distinctions: they are key players in many havens around the globe, and key enablers of the global tax injustice system.

It is interesting to note that despite choppy markets the rank order at the top of the private banking world has been remarkably stable – key recent trends have been for an increased role for independent boutique money managers and hedge funds, and a shift toward banks with a strong Asian presence.

Offshore investor portfolios

Based on a simple model of offshore investor portfolio behavior, data from the Bank for International Settlements (BIS), and interviews with private bankers and wealth industry analysts, this yields a 'scale-up' factor that is also consistent with the aggregate range for 2010 noted earlier.

A simple model, based on a combination of BIS data on cross-border deposits and other asset holdings by 'non-bank' investors, an analysis of portfolio mix assumptions made by wealth industry analysts, and interviews with actual private banks, suggests an overall multiplier of 3.0 to scale up our cross-border deposits figure to total financial assets. This is very conservative.

New revenue sources for global needs

Finally, if we could figure out how to tax all this offshore wealth without killing the proverbial Golden Goose, or at least entice its owners to reinvest it back home, this sector of the global underground is also easily large enough to make a significant contribution to tax justice, investment, and paying the costs of global problems like climate change.

Other estimates

In compiling the evidence for this paper, we've had a chance to examine other recent work by analysts. We find a number of shortcomings, particularly in methods that rely heavily on studies of intra-company transfer pricing.[40]

July, 2012

Tax Dodging and Inequalities in the UK

Danny Dorling

Most people pay all their tax. They pay Value Added Tax on most things they buy. If they earn, they pay income tax – as they earn. If they buy a home they pay stamp duty.

Some people dodge a little tax. They buy some cigarettes on the side in the pub, they take care of a friend's child and don't declare it, or they pay a builder cash in hand for a repair (£1.8bn a year is lost due to 'moonlighting').[41]

Corporate tax avoidance (dubious but not strictly illegal) was estimated by the TUC (Trade Union Congress) to be £12bn for the year 2008. Tax avoidance by individuals is believed to cost the Treasury £13bn a year Illegal corporate tax evasion comes to £70bn a year and unpaid corporate taxes to £26bn a year – a total of £121 bn.[42] Those in charge of UK tax inspectorate claim the figures are lower, but the tax inspectors themselves say, in confidence, that the figures are broadly accurate.[43]

These are considerable sums. But even if tax avoidance and evasion cost as much as £120bn a year, and even if all of it were being undertaken by or on behalf of the wealthiest 1% in society (most of it will be) that avoidance, evasion and refusal to pay accounts for only a very small part of the great inequality that has arisen in British society. Ending the dodging would certainly curtail the rise in inequality, but it would not reverse it. This is because the richest 1% are now so incredibly rich and powerful. Tax dodging must be reduced but reducing it alone would not be sufficient to reverse the trends in inequalities to even get us back to where we were in the 1980s in terms of how unfair and unequal a nation Britain has become. We know how unfair we now are because inequalities are nowadays more carefully measured.

In January 2010 the National Equality Panel used data from the Office of National Statistics to reveal just how unequal Britain had become. If all wealth is included then the-least-well-off-of the-richest-1%-of-people had £2.6 million or more while the person in the middle of the whole distribution had £204,500.[44] However that figure includes the future estimated value of any pension entitlements you might have and any equity in your home.

The National Equality Panel elaborated to get us a better idea of 'marketable' wealth. If future pension benefits are excluded, then the poorest of the best-off 1% still had wealth in excess of £1.5 million or more while median wealth fell to £145,420.[45] Exclude also the estimated equity in the home people lived in and then the poorest of the 1% wealthiest of the population of Britain, had wealth of £665,650 or more, and the median holding was reduced to £42,270.[46] Meanwhile the mean marketable wealth of the average person in the richest 1% was 175 times high than that median marketable wealth of the population.

To work out the mean marketable wealth of the richest 1% we need to estimate the wealth of everyone richer than the poorest of the 1% richest. The *Sunday Times* Rich list of 2010 showed the best-off 1000 people in Britain, headed by Lakshmi Mital, had a wealth of £335.5bn around that time. The best-off 10 of those 1000 held £69.9bn or 20% of that wealth. If that inequality curve continues down within the richest 1% then the average wealth of someone in the top 100,000 but not the top 1000 would be £13.5mn; the total wealth of the top 100,000 would be £1342bn; and the best-off 1% in total have an average of £7.4mn each (175 times £42,270). That's everyone from Mr-poorest-of-the-1% to Lakshmi inclusive. It's a guestimate. Wealth is secret.

Eliminating tax dodging would reduce inequalities in wealth, but not to the levels seen prior to 2006. High income curtailment is also required. No one in the public sector or any private sector body tendering for public sector work should be paid 20 times more than another person. It is a waste of tax-payers' money. Imposing that limit would have a concertina effect down the distribution.

However, even then, and with tax dodging eliminated, the top 5% will still hold half of all wealth by 2028 (they hold 63% today). And most of that top 5%, maybe up to 80% of them or more, will not feel wealthy because they have so little compared to the other 20%.

More progressive income tax is required. Research shows that high rates of income tax do not inhibit economic activity.[47] A land tax might also be needed if wealth redistribution is to be returned to what it was in 1986 – the last time the poorest half of people in the UK had recourse to as much as a tenth of all wealth. (Table 1) A citizen's income may also be needed.

Changes in tax rates have had an even bigger impact on the amounts the rich pay than evasion, avoidance and non-payment of sums due. The wealthiest 1% have secured a series of changes in government policy. Just quite how they manage this is open to many interpretations, from the influence of press barons to the revolving door between government and the financial sector. But the evidence that this has occurred is easy to see. In countries like Britain where the richest 1% take so much, effective taxes on the richest are low and falling. It is not just that income tax on the richest 1% is being reduced on earnings over £150,000, from 50% to 45%, Corporation tax rates were as low as 28% in 2010 and are set of be reduced to 23% by 2013. In itself this is the same in lost revenue as dodging 18% of all that tax.

Manipulating the political process to create a favourable tax regime is only possible when the rest of the population feels it is getting better off. As median incomes and wealth fall, as even the poorest of the best-off 5% begin to feel the pinch, properly taxing the rich becomes possible again. And the wealthy know that.

The wealthy know that many of the options just listed are possible. That is part of the reason they hide so much of their wealth. It is not just to avoid tax. They fear retributive redistribution for the theft of the common wealth over the course of the last generation. The very wealthy often wonder when the 99% of us who have not done so well out of government policy will wake up and do something. They might think we are stupid, but they don't think we are that stupid. If they thought we were really stupid they'd keep all their money in Britain:

In March 2009 a Swiss banker quoted in the Financial Times said he believed that half of all funds deposited in that country would leave if bank secrecy was abolished – implying they must be tainted by tax evasion – and that the bankers know it.[48]

July, 2012

How Much Should the Rich Pay in Taxes?

Thomas Piketty, Emmanuel Saez and Stefanie Stantcheva

In the United States, the share of total pre-tax income accruing to the top 1% has more than doubled from less than 10% in the 1970s to over 20% today.[49] Income concentration has increased substantially in a number of other OECD countries, especially English speaking countries, but only modestly in continental Europe or Japan.[50] This heterogeneity across countries implies that, contrary to a widely held view, new technologies or globalization, which have affected all OECD countries, cannot explain those changes.

At the same time, top income tax rates on upper income earners have declined significantly since the 1970s in many OECD countries, again particularly in English speaking ones. For example, top marginal income tax rates in the United States or the United Kingdom were above 70% in the 1970s before the Reagan and Thatcher revolutions drastically cut them by 40 percentage points within a decade. At a time when most OECD countries face large deficits and debt burdens, a crucial public policy question is whether governments should tax high earners more. The potential tax revenue at stake is now very large. For example, doubling the average US individual income tax rate on the top 1% income earners from the current 22.5% level to 45% would increase tax revenue by 2.7% of GDP per year,1 as much as letting all of the Bush tax cuts expire. This simple calculation is static however and such a large increase in taxes might affect the economic behavior of the rich and the income they report pre-tax, the broader economy, and ultimately the tax revenue generated. We have analyzed this issue both conceptually and empirically using international evidence on top incomes and top tax rates since the 1970s.[51]

There is a strong correlation between the reductions in top tax rates and the increases in top 1% pre-tax income shares from 1975-9 to 2005-10 across 18 OECD countries. For example, the United States experienced a 35 percentage point reduction in its top income tax rate and a very large 10 percentage point increase in its top 1% pre-tax income share.

In contrast, France or Germany saw very little change in their top tax rates and top 1% income shares.[52] Hence, the evolution of top tax rates is a good predictor of changes in pre-tax income concentration. There are three scenarios to explain this strong response, which can be tested and have very different policy implications.

First, higher top tax rates may discourage work effort and business creation among the most talented- the so-called supply-side effect. Accordingly, lower top tax rates would encourage economic activity among the rich and hence economic growth. If the correlation noted above were due entirely to such supply-side effects, the revenue-maximizing top tax rate would be 57%. This implies that the United States still has some leeway to increase taxes on the rich, but many European countries have not.

Second, higher top tax rates can increase tax avoidance. In this scenario, increasing top rates in a tax system riddled with loopholes and tax avoidance opportunities is not beneficial. Instead, a better policy would be to first close loopholes, eliminate most tax avoidance opportunities and only then increase top tax rates. With sufficient political will and international cooperation in tax enforcement, it is possible to eliminate most tax avoidance opportunities, which are well known and documented. With a broad tax base offering no significant avoidance opportunities, only real supply side responses would limit how high the top tax rate can be set.

Third, while standard economic models assume that pay reflects productivity, there are strong reasons to be sceptical, especially at the top of the income distribution where the actual economic contribution of managers working in complex organisations is particularly difficult to measure. In this scenario, top earners might be able to partly set their own pay by bargaining harder or influencing compensation committees.

Naturally, the incentives for such 'rentseeking' are much stronger when top tax rates are low. In this scenario, cuts in top tax rates can still increase top income shares – consistent with the observed trend noted above – but the increases in top 1% incomes now come at the expense of the remaining 99%. In other words, top rate cuts stimulate rent-seeking at the top but not overall economic growth – the key difference with the first, supply-side, scenario.

To tell these various scenarios apart, we need to first analyse to what extent top tax rate cuts lead to higher economic growth. Our research shows that there has been no correlation between cuts in top tax rates and average annual real GDP-per-capita growth since the 1970s. For example, countries that made large cuts in top tax rates such as the United Kingdom or the United States have not grown significantly faster than countries that did not, such as Germany or Denmark.[53]

Hence, a substantial fraction of the response of pre-tax top incomes to top tax rates may be due to increased rent-seeking at the top rather than increased productive effort. Naturally, cross-country comparisons are bound to be fragile, but by and large, the bottom line is that rich countries have all grown at roughly the same rate over the past 30 years – in spite of huge variations in tax policies. Using our model and mid-range parameter values where the response of top earners to top tax rate cuts is due in part to increased rent-seeking behaviour and in part to increased productive work, we find that the top tax rate could potentially be set as high as 83% as opposed to 57% in the pure supply-side model.

To complement our macro evidence, we also directly analyze CEO compensation in the US. We first ask to what extent CEOs are rewarded for outcomes that are the result of 'luck' rather than of their own efforts. This is a form of rent seeking and bargaining because if CEOs were paid according to their real performance, luck shocks should be filtered out. Using a methodology pioneered by Bertrand and Mullainathan (1991), we find that CEOs are consistently rewarded for good outcomes (such as increases in Shareholder wealth, Net income or Return on Equity) which are directly due to a good industry-wide climate, and are hence not achieved by hard work. Furthermore, we find that 'pay for luck' is strongly affected by top tax rates: higher top tax rates decrease pay for luck and in the low tax years since 1987, 'non-deserved' pay for 'luck' has increased for US CEOs.

In our view, the rent-seeking model is the right framework to account for the very high, quasi-confiscatory top marginal tax rates-80% or more-in the United States and the United Kingdom between the 1940s and the 1970s. That is, policy makers and public opinion at that time probably considered – rightly or wrongly – that at the very top of the income ladder, pay increases reflected mostly greed or other socially wasteful activities rather than productive work effort. The Reagan and Thatcher revolution has succeeded in making such confiscatory top tax rate levels unthinkable since then. But after decades of increasing income concentration that has brought back a new Gilded Age, mediocre growth since the 1970s, and a Great Recession triggered by financial sector excesses, a rethinking of the Reagan and Thatcher revolutions is perhaps underway.

The Occupy movement and its famous 'we are the 99%' slogan reflects the view that the top 1% may have gained at the expense of the 99%. In the end, the future of top tax rates depends on the public's perceptions of whether top pay fairly reflects productivity or rather unfairly arises from rent-seeking. With higher income concentration, top earners have more economic resources to influence social perceptions (through think tanks and media) and policies (through lobbying), thereby creating some reverse causality between income inequality, perceptions, and policies. In addition, tax policy and tolerance for high CEO pay may both be the result of social norms which have evolved over time. We hope economists can enlighten these perceptions with compelling theoretical and empirical analysis.

July, 2012

Where the Money Lives*

Nicholas Shaxson

A person who worked for Mitt Romney at the consulting firm Bain
and Co. in 1977 remembers him with mixed feelings. 'Mitt was ...
a really wonderful boss,' the former employee says. 'He was nice,
he was fair, he was logical, he said what he wanted ... he was really
encouraging.' But Bain and Co., the person recalls, pushed employees
to find out secret revenue and sales data on its clients' competitors.
Romney, the person says, suggested 'falsifying' who they were to get
such information, by pretending to be a graduate student working on
a project at Harvard. (The person, in fact, was a Harvard student, at
Bain for the summer, but not working on any such projects.) 'Mitt said
to me something like "We won't ask you to lie. I am not going to tell
you to do this, but [it is] a really good way to get the information." ...
I would not have had anything in my analysis if I had not pretended.

'It was a strange atmosphere. It did leave a bad taste in your mouth,'
the former employee recalls.

This unsettling account suggests the young Romney – at that point
only two years out of Harvard Business School – was willing to push
into gray areas when it came to business. More than three decades
later, as he tried to nail down the Republican nomination for president
of the United States, Romney's gray areas were again an issue when
he repeatedly resisted calls to release more details of his net worth, his
tax returns, and the large investments and assets held by him and his
wife, Ann. Finally the other Republican candidates forced him to do
so, but only highly selective disclosures were forthcoming.

Even so, these provided a lavish smorgasbord for Romney's critics.
Particularly jarring were the Romneys' many offshore accounts. As
Newt Gingrich put it during the primary season, 'I don't know of any
American president who has had a Swiss bank account.' But Romney

* First published in the August 2012 edition of *Vanity Fair*.

has, as well as other interests in such tax havens as Bermuda and the Cayman Islands.

To give but one example, there is a Bermuda-based entity called Sankaty High Yield Asset Investors Ltd., which has been described in securities filings as 'a Bermuda corporation wholly owned by W. Mitt Romney.' It could be that Sankaty is an old vehicle with little importance, but Romney appears to have treated it rather carefully. He set it up in 1997, then transferred it to his wife's newly created blind trust on January 1, 2003, the day before he was inaugurated as Massachusetts's governor. The director and president of this entity is R. Bradford Malt, the trustee of the blind trust and Romney's personal lawyer. Romney failed to list this entity on several financial disclosures, even though such a closely held entity would not qualify as an 'excepted investment fund' that would not need to be on his disclosure forms. He finally included it on his 2010 tax return. Even after examining that return, we have no idea what is in this company, but it could be valuable, meaning that it is possible Romney's wealth is even greater than previous estimates. While the Romneys' spokespeople insist that the couple has paid all the taxes required by law, investments in tax havens such as Bermuda raise many questions, because they are in 'jurisdictions where there is virtually no tax and virtually no compliance,' as one Miami-based offshore lawyer put it.

That's not the only money Romney has in tax havens. Because of his retirement deal with Bain Capital, his finances are still deeply entangled with the private-equity firm that he founded and spun off from Bain and Co. in 1984. Though he left the firm in 1999, Romney has continued to receive large payments from it – in early June he revealed more than $2 million in new Bain income. The firm today has at least 138 funds organized in the Cayman Islands, and Romney himself has personal interests in at least 12, worth as much as $30 million, hidden behind controversial confidentiality disclaimers. Again, the Romney campaign insists he saves no tax by using them, but there is no way to check this.

Bain Capital is the heart of Romney's fortune: it was the financial engine that created it. The mantra of his campaign is that he was a businessman who created tens of thousands of jobs, and Bain certainly did bring useful operational skills to many companies it bought. But his critics point to several cases where Bain bought companies, loaded them with debt, and paid itself extravagant fees, thereby bankrupting the companies and destroying tens of thousands of jobs.

Come August, Romney, with an estimated net worth as high as $250 million (he won't reveal the exact amount), will be one of the richest people ever to be nominated for president. Given his reticence to discuss his wealth, it's only natural to wonder how he got it, how he invests it, and if he pays all his taxes on it.

Ironically, it was Mitt's father, George Romney, who released 12 years of tax returns, in November 1967, just ahead of his presidential campaign, thereby setting a precedent that nearly every presidential candidate since has either willingly or unwillingly been subject to. George, then the governor of Michigan, explained why he was releasing so many years' worth, saying, 'One year could be a fluke, perhaps done for show.'

But his son declined to release any returns through one unsuccessful race for the U.S. Senate, in 1994, one successful run for Massachusetts governor, in 2002, and an aborted bid for the Republican Party presidential nomination, in 2008. Just before the Iowa caucus last December, Mitt told MSNBC, 'I don't intend to release the tax returns. I don't,' but finally, on January 24, 2012 – after intense goading by fellow Republican candidates Newt Gingrich and Rick Perry – he released his 2010 tax return and an estimate for 2011.

These, plus the mandatory financial disclosures filed with the Office of Government Ethics and released last August, raise many questions. A full 55 pages in his 2010 return are devoted to reporting his transactions with foreign entities. 'What Romney does not get,' says Jack Blum, a veteran Washington lawyer and offshore expert, 'is that this stuff is weird.'

The media soon noticed Romney's familiarity with foreign tax havens. A $3 million Swiss bank account appeared in the 2010 returns, then winked out of existence in 2011 after the trustee closed it, as if to remind us of George Romney's warning that one or two tax returns can provide a misleading picture. Ed Kleinbard, a professor of tax law at the University of Southern California, says the Swiss account 'has political but not tax-policy resonance,' since it – like many other Romney investments – constituted a bet against the U.S. dollar, an odd thing for a presidential candidate to do. The Obama campaign provided a helpful world map pointing to the tax havens Bermuda,

Luxembourg, and the Cayman Islands, where Romney and his family have assets, each with the tagline 'Value: not disclosed in tax returns.'

Romney's personal tax rate is a particular point of interest. In 2010 and 2011, Mitt and Ann paid $6.2 million in federal tax on $42.5 million in income, for an average tax rate just shy of 15 percent, substantially less than what most middle-income Americans pay. Romney manages this low rate because he takes his payments from Bain Capital as investment income, which is taxed at a maximum 15 percent, instead of the 35 percent he would pay on 'ordinary' income, such as salaries and wages. Many tax experts argue that the form of remuneration he receives, known as carried interest, is really just a fee charged by investment managers, so it should instead be taxed at the 35 percent rate. Lee Sheppard, a contributing editor at the trade publication *Tax Notes*, whose often controversial articles are read widely by tax professionals, is nonplussed that the Obama campaign has been so listless on the issue of carried interest. 'Romney is the poster boy, the best argument, for taxing this profit share as ordinary income,' says Sheppard.

In the face of such arguments, Romney's defense is that he never broke the rules: if there is a problem, it is in the laws, not in his behavior. 'I pay all the taxes that are legally required, not a dollar more,' he said. Even so, 'When you are running for president, you might want to err on the side of overpaying your taxes, and not chase every tax gimmick that comes down the pike,' says Sheppard. 'It kind of looks tacky.'

The assertion that he broke no laws is widely accepted. But it is worth asking if it is actually true. The answer, in fact, isn't straightforward. Romney, like the superhero who whirls and backflips unscathed through a web of laser beams while everyone else gets zapped, is certainly a remarkable financial acrobat. But careful analysis of his financial and business affairs also reveals a man who, like some other Wall Street titans, seems comfortable striding into some fuzzy gray zones.

The Caped Avoider!

One might perhaps accept an explanation by Romney's campaign spokeswoman, Andrea Saul, that the candidate's failure to include his Swiss account in earlier financial disclosures was merely a 'trivial inadvertent issue.' But deeper questions do emerge.

All the assets on Mitt's financial disclosures are in blind trusts or retirement accounts held by him and Ann. Blind trusts are designed to avoid conflicts of interest for those in public office by having politicians' assets managed by independent trustees. The Romneys' blind trust was created when Mitt was elected governor of Massachusetts. Curiously, the Romneys appointed Bradford Malt as their trustee. It's certainly true that under Malt the trusts don't appear to be as blind as they might be: for instance, in 2010 the Romneys invested $10 million in the start-up of the Solamere Founders Fund, co-founded by their eldest son, Tagg, and Spencer Zwick, Romney's onetime top campaign fund-raiser; Solamere is now in the Ann Romney blind trust. Malt has said he invested in Solamere without consulting Mitt or Ann and explained he liked Solamere because of its diversified approach and because he knew the founders and had confidence in them.

Likewise, the Romneys were reported to have invested at least $1 million in Elliott Associates, L.P., a hedge fund specializing in 'distressed assets.' Elliott buys up cheap debt, often at cents on the dollar, from lenders to deeply troubled nations such as Congo-Brazzaville, then attacks the debtor states with lawsuits to squeeze maximum repayment. Elliott is run by the secretive hedge-fund billionaire and G.O.P. super-donor Paul Singer, whom *Fortune* recently dubbed Mitt Romney's 'Hedge Fund Kingmaker.' (Singer has given $1 million to Romney's super-pac Restore Our Future.)

It is hard to know the size of these investments. Romney's financial disclosure form lists 25 of them in an open-ended category, 'Over $1 million,' including Solamere and Elliott, and they are not broken down further. Romney hides behind a disclaimer that the fund managers 'declined to provide such information' about their underlying assets. Many of these funds are set up in tax havens such as the Cayman Islands, where a confidentiality law states that you can be jailed for up to four years just for *asking* about such information.

Andrea Saul said of these investments, 'Everything … was reported correctly.' Joseph Sandler, a Democratic lawyer who has worked with candidates on disclosures for more than two decades, is skeptical. 'The law is the law,' Sandler says. '[Romney] says, "Well, you know, they won't tell me." But when you run for office in the U.S. and are not prepared to comply with disclosure requirements, you should either divest yourself of the assets or don't run.' *The Washington Post* summarized the opinions of experts across the political spectrum by saying Romney's disclosures were 'the most opaque they have encountered.'

Mysteries also arise when one looks at Romney's individual retirement account at Bain Capital. When Romney was there, from 1984 to 1999, taxpayers were allowed to put just $2,000 per year into an I.R.A., and $30,000 annually into a different kind of plan he may have used. Given these annual contribution ceilings, how can his I.R.A. possibly contain up to $102 million, as his financial disclosures now suggest?

The Romneys won't say, but Mark Maremont, writing in *The Wall Street Journal*, uncovered a likely explanation. When Bain Capital bought companies, it would create two classes of shares, named A and L. The A shares were risky common shares, to which they would assign a very low value. The L shares were preferred shares, paying a high dividend but with the payoff frozen, and most of the value was assigned to them. Bain employees would then put the exciting A shares in their I.R.A. accounts, where they grew tax-free. With all the risk of the deal, the A shares stood to gain a lot or collapse. But if the deal succeeded, the springing value could be stunning: Bain employees saw their A shares from one particularly fruitful deal grow 583-fold, 16 times faster than the underlying stock.

The Romneys won't tell us how, or even if, they assigned super-low values to the A shares, but there are a couple of ways to do it. One is to use standard options models to price the shares – then feed inappropriate assumptions into those models. Romney could alternatively have used a model called liquidation valuation, which Kleinbard says would have been 'completely inappropriate.' Without seeing the assumptions used on Romney's tax returns from the years when those lowball A shares were squirted into his I.R.A., we cannot know how he did it. Whatever methods he used, however, the valuations were, according to Andrew Smith, of Houlihan Capital in Chicago, "pushing the envelope." (Andrea Saul retorts, 'Why should successful investments be criticized?')

Mitt's and Ann's I.R.A.'s have also been receiving profit interest

from (mostly Cayman Island–based) Bain Capital funds that were
set up long after he had left the company, in 1999. For example, the
2010 return reveals a profits interest in a Cayman-based fund called
Bain Capital Partners (AM) X LP, which was transferred to the Ann
D. Romney trust in October 2010. An attachment to the return says
the Ann D. Romney trust is 'performing services' to the partnership,
which is boilerplate language for these kinds of filings. Her blind
trust could receive lightly taxed income from Bain Capital for years
to come, well into the presidential term her husband hopes to win.

But administrative guidance says you can do this kind of thing
only if the compensation is in recognition of past services you have
provided. 'This should not mean retired from the mother ship 10
years out and getting profits you had nothing to do with,' Sheppard
says, adding that Romney can get away with it because of excessive
'administrative indulgences' that have allowed a 'perversion of the law
in favor of a small class of overcompensated investment managers.'

Romney's I.R.A. also appears to have invested in so-called blocker
corporations in the Cayman Islands and elsewhere. U.S. pension
funds, foundations, and even I.R.A.'s routinely use offshore blocker
corporations to avoid something called the Unrelated Business
Income Tax, which was designed to keep nonprofits from competing
with ordinary companies in areas outside their core purpose: if you
invest directly you get hit with the tax, but if you invest in a blocker,
which then invests in the U.S. business, you escape it. Romney's I.R.A.
appears to have employed this lawful escape route, and his campaign
has used language suggesting that it has. But that would mean the
Romney camp's claim that Mitt's tax consequences of investing via
the Cayman Islands is 'the very same' as it would have been had he
invested directly at home is simply not true. (Romney spokesperson
Andrea Saul says Romney 'gets the same benefit anyone would get
from an I.R.A.,' but she did not respond to questions on whether his
I.R.A. had used blockers or avoided taxes by investing via tax havens.)

A Deutsche Bank analysis of 68 Bain deals Romney was involved
in calculated an internal rate of return – a standard private-equity
benchmark – at a staggering 88 percent annually (though after fees
and inflation, investor performance may have been little more than
half that). It is substantially on this stellar record that Romney is now
running for president. His work at Bain was unquestionably good

for himself and for Bain, but was it also good for the businesses he acquired, for their workers, and for the economy, as he claims?

A report by Bain and Co. itself, looking at the period from 2002 to 2007, concluded that there is 'little evidence that private equity owners, overall, added value' to the companies they took over: nearly all their returns are explained by broad economic growth, rising stock markets, and leverage. Josh Kosman, who researched the subject of private equity for his book *The Buyout of America*, singles out Bain Capital in particular. 'They take pride in pushing the leverage envelope [i.e., use of borrowed money, which magnifies returns, while off-loading the risks onto others] more than their peers,' he says. 'I have heard that from limited partners in Bain's funds. I have heard that from bankers who lend money to finance their leveraged buyouts. Bain always prided itself on "We'll push leverage more than the others." They brag about that, behind closed doors.'

Dade Behring is a *cause célèbre* for Romney's and Bain's critics, and it illustrates the leverage problem clearly. In 1994, Bain bought Dade International, a medical-diagnostics company, then added the medical-diagnostics division of DuPont in 1996 and a German medical-testing company called Behring in 1997. Former Dade president Bob Brightfelt says the operation started well: the Bain managers were 'pretty smart guys,' he recalls, and they did well cutting out overlap, and exploiting synergies.

Then brutal cost cutting began. Bain cut R&D spending to an average of 8 percent of sales, a little more than half what its competitors were doing. Cindy Hewitt, Dade's human-resources manager, remembers how the firm closed a Puerto Rico plant in 1998, a year after harvesting $7.1 million in local tax breaks aimed at job creation, and relocated some staff to Miami, then the company's most profitable plant. Based on reassurances she had received from her superiors, she told those uprooting themselves from Puerto Rico that their jobs in Miami were safe for now – but then Bain closed the Miami plant. 'Whether you want to call it misled, or lied, or manipulated, I do not believe they provided full information about what discussions were under way,' she says. 'I would never want to be part of even unintentionally treating people so poorly.'

Bain engaged in startling penny-pinching with the laid-off employees. Their contracts stipulated that if they left early they would

have to pay back the costs of relocating to Miami – but in spite of all
that Dade had done to them, it refused to release the employees from
this clause. 'They said they would go after them for that money if they
left before Bain was finished with them,' Hewitt recalls. Not only
that, but the company declined to give workers their severance pay in
lump sums to help them fund their return home.

In 1999, generous pensions were converted into less generous
benefits, wages were cut, and more staff members were laid off. Some
employees contacted Norman Stein, then the director of the pension-
counseling clinic at the University of Alabama law school, with a
view to challenging the conversions. Stein says the employees were
'extraordinarily nervous,' so fearful, in fact, that they refused to let
lawyers even make copies of pension documents. 'I have been dealing
with pensions issues for over 25 years and I never saw anything like
this,' recalls Stein. The spooked employees did not go to court. Stein
says that, while breaking pension contracts like this was not unheard
of, the practice at that time was 'questionable,' adding that Dade may
have saved $10 to $40 million from converting its pensions.

The beauty – or savagery – of leverage is that it can magnify any
and all cash-flow boosts, such as this one. Take $10 to $40 million
squeezed from a pension pot, then use that to create new, rosier
financial projections to borrow several times that amount, and
then pay yourself a big special dividend from the borrowed funds,
many times the size of the pension savings. That is just what Bain
Capital did: the same month it converted the pensions, it created
new financial projections as a basis to borrow an extra $421 million
– from which Bain, its co-investor Goldman Sachs, and top Dade
management extracted $365 million in dividends. According to
Kosman, 'Bain and Goldman – after putting down only $85 million
… made out like bandits – a $280 million profit.' Dade's debt rose to
more than $870 million. Romney had left operational management
of Bain that year, though his disclosures show that he owned 16.5
percent of the Bain partnership responsible for the Dade investment
until at least 2001.

Quite soon, however, a fragile Dade faced adverse conditions
in the currency markets, and it had to start in effect cannibalizing
itself, cutting into the core of its business. It filed for bankruptcy
in August 2002 and Bain Capital departed. When Dade emerged

from bankruptcy, its new owners invested in long-term R&D, and it flourished again.

Nor was this an isolated incident: Kosman lists five other 'formerly healthy' companies – Stage Stores, Ampad, GS Technologies, Details, and KB Toys – Bain helped drive into bankruptcy, while making big profits. (Despite numerous entreaties from *Vanity Fair* to Bain Capital to address on the record points in this article with which it might disagree, the firm refused to do so and instead provided this statement: 'When politics overwhelm fact, some will distort or cherry-pick our record and launch unfounded allegations and insinuations. The truth and the full record show that Bain Capital operates with high standards of integrity and excellence in compliance with all laws. Any suggestion to the contrary is baseless.')

Tax Haven U.S.A.

The term 'financialization' describes two interlocking processes: a disproportionate growth in a country's deregulated financial sector, relative to the rest of the economy, and the rising importance of financial activities with a focus on financial returns among industrial and other non-financial corporations, often at the expense of real innovation and productivity.

Some see the rising influence of finance and financial models in epochal terms. Author of *Financialization and the U.S. Economy* Özgür Orhangazi summarizes academic literature that sees financialization 'as one of the indicators of the decline of the hegemonic power': imperial Venice, Genoa, Holland, and Britain all saw their power rise on the back of productive industrial capitalism, followed by domination by the financial sector, which eventually began to cannibalize the productive sector in pursuit of financial returns – a process that ended in weakness and collapse.[54]

Little noticed in the academic discussions of financialization is the role of offshore tax havens, one of the big reasons the financial sector has become so powerful. In 1966, Michael Hudson, a young Chase Manhattan balance-of-payments economist, was in a company elevator when he was handed a memo by a former State Department operative. The memo came from the U.S. government, and Hudson was tasked with figuring out how much foreign money the U.S.

might attract. 'They were saying, "We want to replace Switzerland," ' Hudson explains. 'All this money will come here if we make this the criminal center of the world. We wanted foreign criminal money, which was patriotic, but not American criminal money.'

In the years since then, almost unknown to most Americans, the United States has turned itself into a giant tax haven for foreigners, just as the memo suggested. Federal and state tax laws have been deliberately shaped to give foreigners special tax exemptions unavailable to Americans, plus financial secrecy and exemptions from regulatory restraints. 'We have criticized offshore tax havens for their secrecy and lack of transparency,' said Senator Carl Levin. 'But look what is going on in our own backyard.'

In this grand scenario, tax havens such as the Caymans serve as feeders of foreign savings into Tax Haven U.S.A. from abroad, providing foreign investors with additional ways to skip around tax, disclosure, and regulatory requirements that they might trigger if they invested directly.

The money sucked into Tax Haven U.S.A., often via the 'feeder' tax havens, is frequently tax-evading and other criminal foreign money, in the spirit of Hudson's 1966 memo, and it is predominantly channeled not into productive investment but into real estate and financial business.

One cannot properly understand Wall Street's size and power without appreciating the central role of offshore tax havens. There is absolutely no evidence that Bain has done anything illegal, but private equity is one channel for this secrecy-shrouded foreign money to enter the United States, and a filing for Mitt Romney's first $37 million Bain Capital Fund, of 1984, provides a rare window into this. One foreign investor, of $2 million, was the newspaper tycoon, tax evader, and fraudster Robert Maxwell, who fell from his yacht, and drowned, off of the Canary Islands in 1991 in strange circumstances, after looting his company's pension fund. The Bain filing also names Eduardo Poma, a member of one of the '14 families' oligarchy that has controlled most of El Salvador's wealth for decades; oddly, Poma is listed as sharing a Miami address with two anonymous companies that invested $1.5 million between them. The filings also show a Geneva-based trustee overseeing a trust that invested $2.5 million, a Bahamas corporation that put in $3 million, and three corporations in the tax haven of Panama, historically a favored destination for Latin-American dirty money – 'one of the filthiest money-laundering sinks in the world,' as a U.S. Customs official once put it.

Bain Capital has said it did everything required by the U.S. government to check that the investors were not associated with unsavory interests. U.S. law doesn't require Bain to enforce the tax laws of its investors' home countries, but the presence of Swiss trustees, Bahamas trusts, and Panama corporations would raise red flags with any tax authority.

Many Americans might react with a shrug to the idea of shady foreign money such as Robert Maxwell's being invested here. But, says Rebecca Wilkins, of the Washington, D.C.-based nonprofit Citizens for Tax Justice, 'It is shocking that a presidential candidate should think that is O.K.'

August, 2012

The Finance Curse: Introduction

Nicholas Shaxson and John Christensen[55]

It is now well known that many countries which depend on earnings from natural resources like oil have failed to harness them for national development. In many cases it seems even worse than that: for all the hundreds of billions of dollars sloshing into countries like oil-rich Nigeria, for instance, such places seem to suffer more conflict, lower economic growth, greater corruption, higher inequality, less political freedom and often more absolute poverty than their resource-poor peers. This paradox of poverty from plenty has been extensively studied and is known as the Resource Curse.

This book asks whether some countries with oversized domestic financial centres may be suffering from a similar, and related, phenomenon.

We find strong evidence that the answer is yes – and not just for reasons related to the global financial crisis that erupted in 2007/8. Perhaps more surprisingly, this phenomenon that we are calling the Finance Curse is similar in many ways to the Resource Curse: there are big overlaps in both their causes and their effects.

The Finance Curse has been evident for decades – and if untreated it may well endure for years or even decades after the latest crisis has blown over.

Every economy needs its financial plumbing, and for decades academic studies suggested that bigger is generally better when it comes to financial sector growth. The crisis has called all that research into question. New evidence is starting to emerge from the IMF, the Bank for International Settlements and others, revealing that above a certain size, finance turns bad.

Our book, drawing on our many years of hands-on experience of both resource-dependent countries and finance-dependent ones, goes far beyond the boundaries of their research to create an unprecedented comprehensive body of evidence about the perils of oversized finance.

Despite the trillions flowing into and through the City of London, for instance, Britain performs worse on major human development indicators – inequality, infant mortality, poverty, and more – than Germany, Sweden, Canada and most of its other rich-country peers. Each ailment has many explanations, but oversized finance appears to be a major contributor.

Country capture

The Finance Curse is a story about 'Country Capture' – where an oversized financial sector comes to control the politics of a finance-dependent country and to dominate and hollow out its economy. Some elements of this 'capture' are already well understood but our book introduces a wide range of new ideas and analysis.

In large finance-dependent countries such as Britain or the United States, the Finance Curse's causes and effects are masked by background noise in large, raucous democracies. But in the small finance centres and tax havens such as the Cayman Islands or Cyprus, these complexities are stripped away and the phenomenon is laid bare in purer, more crystallised forms which are easier to see and understand.

The tax havens, which we have studied extensively, carry important lessons – and warnings – for larger finance-dependent countries.

The book

This book starts with a brief overview of the Resource Curse. The main sections that follow, on the Finance Curse, start by looking at the most important and most widely publicised claims made by defenders of large financial sectors.

We then examine these claims in turn and reveal why nearly all of them are wrong. Along the way we expose catastrophic errors in studies that claim to demonstrate to policy makers the 'contribution' of finance.

Next, we show that not only is the 'contribution' of finance usually much smaller than advertised, but it is worse than that: a wide and diverse range of harms flow from having an overly large financial centre. One can plausibly say that for many countries, the net 'contribution' of finance is likely to be negative – in some cases strongly so.

The picture is – of course – not a simple one. Many of these effects, particularly the political ones, cannot be quantified. The political damage is probably more acute in small countries hosting financial centres, while in larger countries such as Britain or the United States the damage is probably felt more heavily in economic terms.

And just as some resource-rich countries like Norway or Chile seem to have successfully avoided or managed the Resource Curse, some finance-dependent countries like Switzerland or Luxembourg seem to have tempered or even avoided the Finance Curse.

But some countries such as Britain and the United States genuinely do seem cursed by their oversized financial centres. A sector widely regarded as the Goose that Lays the Golden Eggs often turns out to be a very different bird: a Cuckoo in the Nest, crowding out, hollowing out and undermining other economic sectors. Very often, the interests of the financial centre conflict directly with the national interest.

Our analysis has profound implications. Financiers routinely cry 'don't tax or regulate us too much or you will be "uncompetitive" and we will run away to Geneva or London or Hong Kong' – and far too often the politicians quail and give them what they want. These threats and fears are perhaps the most important reasons why it is so hard to regulate finance appropriately, and why big banks are bigger and potentially more dangerous today than before the crisis erupted.

Our Finance Curse thesis cuts through this Gordian knot. Taking it on board puts power right back in the hands of democratically elected officials. If too much finance is harmful, then it makes clear political and economic sense to regulate and tax this sector appropriately. If the end result is less financial activity, then that will be beneficial. It is therefore absolutely not necessary to participate in the 'competitive' race on lower standards of financial regulation, and the obvious course of action is national leadership on better standards, even in the absence of collective international agreements.

Finally, this is *not* a book about how global financial centres can transmit damage to other countries, important though that subject is. It is about how an over-sized financial sector can harm its *own* host country.

May, 2013

WIDENING THE TERMS, 2013-2105

Enterprise and Rent-Seeking:
A Mythical Conflation

William Davies

There was a 19-year period, between the fall of the Berlin Wall and the fall of Lehman Brothers, when 'neoliberalism' became virtually invisible to everybody, save for its critics in what was called the 'anti-globalisation movement'. There was no longer a distinct political movement or philosophy that could be referred to as 'neoliberal', and nor were there any obvious ideologues selling the virtues of free markets or enterprise. Rather, the backdrop of unregulated, finance-led, global capitalism was just the reality against which politics and policy seemingly had to happen.

The global financial crisis has changed that. The intellectual and policy roots of our present economic malaises are now thrown into question, and the practices of elites (especially in the finance sector) are being raked over publicly. The term 'capitalism' is common currency in mainstream political debate, in a way that was not true a decade ago. How can we throw off the strictures of neoliberalism? Why are we still so stuck with it? And is there a different capitalism, or even an alternative to it? One small consolation of a protracted economic crisis is that such questions are put on the table, with often enlightening public results.

Inevitably, this hubbub has drawn some of the original 'neoliberals' out from their caves. British think tanks such as the Institute of Economic Affairs (IEA) and The Adam Smith Institute are returning to some of their favourite 1970s tunes, blaming government for everything, arguing that only entrepreneurs can save us. In one of the more outlandish examples of this, a former Conservative Defence Secretary in the British Government, Liam Fox, argued in March of this year that a 'great socialist coup' was responsible for the depression of the UK economy, and that only smaller government could rescue us.

The early neoliberal thinkers of the 1930s and 40s were notoriously paranoid about the threat and reach of socialism. But the tenacity of those such as Fox, in still seeing reds under the beds in this age of spiralling inequality and the near disappearance of private sector unionism, is quite remarkable. Either due to chronic failure of imagination, or sheer nostalgia, the assumption of this revitalised New Right seems to be that Britain is currently experiencing the 1970s all over again, and deregulation will ride to the rescue.

One curiosity of this baroque policy revival is that, in its inevitable anti-tax rhetoric, its target has shifted slightly. Perhaps in view of the political disaster which was George Osborne's cutting of the highest rate of income tax in last year's budget, the main target of the anti-tax movement has shifted from income tax to capital gains tax (CGT).

Osborne himself had raised CGT from 18% to 28% in his emergency 2010 budget. But it was only as low as 18% because Alasdair Darling had abandoned the tapering system in 2007, which saw CGT vary between 10% and 40%, depending on how long the asset was held for. Income tax is such a politically charged area of fiscal policy, that politicians are fearful to make very significant changes. Large amounts of political capital can be expended, in exchange for relatively small increases in tax revenue. CGT, on the other hand, is a far more fluid area of policy, which allows the Right to become more ideologically exercised and vocal.

The Adam Smith Institute put out a report attacking the level of CGT in February. Philip Booth of the IEA wrote a piece for *Prospect* in the same month attacking CGT, inheritance tax and stamp duty, as impediments to growth. Then, in a speech to the IEA, Fox demanded that CGT be abolished altogether, in order to get the economy moving again. While Conservatives of a neoliberal persuasion like to talk up the benefits of hard work, they are looking to treat the proceeds of speculation, rent-seeking and asset price inflation more favourably.

While it seems highly implausible that even a Conservative Chancellor will adopt any of these proposals, what is being showcased here is a fundamental oversight in neoliberal thinking, that was present throughout the genesis of the New Right on both sides of the Atlantic. What Fox et al strategically – or blindly – elide, in their attacks on CGT, is the distinction between constructive entrepreneurship and a form of rentier capitalism dominated by asset speculation. The rhetorical trick of neoliberalism, both in its long period of exile as a critique of Keynesianism and socialism, and in its applied phase of the 1980s and 90s, is to use the language of 'enterprise' to defend the freedoms of speculators and asset-strippers.

May, 2013

The Ills of Financial Sector Dominance

Doreen Massey

Societies take different shapes in different eras. They are framed by distinct forms of economy, specific social and political arrangements, and particular common understandings of how the world works. These are expressed too in distinct geographies, which in turn feed back into the way in which the country develops.

Since the undermining of the social-democratic settlement of the post-war years, UK economy and society has been framed by what we have come to call 'neoliberalism'. This was not inevitable; other alternatives were available; the victory of neoliberalism was an outcome of political and social contest.[56] And central to that victory, and to neoliberalism in its widest sense, was the triumph of finance. 'Finance', in the current era, is not just a sector of the economy; it is at the core of a new social settlement in which the fabric of our society and economy has been reworked. There is a long history in the UK of 'the City' having an important and often harmful role, but this time is different. Finance and financialisation now mould our economy, geography, ideology and politics to a degree that is not only astonishing but deeply negative.

Some of the dismal results of this dominance at national level are well documented: the vicious exacerbation of economic inequality; the crowding-out of other sectors of the economy (far from being the golden goose, the dominance by finance makes life much more difficult for other sectors); the pervasiveness of individualism and competitive greed. But the way these things work out on the ground in different places highlights even more the contradictions inherent in this social settlement.[57]

London itself, the pinnacle of finance's success, is riven with contradictions. A city once known for its variety of small industries is seeing that rich ecology erased, especially in the area around the City, by the power of finance as it either buys up, or simply has the effect of raising the price of, land and property. Small companies, perfectly viable in production terms, cannot survive – a real irony given the ritual political invocation of small businesses as the hope for the future.

London is also the most unequal city in the country, and this too produces problems. It exacerbates the poverty of the poor, especially through house-prices. In its most bizarre recent manifestation local councils are 'decanting' their benefit-claiming poor to other regions. The whole social reproduction of the city is made more difficult.

Meanwhile 'the regions' also suffer from the dominance of finance. It is not only that this sector itself, and its wealth, are located in London. It is that its dominance of the national economy (and polity – see later) actively undermines regional growth.

Thus the City sucks in graduate labour from other regions, depriving them of a stratum from which economic growth might spring. (Meanwhile politicians castigate them for a lack of skills!) If the golden goose argument worked there'd be a geographical 'trickle-down' to the rest of the country. The truth is that the opposite happens. Meanwhile the degree of national inequality is exacerbated, through the regional dimension, as owner-occupiers in London and the South East 'make' more from increases in house-prices than they earn from their jobs.

One response from the London financial elite is that there is a fiscal transfer from London to the regions. Not only does this not address the dynamics of regional growth, it is a carefully calibrated fiction.[58] It is a political slogan based on very narrow criteria, which fails to take account of a host of ways in which London (and finance specifically) benefit from national policy. And it provokes damaging antagonisms, dividing the nation on regional lines when hostility should really be addressed to finance and the super-rich.

So we have a dysfunctional capital city, ferocious inequalities both within that city and between a vortex of growth in the South East and a land often referred to as 'the Rest of the Country', and an economic path that is detrimental to balanced growth. And all these are problems arising, not from the *crisis* of finance and the way that has been addressed, but from its *growth*, its dominance. It is imperative that we construct a different settlement.

One reason this bizarre arrangement exists is that finance dominates not only the economy but also politics and ideology. Its political influence is widely documented, yet somehow unseen or simply accepted (compare with the outrage at any hint of influence by trades unions). Yet in fact it is extremely active: it funds endless research projects that confirm its status as the golden goose, it is seen as a source of unbiased expertise, there are revolving doors with government … and it doesn't even have to 'lobby' very explicitly, since it is cosily part and parcel of the social world of the elites. Policies across the range reflect the interests of finance, whose upper échelons are at the core of an elite whose spatial concentration in the South East consolidates their mutual support. There is a grossly unequal geography, as well as class configuration, of democracy and of voice in this country. And the City puts in a lot of work to keep it thus.

Less routinely recognised is how 'finance thinking' has become hegemonic ideologically. Finance may be a global industry but part of its power lies in the fact that it is intimate too – it gets inside our heads.[59] People from finance are interviewed as 'experts' in the media, as though they had no interests at stake. Economics is thus removed from political contestation. Competitive individualism is taken for granted. Distinctions are forgotten (erased) between earned and unearned, between value creation and value extraction (convenient, since finance's growth has depended so much on the latter – hence the burgeoning inequality from which we began this thumb-nail sketch of the state of the nation). In this society that celebrates choice we are told there is no alternative. This truly is hegemonic common sense, and it is at this level that social settlements are consolidated. It is at this level, therefore, that a challenge must be launched. This means not just contesting individual policies and issues (though that must be done) but even more importantly challenging the whole framework, the very language, that has become our society's common sense, and that both obscures the injustice that is being done and lulls us into acceptance that it is all inevitable.[60]

Moreover if this challenge is necessary because of the effects 'at home', it is equally so because of the UK's role in the wider world. As the Tax Justice Network has tirelessly pointed out, the existence of tax havens, and the practices of tax evasion and avoidance, are a means of redistribution from global poor to global rich and a key cause of world poverty. London's finance sector is a prime node in these arrangements. Could we develop what I have called 'a politics of place beyond place', addressing our responsibilities for the global effects of our economy?[61] Indeed the internal and external politics of place are linked – the poverty in London is an element in the same dynamics as the poverty in the global South. Indeed, to take us back to the initial argument, London's finance sector was one of the crucial birthplaces of, and is now a key place of diffusion of, global neoliberalism, with its practices of cutting back state services, privatisation and deregulation. These are among our main exports.

We are living a strange situation – a populace guided by a hegemonic discourse that prevents escape from neoliberalism and yet a wide range of disparate groups whose interests potentially range them against the dominance of finance. There has been an economic (financial) crisis, but the ideological carapace has not cracked. Is it possible to build alliances, perhaps as suggested in the Green New Deal, and to break out of the common sense of this finance-dominated social settlement?

September, 2013

More Than A Lobby: Finance in the UK

Tamasin Cave

Lord Sassoon, until January this year economic secretary to the Treasury, is a man who bestrides the worlds of government and finance. In 2012 he delivered the inaugural summer lecture of the British Bankers Association. He began by thanking the outgoing head of the BBA, Angela Knight for her services to Britain: 'Angela, the country owes you a debt of gratitude', he said, praising her for her steady calm presence during the Northern Rock crisis of 2007, for her masterful lobbying to defend the City in Brussels, and for rebuilding banking's relationship with the UK government and with the industry's customers.[62]

Sassoon went on to explain how, as early as 2003, the Bank of England financial stability team had already identified 'some of the key issues that would be at the heart of the crisis, for example, the over reliance of Northern Rock on wholesale funding, the extent of Bradford and Bingley's exposure to the buy-to-let market, RBS's increasing exposures in Germany and elsewhere'.

He talked of how in 2005, Andrew Large, who was deputy governor of financial stability at the Bank, was 'ringing alarm bells', one of two people identified by Sassoon at 'the top global table that were standing out against the orthodoxy'. 'Sadly we all listened but took no action,' said Sassoon.

According to Lord Sassoon, this is a government 'utterly committed to ensuring the UK is open to business and that London continues to thrive as a global economic centre… A government with a number of bankers in its ranks, led by a Prime Minister who is proud to say he comes from a stock broking family'. Sassoon's remarks echo the sentiments of the Labour Party's Ed Balls a few years earlier. In 2006 Ed Balls told an audience at the BBA that 'when the WorldCom accounting scandal broke in the US, we resisted pressures from commentators for a regulatory crackdown'. He went on to say that the UK government had a 'specific and clear interest' in safeguarding 'the light touch and proportionate regulatory regime that has made London a magnet for international business'. Of course it was this same 'light touch' regulatory regime that allowed Northern Rock, Bradford and Bingley and RBS – finance as a whole – to engage in a frenzy of risky business.

Lord Sassoon is only one of many former bankers to have served in the current government. In the current Cabinet both David Laws and Oliver Letwin worked in investment banking before they entered Parliament. In fact the UK comes second only to Switzerland for the number of people moving through the 'revolving door' between the finance sector and officialdom according to a report by the OECD.[63] Baron Green of Hurstpierpoint, previously Chairman of HSBC is currently a Minister at both the Department for Business Enterprise and Skills and the Foreign and Commonwealth Office. In May 2013 the former Chairman of Goldman Sachs, Richard Sharp, joined the Bank of England's Financial Policy Committee, the new watchdog set up to protect the public from another financial meltdown.[64] Two months later another former Goldman Sachs banker, Mark Carney, became the governor of the same institution. Current and former employees of the investment bank also known as 'the vampire squid' have donated £8.8 to Britain's political parties in the last decade. Sharp himself donated £400,000 during that period. And this is only a fraction of what the sector gives. In 2011, hedge funds, financiers and private equity made up over a quarter of Conservative Party funding, with the City as a whole contributing more than half of its donated income.

The global accountancy firms – the so-called 'Big Four', PWC, KPMG, Deloitte and Ernst & Young – are also deeply embedded in the British state. They earn hundreds of millions of pounds a year from government business while loaning their staff to government departments and political parties, where they advise on everything from tax law to privatisation programmes.

All four companies insist that their involvement is limited to providing 'technical insight' into proposed polices. But at the same time they actively lobby government for changes in tax legislation. Ernst & Young's Tax Policy Development team, for example, says that it 'works with clients to develop proposals for changes in tax policy that can be taken to government'.

'Unlike a traditional lobbying service,' the pitch reads, Ernst & Young's team will work with its clients to develop 'technical policy options in a form that is used inside Government today'. Put simply, this means it uses its knowledge of the workings of government to lobby for clients. This, it says, means that tax changes can be 'implemented with the minimum of delay', and makes sure that 'the concerns of policy-makers are addressed'. This gives proposed tax breaks 'the maximum chance of adoption'. In this respect, the insider status of E&Y is clearly of benefit to its clients.

The advantages to clients of lobbying for tax policy changes – as opposed to tax planning – are clearly explained in Ernst & Young's pitch: 'In an era where the government is focusing on actively identifying and countering tax avoidance, and where there has been considerable media coverage on particular "tax avoiders", policy development offers a low risk alternative.' In other words, 'policy development' – lobbying for changes in the law – offers its corporate clients a less risky way to reduce their tax bill.

Incidentally, Ernst & Young's lobbying team would not be covered by the government's proposed register of lobbyists, which is making its way through Parliament. If it passes in its current form, the register will include only a tiny fraction – 5 per cent on some estimates – of the £2billion UK lobbying industry.

Former politicians and advisers beat a well-trodden path in other direction. Tony Blair and his lieutenant Jonathan Powell both took jobs at Morgan Stanley when they left Downing Street. They are members of a group too numerous to name here. But some idea of the scale of what's happening can be grasped if we restrict ourselves to former Ministers in the Department of Health during the New Labour years. Alan Milburn is now an advisor to Bridgepoint, a private equity firm and has also worked for PWC. Norman Warner has been an adviser to Apax Partners, another private equity firm. And Patricia Hewitt has advised Cinven, yet another private equity group.

And then there is the current Prime Minister. As Lord Sassoon notes, David Cameron comes from a stock broking family. This underplays things a little. His father co-founded the Panamanian investment company Blairmore Holdings and was the chairman of Close International Asset Management, based in Jersey. Unlike Tony

Blair, who only began to make extensive use of tax havens on leaving office, Cameron is part of an offshore dynasty. Blairmore indeed.

Through the revolving door that takes politicians into lucrative employment and financiers into government, through party donations, and through the informal mechanisms of finance's lavish hospitality, the political class is integrated with the sector to the point where it can be difficult to see where one stops and the other starts. Ambitious politicians have been eager to associate with investment bankers and others from the sector. There's money to be made, of course, but also the seductive sense that they are in the room with the people who understand how the world really works, with the winners. Billions in taxpayers' money seems like a small price to pay for such company. And the pervasive secrecy and clannishness of British politics only compounds the problem. We do not know, for example, how much money finance contributes to the free market think tanks that enjoy such sympathetic coverage in the UK media.

Given the degree of overlap, and the shared commitment to London as a world financial centre, the organized lobbies for finance do not have to spend much time persuading the government to promote their interests. Instead, in the words of the then-Chancellor and later Prime Minister Gordon Brown, they work together to 'promote the City and its financial service expertise throughout the world'. It is hardly surprising that the few warnings that reached Sassoon's 'the global top table' went unheeded. The British government no longer sees the financial sector as one lobby among others. It sees itself as a lobbyist for finance. This was, and is, a recipe for trouble.

September, 2013

The Metropolitanisation of Gains, The Nationalisation of Losses

Adam Leaver

A recent 800-page report highlighted just how unequal the UK regional economic landscape has become.[65] In ratio terms, the UK's largest 2nd tier city generates around 10% of the output of London – the second highest capital to 2nd tier city output inequality within the EU. In terms of the regional concentration of GDP creation, we have more in common with a Hungary, Bulgaria, Romania or Greece than a Germany, Netherlands or Sweden. And while there is evidence to show that the UK's 2nd tier cities were growing faster than the capital pre-crisis (from a lower base), that trend is now being undone as austerity cuts bite into the non-metropolitan North and West.

At one level it is no surprise that the UK coalition government's immediate post-election rhetoric about rebalancing has been abandoned, to be replaced by a new, morally-laden discourse about the unfair subsidies received by the regions and the rights of Londoners to keep more of 'their' income.[66] UK recessions encourage internecine squabbles over resources and London's position as both political and economic centre mean there was only ever likely to be one clear winner. But as Londoners and their informal representatives look on jealously as the bank notes seem to disappear to the non-metropolitan North and West, it is perhaps worth revisiting how we got here. This is a complex issue that requires balance and open-mindedness if we are to understand the diversity of flows in a national economy.

In terms of the UK national growth model, two processes have cemented London's dominance within the economy. First we now rely less on the manufacture of things and more on the manufacture of credit. We have bought into a growth model that depends on the ability of our banks to lend against assets, and for households (and businesses) to convert the capital gains from those rising asset prices into expenditure. It is a startling fact that the real value of housing equity withdrawal under Thatcher and Blair was marginally higher than the real value of GDP growth.[67] This national model significantly empowers London's form of 'gentlemanly capitalism': the historically entrenched culture and interests of land and finance within the UK which prioritise the making of money from money over the making of money from industrial enterprise. The political and economic spheres mutually reinforce each other: finance has access to the charmed circle of policy formation because of the great wealth and prestige bestowed upon them by a credit-fuelled, asset based growth regime.

Second, the broader process of privatisation and the extension of public-private partnerships disproportionately benefit a global city like London. London does attract capital, but it does so because it is a kind of conversion machine, taking national and international assets, converting them into revenue streams from which well-placed individuals skim high pay. In other words. London attracts capital because it is also *extractive*. Let's take the UK's Private Finance Initiative (PFI)[68] as an example. The PFI is a form of Public Private Partnership (PPP) where public infrastructure projects are funded, built and managed by the private sector to a public specification. Generally PFI contracts last a minimum of 25 years, during which the private sector receive payments in exchange for bearing the project risk. Notionally private sector participants are paid only if services are delivered according to the negotiated concession agreement. The decomposition of activities around a contracted-out infrastructure project leads to a fragmentation of corporations around specialised functions, so that one company may provide the finance, another may build the school or hospital, another may manage the services. In theory some of these functions need not be located on the site of the project. And certainly the revenue streams do not all circulate regionally: the finance company probably has its operating office in London, as might the service management office. Even the building firm might be co-ordinated from London using local contractors on site. Overseas companies that invest in infrastructure funds are also likely to have an office in London, and those senior workers are likely to be extremely well paid.

Fragmentation has led to a concentration of certain functions like financing and asset management in London. This has diminished capacity in the regions through the withering of broad competences, the destruction of joined up supply chains, and skills drift as talent is forced to relocate down South to find a job. State-sponsored investment projects across the country have benefited private sector growth in London and the South. The obvious counterfactual – a publicly funded and organised infrastructure development programme – would result in a greater proportion of project revenue streams accruing to the region around the development site, kicking in multipliers that would further benefit the local economy.

These two developments tell us something about modern day capitalism in the UK. Contrary to the fantasies of free-market proponents, the success of London has much to do with an active UK state and its willingness to take on or underwrite private sector liabilities. The banking sector, for example, is a net recipient of state funds which the whole country must pay for, even though the private gains are largely realised in London. By our calculations, the Treasury received taxes of £203 billion over five years up to 2006/7; substantially less than the cost of the UK bank bailouts, estimated at between £289 billion to £1,183 billion by the IMF.[69] If we factor in the impact of government bailout guarantees on bank borrowing rates, then the longer term subsidies are even higher.[70] And all this is before we consider the costs of mis-selling and other predatory habits

Liabilities are also underwritten at public expense in the case of PFIs. Typically PFI consortia leave the maximum contractual risk with the local state or cost at a premium any risks that cannot be offloaded. So the flipside to the revenue streams clipped by metropolitan elites is a series of costs and liabilities passed onto non-metropolitan areas. There are also many hidden, contingent liabilities – as when NHS Trusts cannot repay their PFI loans, or unwieldy contracts produce inefficiencies and exorbitant penalty clauses which are costly to renegotiate. And this is before we discuss the many contracts that overshoot their original estimates.

All of these interventions should be thought of as state subsidies; received mainly by private subsidiaries operating in the capital, and paid for by taxpayers the length and breadth of the country. This quiet cross-subsidy from North and West to South East has been running un-noticed for a long period of time. Its unanticipated result is a kind of regional moral hazard: the metropolitanisation of gains, and the nationalisation of losses.

But we have arguably reached the limits of that model. Despite the current political spin that a 3% rise in house prices (driven mainly by an 8% rise in the capital) marks the end of our problems, there is a limit to how far asset prices can rise when wages and growth are stagnant. We just aren't growing fast enough to take on the liabilities to fuel the asset price rises, and we aren't paying people enough to allow them to take on larger interest repayments. If debt is a claim on our future growth, there comes a tipping point where the scale of debt repayments act as a drag on growth, crowding out investment and consumption.

From this perspective, a genuine rebalancing of the economy to a more sustainable model will involve a lot more than devolution. It will involve a lot more than encouraging private sector growth in the regions. It will require a fundamental rethink of the corporate welfare apparatus that has so benefitted the London area in recent years.

September, 2013

Illicit Financial Flows, Poverty and Human Rights[71]

Lloyd Lipsett

In October 2013, the International Bar Association's Human Rights Institute (IBAHRI) published an innovative new study, *Tax Abuses, Poverty and Human Rights*. The publication was the result of over a year of research and international consultations by a Task Force on Illicit Financial Flows, Poverty and Human Rights. Although tax abuses have been rising in prominence on the global political agenda in recent years, the issues have rarely been framed in terms of human rights. From the early feedback on the IBAHRI Task Force's work, an explicit human rights analysis is a welcome contribution to the global debates on tax justice, and further research and discussion is required in order to provide more practical guidance to policy-makers and practitioners.

The Task Force found that tax abuses have considerable negative impacts on the enjoyment of human rights. Simply put, tax abuses deprive governments of the resources required to provide the programmes that give effect to economic, social and cultural rights, and to create and strengthen the institutions that uphold civil and political rights. Actions of states that encourage or facilitate tax abuses, or that deliberately frustrate the efforts of other states to counter tax abuses, could constitute a violation of their international human rights obligations, particularly with respect to economic, social and cultural rights.

In the context of the developing world, the tax abuses of greatest concern to the Task Force included transfer-pricing and other cross-border intra-group transactions; the negotiation of tax holidays and incentives; the taxation of natural resources; and, the use of offshore investment accounts. Secrecy jurisdictions are also a concern because of their role in facilitating tax abuses.

The Task Force's human rights analysis also underscores the link between human rights and extreme poverty. For instance, the UN Human Rights Council had recently adopted *Guiding Principles* on *Extreme Poverty and Human Rights* that describe how poverty is connected as a cause or consequence of violations of 14 different human rights and all the key human rights principles – ranging from the right to food, the right to health, the right to education, the right to social security, to the principle of transparency.

Building on its review of international human rights law, the Task Force's report presents a number of conclusions and recommendations for governments, business enterprises and the legal profession:

Conclusion #1: States have obligations to counter tax abuses at the domestic and international level, including through cooperation in multinational institutions. While it must be recognized that international human rights treaties do not address tax abuses in an explicit manner, the Task Force concludes that States' legal obligations related to economic, social and cultural rights can be applied to the question of tax abuses, in terms of their actions at the domestic level, in their international cooperation efforts and in their participation in multilateral institutions.

Conclusion #2: Business enterprises have a responsibility to avoid negative impacts on human rights caused by tax abuses. The emerging human rights guidance for business enterprises suggests that all business enterprises, including corporate legal advisors and bankers, should exercise due diligence on the potential negative impacts of their operations – including with respect to the impacts of their tax planning strategies. Indeed, tax abuse is poised to become an important issue for business enterprises in terms of corporate social responsibility, reputational risk and human rights.

Furthermore, the estimated scale of corporate tax abuses also undermines some of the claims that foreign investment and private enterprise are major drivers of sustainable development. While there is undeniable evidence that foreign investment and private enterprise is – and can be – a powerful force for development and positive human rights impacts, evidence about the extent of tax abuses by multinational enterprises serves to reinforce criticism and cynicism about the role of the private sector in development.

Conclusion #3: The legal profession has an important role in assisting states and business enterprises in confronting the negative impacts of tax abuses on human rights. There was widespread agreement in the interviews that lawyers must balance their obligation to defend their client's interest with the underlying role of the tax system in society. One stakeholder stated that 'we also need to encourage positive performance and the positive leadership role that lawyers can play in creating rules and regulations. Lawyers need to decide what is acceptable behaviour for their profession and to take the issue [of tax abuses] outside an individual decision for an individual lawyer.'

Early Reactions and Next Steps

Not surprisingly, the early reaction to the Task Force's report has been varied. Tax justice advocates and human rights organizations have welcomed the linking of tax abuses and international human rights law – which provides an additional rationale for action on these important issues. Tax practitioners have raised valid questions about the need for more precise criteria to delineate legitimate tax planning and the tax abuses that fall afoul of human rights standards. Some commentators have stressed the need for additional research to better understand the magnitude of tax abuses and their impacts on developing countries.

The IBAHRI Task Force welcomes these comments and is also encouraged to see new initiatives and conferences that are delving into different aspects of the issues raised by the publication. While the Task Force's publication succeeded in providing a broad framing of issues and stakeholder feedback in terms of international human rights standards, the details of abusive tax schemes and practices also need to be analysed at a more microscopic level. The development of further case studies can help to provide concrete and nuanced illustration of the links between tax abuses and their negative impacts on human rights. The development of practical guidance can help policy-makers and practitioners to think through the human rights implications of their actions and advice.

The Task Force's publication on tax abuses and human rights therefore should be viewed as a starting-point for a global conversation between states, business enterprises, civil society organizations and the legal profession about ensuring that the human rights dimension of taxation is increasingly understood and more fully respected.

May, 2014

Human Rights and Just Taxation

Thomas Pogge

The most widely underfulfilled human rights, by far, are social and economic ones, such as the right to a standard of living that is adequate for the health and well-being of oneself and one's family, including food, clothing, housing and medical care and necessary social services, and the right to security in the event of unemployment, sickness, disability, widowhood, old age or other lack of livelihood in circumstances beyond one's control.[72] About half of all human beings suffer serious deprivations of one such kind or another and have no access to the necessary social services that would protect them.

The first-line responsibility for these unfulfilled human rights lies with the governments of the countries in which the poorer half live. But these governments are also poor. While the industrialized states have annual revenues in the order of $20,000 to $50,000 per person, India has annual revenues of barely $200 per person and many other governments are poorer still. These large international discrepancies are due to two factors: the *per capita* gross domestic products of poor countries are much smaller; and they also raise a much smaller proportion of their GDPs as government revenues, typically under 20% as compared to an OECD average of well over 40%.

It is difficult for poor-country governments to raise income or consumption taxes from the poor majority of their population – such taxes are unpopular, costly to collect and aggravate the very human rights deficits they are supposed to alleviate. But such governments also encounter difficulties in imposing taxes on those who could pay. Through sophisticated efforts, wealthy citizens of these countries, and corporations operating within them, escape taxation to an extent that would be unthinkable in an affluent country with political clout and a highly sophisticated and well-funded tax administration. Boston Consulting Group estimates that 33.3% of all private financial wealth owned by people in Africa and the Middle East and 25.6% of such wealth owned by Latin Americans – some $2.6 trillion – is kept abroad; while the analogous estimates for North America and Europe are 1.8% and 7.9%, respectively.[73] To raise taxes on the income and capital gains produced by this wealth, poor countries must largely rely on the honesty of their taxpayers as they lack access to information about their citizens' overseas holdings.

Multinational corporations (MNCs) also massively escape taxation, typically by creating additional subsidiaries in tax havens and then instructing their poor-country subsidiaries to contract with their tax-haven subsidiaries into money-losing arrangements involving trade misinvoicing, abusive transfer prices as well as inflated consulting and trademark fees.[74] These arrangements diminish the taxed profits of the poor-country subsidiaries while increasing the untaxed profits of the tax-haven subsidiaries. Global Financial Integrity estimates that corporate tax abuse accounts for 80% of all illicit financial outflows from less developed countries, or about $4.7 trillion during the 2002–11 period and $760 billion in 2011 alone.[75] This is five or six times the sum total of all official development assistance flowing into these countries during the same periods.[76] Christian Aid calculates that, through these profit- and tax-diminishing capital outflows, governments of less developed countries have lost tax revenues in the order of $160 billion annually – or about $2.5 trillion for the Millennium Development Goals period (2000–2015). 'If that money was available to allocate according to current spending patterns, the amount going into health services could save the lives of 350,000 children under the age of five every year.'[77]

Four groups of agents bear responsibility for the human rights deficit that results from poor countries' inability fully to collect reasonable taxes. First, the secrecy jurisdictions and tax haven countries (including Switzerland, Ireland, the UK and the US) which structure their tax and legal systems so as to encourage tax abuse and also typically protect bank secrecy against the tax authorities of less developed countries. Second, the individuals and corporations that erode the tax base of poor countries by using tax havens to hide their wealth and profits. Third, the bankers, lawyers, accountants and lobbyists who devise, implement and 'legalize' these schemes. Fourth, powerful rich-country governments which facilitate the tax dodging of their MNCs abroad[78] and get tax havens to cooperate with their own tax enforcement efforts without ensuring that poor-country governments receive similar cooperation.[79]

The key to reducing the tax gap and consequent human rights deficit in the poor countries is global financial transparency: the abolition of shell companies and anonymous accounts, automatic exchange of tax information worldwide, and the requirement that, in their audited annual reports and tax returns, MNCs report their sales, profits and taxes paid country by country for each jurisdiction in which they operate. Such financial transparency would not merely advance tax justice but additionally protect human rights by also curtailing the activities of criminals such as terrorists, money-launderers, and traffickers in persons, drugs and weapons.

These changes must be implemented by the governments of tax havens and other rich countries, which will continue to move forward so long as there is sufficient pressure and support from their populations. Tax dodgers and their bankers, lawyers, accountants and lobbyists can help by not opposing or subverting the needed reforms and by collaborating toward the formulation and acceptance of ethical standards governing, for example, the conduct of MNCs or of international tax lawyers and accountants. A major break-through for financial transparency is now within reach. Let us ensure that the populations of the poor countries, whose basic human rights are at stake, participate fully.[80]

June, 2014

Taxation for Human Rights

Magdalena Sepúlveda

What does tax have to do with human rights? Why is tackling tax evasion an ethical and legal obligation as well as a necessity for good governance? What do human rights obligations tell us about how States should design tax systems? How can good tax policies help us eradicate poverty and improve the enjoyment of human rights? These are all issues I hope to illuminate in my next report to the Human Rights Council.[81]

Historically, human rights professionals and monitoring bodies have shown hesitation in addressing fiscal policies and their impact, but thankfully this is now beginning to change. During my country missions – for example to Paraguay and Ireland – I have seen firsthand the extremely unjust effects of taxation and spending policies that do not take human rights into account. It has become evident from the work of academics, practitioners, economists, NGOs and the UN, that examining fiscal and tax policies is a crucial component of assessing States' compliance with human rights obligations. In particular, recent work has illuminated the relevance of these policies to with regard to tackling inequality and in providing for the realization of human rights. Governments' rhetoric about eliminating poverty and realizing human rights is rendered meaningless without an effort to collect the funds necessary to pay for hospitals, piped water, schools, social security or legal aid. Without adequate tax revenue, the availability and quality of public services suffer, with a direct negative impact on the enjoyment of rights such as education and health of the poorest people in society. This in turn perpetuates inter-generational poverty.

A rights-based approach provides guidance on how, and from whom, States should collect taxes. Often, due to their limited political voice, people living in poverty are required to pay more than their fair share in taxes, while their needs are overlooked when resources are allocated. For example, on my mission to Paraguay, I found that there was no income tax and the government largely relied on sales tax for revenue. This had profoundly discriminatory effects: the poorest 10 per cent of the population was paying 18 per cent of their income in VAT while for the richest 10 per cent of the population, VAT represented only 4.6 per cent of their income. [82] As well as running afoul of the right to non-discrimination, by disproportionately cutting into their already small income, this also denied the poorest their rights to food, health and an adequate standard of living, among others.

The International Covenant on Economic, Social and Cultural Rights obliges its 161 signatory states to use the 'maximum available resources' to secure the economic, social and cultural rights of its population. These maximum available resources include those that could *potentially be collected* through taxation. Therefore, if a State has a small tax base or overlooks widespread tax evasion while its people go hungry or homeless, it may in fact be in violation of this obligation.

Tax evasion, which is a particularly high-profile issue at the moment, has been estimated to result in annual revenue losses of USD $285 billion to developing countries, [83] and Africa loses twice as much in illicit financial outflows (including tax evasion) as it receives in aid. The problem is not just limited to the developing world; tax evasion in Spain is estimated to have resulted in a loss equivalent to EUR 88 billion in 2010. This greatly exceeds the total budget cuts made in 2012 as part of devastating austerity measures, which severely impacted human rights enjoyment in the country. [84] A state that does not take strong measures to collect all taxes owed cannot be said to be devoting the maximum available resources to the realization of economic, social and cultural rights.

It is important, now more than ever, for human rights advocates to get ahead of the cost argument rather than avoiding it. The devastating spread of austerity measures – including taxation and fiscal policy reforms – is hitting the poorest people hardest and in many cases threatens their health, livelihood and very survival. Time and again, the poorest and most disadvantaged people (such as women, single parents or persons with disabilities) are being asked to pay more proportionally, while wealthy persons and corporations are escaping without paying their fair share. All too often, when governments face human rights bodies they use the defense of resource constraints; for instance claiming that the financial crisis leaves them no choice but to cut welfare benefits and services that those living in poverty rely on. Politicians, diplomats and policy-makers wheel out these excuses repeatedly, in media interviews and in reaction to the criticism of human rights bodies. In fact, in nearly every country of the world it is not a question of lack of resources, but rather of a lack of political will to collect and marshal these resources in a manner that is compliant with human rights – even though these states have voluntarily committed themselves, through international treaties, to precisely this responsibility.

Thankfully, more and more people are looking at tax through the lens of human rights. I warmly welcome this timely edition of *Tax Justice Focus* for bringing the human rights imperative to the fore, because there has never been a greater need to work together to demystify the idea that fiscal and macroeconomic policies are outside the reach of international human rights law. In the vital work of clarifying and communicating the social, economic and ethical imperative for a new global paradigm around tax, human rights and tax justice advocates are strategic allies.

June, 2014

Public Duty, Private Gain: Professional Ethics and Tax

Atul K. Shah

Many features distinguish professionals from other groups like merchants, traders or labourers. Professionals are generally seen as having a strong sense of integrity, responsibility and accountability to the public interest. For example, auditors are required by law to use their professional training, independence and judgment to give a 'true and fair' opinion on the financial statements of companies. In this case, the state has given professionals not only the right, but also the responsibility, to supervise private enterprises using their expertise.

Both the accountancy and the legal professions are therefore vulnerable to challenge on public interest grounds, because they earn their professional privileges in the expectation that they will use them to serve the public good. Their professional status is not purely based on their ability to perform well in the service of their clients' interests and to earn a great deal of money as a result. Many professional firms have recognised that they risk their long-term commercial prospects if they lose sight of the public duty at the origin of their professional privileges. However, the actions that they have taken to date to mitigate these risks have been focused on public relations rather than on substance.

Today, the Big 4 accounting firms, Deloitte, PWC, KPMG and EY, are faced with a fundamental cultural and professional dilemma: do they serve the dollar or their professional code of ethics and responsibility? Past scandals point to instances where this tension has unravelled in spectacular fashion, such as the demise of Arthur Andersen after its unethical and highly conflicted auditing of Enron.

In the area of taxation, this conflict between public and private interest is particularly acute. Protecting the public interest would require the Big 4 firms to ensure that their clients pay a fair amount of taxes. The commercial reality, however, is that they often go out of their way to help clients minimise their tax liabilities. They have offices in 179 of the 223 secrecy jurisdictions identified by Tax Research in a 2009 survey and they proactively help clients to reduce taxes through these secrecy jurisdictions.

Tax is an obligation to pay a proportion of earnings to support the state in its role as a provider of public services. It is a duty, not a choice. In the nineteenth century, John Ruskin wrote in 'Unto This Last' that most businessmen know nothing about political economy, and that all they know is how to count their revenue and costs. Ruskin observed that they did not appreciate the vital enabling role of the state in this process, preferring to take personal credit for their earnings. There seem to be echoes of this myopic worldview in the refusal of many tax professionals to acknowledge that using their expertise to undermine rather than adhere to principles of tax compliance is at odds with their values of integrity and responsibility.

Even though new recruits are trained and examined on the subject of ethics, the culture and values of the Big 4 firms are in many ways contrary to those ethical values. Instead of charging for tax advice on the basis of employee time, they charge in terms of money saved to the client, so it is much more lucrative to help clients to pursue aggressive tax strategies. Their internal codes of ethics often place the burden onto the employee to raise any issues of concern. And because these firms work with large clients, individual employees generally only deal with one aspect of a piece of client work, and rarely see the whole picture of what the firm is doing on behalf of its clients. The partners at the top may have a clearer overview, but it is likely that by the time they reach that stage, they have already been socialised into the culture. Those who might have challenged the system would not have reached the top, and so strongly ethical behaviour is filtered out.

The Institute of Chartered Accountants in England & Wales (ICAEW), the world's oldest professional body of accountants, has not sanctioned any Big 4 firms for their tax avoidance schemes or advice. Neither have the Chartered Institute of Management Accountants (CIMA) or the Association of Chartered Certified Accountants (ACCA), bodies which are equally global and perhaps even more so. On the contrary, these professional bodies often applaud the Big 4 and act as their choirmasters. The Big 4 routinely take advantage of legal loopholes to undermine the fundamental spirit of corporate and private tax regimes. In reaction to public criticism, the ICAEW recently published a 'technical release' on professional conduct and taxation. The section on ethics and values does not mention the duty of accountants to protect the public interest. Instead, the document provides its members with advice about how to deal with tax avoidance issues and communicate with HMRC. The ICAEW claims that it is clients who want to undertake aggressive tax avoidance schemes, and that some profiteering barristers are sanctioning aggressive tax avoidance. This is blame-shifting.

Recent public scandals about tax avoidance at large companies like Google, Starbucks and Apple prompted the ICAEW to complain about the negative publicity for large companies and to put the blame on government for the lack of clear tax rules and guidance. Its actions suggest that, instead of "protect[ing] the quality and integrity of the accountancy and finance profession", it is defending the Big 4 firms from accusations made about lapses in that quality and integrity.

What is needed is for members of professional bodies such as CIMA, ACCA and ICAEW to raise their concerns about unethical practices with those bodies, and for a wider movement to encourage the strengthening and enforcement of ethical codes by professional firms in relation to tax advice. This is not to underplay the role of government in responding more robustly to misdemeanours, and revoking licences to practice in the most extreme cases.

November, 2014

Women and Taxation: From Taxing for Growth and Tax Competition to Taxing for Sex Equality

Kathleeen Lahey

The Convention on the Elimination of All Forms of Discrimination against Women (CEDAW) was ratified in 1982, and the Beijing Platform for Action was adopted to accelerate the implementation of CEDAW in 1995. Despite the many steps taken around the world to put these international agreements into effect, women continue to experience significant economic inequality everywhere.

Many more women are poor than men. Very few women anywhere are as wealthy as men. As a result, political claims that tax cuts, low tax rates, and tax competition are essential for sustained economic growth have particularly undercut women's progress toward economic equality. Even in tax cut and low tax regimes, every component of 'taxing for growth' formulas increases tax burdens on women because they ignore women's economic realities: globally, with no exceptions, women have lower incomes, more unpaid work, more precarious and low-paid work, less income security, and less political stature than men in their countries.

How has this happened? It has happened because fiscal policies are constructed around one goal – taxing for growth – and largely ignore taxing for social needs. Advocates of market fundamentalism and free trade have promoted unregulated exploitation of domestic resources in search of higher business profits and privatization of government functions. Multinational corporations have exploited this policy climate by demanding that host countries give them special tax cuts, set up export production and tax free trade zones, and even donate lands, water, cheap mineral rights, and unregulated labour to induce them to set up operations in their borders.

The mantra of 'taxing for growth' has been promoted by the World Bank, the IMF, the OECD, the EU in making fiscal recommendations for high- and low-income countries alike. Their country-specific tax policy recommendations are adapted to national conditions, but the basic formula for 'tax cuts for growth' has been virtually the same everywhere: cut graduated individual and corporate tax rates, which generally range from low or zero tax rates on those with low incomes to high rates on the wealthy; raise more revenue with high-rate with 'flat' consumption taxes like the VAT and commodity taxes; give special tax breaks on investment incomes, savings, and capital gains; cut taxes on the rich; increase taxes on the poor.

In high-income countries, the result has been falling tax ratios (tax revenues as a share of GDP). This in turn has led to continued budget cuts to government services and programs – literally, permanent government austerities. In low-income countries, even those with increasing tax ratios, the result has been heavy reliance on gender and income regressive VAT and commodity taxes that are particularly hard on the poorest.

Globally, the end result of taxing for growth regimes has been increasing concentration of incomes and wealth in the hands of small numbers of very wealthy individuals and large corporations. Growing income inequalities between the Global North and South, between the rich and everyone else, and between women and men have reached crisis levels in countries at every level of development.

Revisioning fiscal systems around taxing for sex equality

There are no easy solutions to the growing gender and income inequalities resulting from growth and tax competition regimes. The negative effects of taxing for growth on the status of women, poverty levels, and human development has been pervasive and profound. Politicians now routinely think in terms of what remaining taxes can be cut, how remaining public programs and institutions can be further trimmed or transferred to the private sector to cut government spending or pay down deficits, and how to increase foreign direct investment in their countries by reducing taxes, business regulation, and labour costs.

Revisioning this discourse requires people to restate the fundamental principle that governments and taxes exist to meet the basic needs of all people – not just the wealthy. And of both women and men – not just men. In order to do this, both the technical mechanics of tax laws and of underlying economic policies have to be reframed around pursuing gender and income equality to secure the wellbeing of all.

Taxing for sex equality involves two vital steps. First, no jurisdiction should enact any new tax or spending laws, programs, or practices that increase market or after-tax income gender gaps. Second, the negative gender effects of all existing tax, spending, and other fiscal laws should be corrected as a matter of urgency.

On the spending side of government budgets, 'taxing for equality' calls for producing enough revenue to increase government investments in education and skills, care resources, transportation, health, food security, and housing resources in order to reduce women's markedly unequal shares of unpaid work and increase women's shares of market incomes, after-tax incomes, and political authority.

On the tax side of budgets, flat-rated and minimally graduated rates of personal and corporate income and capital taxes should be converted immediately to graduated income tax structures – 'progressive' tax structures – that base tax liability on ability to pay. Revenue systems designed to 'tax for sex equality' should have all these features:

- progressive personal and corporate income taxes generating at least 60% of all domestic revenues;
- supplementary allowances for all individuals in paid work earning less than above-poverty incomes;
- income supplements designed to promote not just part-time or occasional paid work, but fulltime permanent decent paid work;
- tax exemptions that ensure that no income taxes can tax individuals back into poverty;
- income tax rates that enable governments to redistribute market incomes from those with the highest incomes to those with the lowest incomes;
- cost of living mechanisms that keep progressive income tax rates in sync with actual costs of living;
- tax exemptions that do not tax anyone living below poverty levels combined with food, housing, education, and income supplements that raise everyone above poverty levels;
- tax all adults as individuals
- ensure that all tax benefits, cash benefits, and in kind government

services are given to women as individuals in order to protect their financial autonomy;

- provide adequate tax-free allowances for dependent children during all schooling years;
- eliminate any provisions that deliver tax benefits in lieu of public or direct grants (i.e., eliminate all tax expenditures, which do not generally reach those with low incomes);
- repeal all tax, cash, and in kind benefits that subsidize women's unpaid work;
- eliminate use of presumptive or imputed incomes as the basis for taxation at all but moderate and high income levels;
- especially in low-income countries, restructure income security measures as direct contributory systems funded largely by employers and governments for all those unable to accumulate sufficient capital to provide for their own lifelong income security;
- reward workers and businesses entering the formal reported economy with meaningful supports, but prohibit the use of punitive tax compliance and regulatory measures.

Free trade agreements, globalization, and 'taxing for growth' formulas have all contributed to increased use of flat-rate VAT, commodity, property, and sales taxes in countries at all levels of development. Such taxes are all gender and income regressive, and, when continued in use at all, should be restructured to provide, as a minimum:

- full exemptions for all goods, services, lands, buildings, institutions, rights, and inputs into education, care, health, community and other public facilities, and government processes;
- such exemptions to include foods, medicines, personal care items, clothing, personnel, books, writing equipment, and other items typically used in those sectors;
- total revenues raised by such taxes should be at least 20% less in total value than the combined revenue raised through income and capital taxes.

Tax systems should also provide for progressive wealth and inheritance taxes payable only by the wealthiest (top 15%), with these features:

- limited opportunities for evasion;
- guaranteed life estates for surviving family members during educational, disability, and final years;
- abolition of the use of charitable foundations and donations beyond specified modest limits.

Tax systems should produce enough revenue to meet all of a country's infrastructure, social, human welfare, and economic development needs. Countries with natural resources should sequester nonrenewable and volatile renewable resource revenues in independent trusts that provide no more than 3% of annual trust incomes to annual national budgets.

Women's fiscal equality is fundamental to all human rights. Governments around the world are presently negotiating the terms of the new Sustainable Development Goals (SDGs) to replace and expand the Millennium Development Goals that expire in 2015. SDG Goal 5 calls on all governments and international organizations to 'Achieve gender equality and empower all women and girls, and Goal 10, to 'Reduce inequality within and among countries'. All the SDGs in turn depend on achieving Goal 17, to 'Strengthen the means of implementation and revitalize the global partnership for sustainable development.'

The Universal Declaration of Human Rights declares that 'everyone is entitled to all the rights and freedoms set forth without distinction of any kind, including distinctions based on sex' (Article 28), and CEDAW recognizes the 'the equal rights of men and women to enjoy all economic, social, cultural, civil, and political rights' (preamble).

Now is the time to demand full endorsement of the SDGs as well as explicit reference in them to national and international obligations to raise the revenues necessary to realize these goals, to spend such revenues in ways that eliminate longstanding economic inequalities between women and men, between the politically disenfranchised and powerholders, and among countries at dramatically divergent levels of development and economic durability.

None of these goals can be achieved without ensuring that women everywhere live on terms of genuine fiscal equality.

May, 2015

Fossil-fuel Subsidies and Taxation: Two Sides of the Same Carbon Coin

Laura Merrill

Governments spent around USD 600 billion last year subsidising the price of petrol, diesel, gas, electricity and coal in order to keep consumer prices below international levels.[85] Governments spend another USD 100 billion annually on subsidies to upstream producers of oil, gas and coal. These subsidies include tax breaks, infrastructure investment (ports and rail tracks in particular), write offs and the like.[86] For the G20 alone such exploration and producer subsidies are estimated to be around USD 88 billion,[87] yet upstream producer subsidy figures are far more opaque and difficult to quantify at the national level (sometimes for good reason). These are the producer subsidies. In the EU consumption and production subsidies combined totalled around USD 40 billion in 2010. This development approach, in which energy systems are built around the use of fossil-fuels, has led to prosperity for some. But we are all paying a high price in terms of climate change and human health.

Fossil-fuel subsidies in an age of climate change drive us in the wrong direction. With lower prices to consumers and lower costs to producers, consumers consume more, producers produce more. This increases the use of fossil-fuels and the levels of pollution in our cities and of carbon in the atmosphere. One piece of research on the historic link between fossil-fuel subsidies and climate change suggests that these subsidies drove 36 per cent of global carbon emissions between 1980 and 2010.[88] An IMF working paper includes the broader costs to society of fossil fuels (such as traffic accidents and pollution, as well as the social costs of climate change) and finds the true cost of fossil fuels amounts to an eye-popping USD 5.3 trillion a year,[89] or USD 10 million a minute.[90]

Studies suggest that such is the scale of these subsidies that their removal could lead to a decrease in global green house gas (GHG) emissions of between 6 and 13 per cent by 2050, compared to business as usual.[91] There is no doubting that such subsidies (even using more restrictive definitions such as those of the WTO) are significant and dwarf government support to renewables and private investment in energy efficiency by a factor of four.[92] They can represent a significant fiscal drain on government budgets. In some Southeast Asian countries they account for between 5 and 30 per cent of government expenditure,[93] far more than levels spent on health or education. In general most subsidies are found in the Middle East and North Africa region (around 50% by total value) followed by Emerging and Developing Asia, and Central and Eastern Europe.[94]

Because of the scale of the subsidies opportunities for rent-seeking and corruption abound. Unsurprisingly, fossil-fuel subsidies (particularly for oil) and countries with weak institutions tend to go hand in hand. Indeed, research finds that there is a link between the ration of subsidies to GDP and measures of 'government effectiveness, rule of law, regulatory quality and freedom from corruption'.[95] There are also strong links between countries that have energy resources and the presence of subsidies, and the view (sometimes enshrined within constitutions) that national fossil fuel resources should be available cheaply to the population. Such subsidies were set up for development and support to the poor but it is now argued that they are maintained in part because governments lack the capacity to pursue policy goals by other means.[96] Industrial interests also play a big part in retaining fossil-fuel subsidies. Fuel smuggling between countries and the adulteration of fuels to exploit subsidies are also a huge problem (for example in Venezuela)[97] where they cause lost revenues to governments and further entrench vested interests. They also no longer achieve their policy objectives and are an extremely inefficient way of targeting the poor – GDP is lower and the benefits of the subsidies are captured mostly by the wealthier sections of society (only 8% benefits the poorest section of society).[98]

Many countries are taking advantage of lower oil prices to remove consumer subsidies without high pass-through costs to consumers. Around 30 countries underwent some form of reform in 2013-2014. Notable recent examples include Indonesia, Egypt and India on consumer subsidies. France also announced the removal of some producer subsidies in the lead up to the Lima Climate Change talks at the end of last year. Whilst some countries have made progress many others such a Nigeria, Mexico, Venezuela and many Middle East and North African countries have far to go. It is not for want of trying: Nigeria has sought to reform the subsidy system thirteen times. An attempt to redistribute fossil fuel subsidies through a shift towards a cash transfer system (SURE-P) was undermined due to persistent governance issues.[99] However, such a move away from fossil fuel subsidies and towards a parallel investment in cash transfers and targeted social safety nets can take place and has done so in Iran, in Ghana and the Philippines. The Global Subsidies Initiative consistently recommend an orderly approach to governments for quitting subsidies: get the prices right, build support for reform and mitigate negative impacts.[100] The bigger ask is for countries to then reinvest savings from subsidy reform into changing the energy mix towards more sustainable energy and transport for all. With the removal of fossil fuel subsidies, countries like Morocco have turned towards the sun and ambitious renewables investment and targets. Others like Ghana have dismantled subsidies but are now attracted by the current low market price of coal to drive development. The world coal price is far below the true cost of power.

On the other hand, the current low oil price also leads producers and state owned companies - often within more developed countries - to seek further public subsidies to support operations. Hidden tax breaks and other benefits from wealthy states are more alarming. Research from last year finds that 'globally, a third of oil reserves, half of gas reserves and over 80 percent of current coal reserves should remain unused from 2010 to 2050 in order to meet the target of 2°C'.[101] Moves to develop new frontiers in exploration such as the Arctic or fracking are 'incommensurate' with the 2°C' target. Fossil-fuel subsidies to production and exploration play a role in ensuring continued access to, and exploitation of, such resources, as GSI found with specific project research commissioned on the Arctic.[102]

However, the good news is that once governments remove fossil-fuel subsidies the potential for revenue collection via the imposition of VAT or GST (Goods and Services Tax) on transport fuels greatly increases. Global revenue gains from the removal of subsidies and the efficient taxation of fossil fuels could be around USD 3 trillion to governments. There is considerable scope to increase the tax take from fossil fuels in Emerging and Developing Asia, the Commonwealth of Independent States, the Middle East, North Africa, Afghanistan and Pakistan. For example the Philippines removed subsidies and now taxes fuel at 12% VAT to pay for the national social safety net and provide incentives to renewables. Taxation and higher prices that reflect the true cost of fossil fuels can encourage greater energy efficiency and the more careful use of fossil fuels. They can also be used to fund safety nets and put renewable and sustainable sources of power at the centre of the energy sector.

July, 2015

APPENDIX: THE DECLARATIONS

Declaration of the Tax Justice Network

Part 1. "Only the little people pay taxes..."

1. Large corporations and wealthy individuals are increasingly avoiding their obligation to contribute to society through taxation. With the aid of governments, they are shifting the tax burden further onto ordinary citizens and smaller businesses. Governments claim that revenues are too low to achieve social justice through decent public goods and services; privatisation and cuts in social expenditure are presented as the only solutions. Instead, we argue for tax justice: to restore the ability to tax the wealthy beneficiaries of globalisation.

2. Tax avoidance now occurs on a massive global scale. Assets held offshore, beyond the reach of effective taxation, are already estimated to equal one-third of total global assets.

3. Around half of all world trade appears to pass through tax haven jurisdictions, as corporations shift profits to where they can avoid tax. Networks of banks, lawyers and accountants create complex and secret financial structures, reducing transparency and enabling tax evasion. Claims of corporate social responsibility are undermined when low corporate tax payments are exposed. Such behaviour is economically inefficient, socially destructive, and profoundly unethical.

4. Developing countries are estimated to lose revenues greater than annual aid flows. An increased return of just half a per cent on global assets held offshore could yield sufficient revenue to finance the UN Development Goals for 2015, halving global poverty. Instead, such

development is under threat from the huge tax breaks offered to attract large corporations, and from the vast outflow of funds from developing countries to tax havens.

5. These trends threaten democracy and development. A process of tax competition at the global level undermines the social contract previously set within the national arena, as states compete to offer tax exemptions to capital. Tax havens grow more numerous, the world's richest financial centres get even richer, taxes paid by large corporations fall, and ordinary citizens bear the cost. We call upon all concerned to meet this challenge, by building global and national campaigns for tax justice.

Part 2. A manifesto for tax justice

1. It is vital to act now, before the process of tax competition becomes even more established in the world economy. Our aims are to achieve the following:

> to eliminate cross-border tax evasion and limit the scope for tax avoidance, so that large corporations and wealthy individuals pay tax in line with their ability to do so;

> increase citizens' influence in the democratic control of taxation, and restrict the power of capital to dictate tax policy solely in its own interest;

> restore similar tax treatment of different forms of income, and reverse the shifting of the tax burden onto ordinary citizens;

> remove the tax and secrecy incentives that encourage the outward flow of investment capital from countries most in need of economic development;

> prevent the further privatisation and degradation of public services.

1. There are of course concerns, reservations, and difficulties in

working towards such aims. However, with sufficient research, democratic dialogue, and a fair distribution of the benefits of progress on this issue, we believe that such problems can be overcome. For example:

Financial secrecy and lack of information currently inhibit the research required to establish the true picture in many states. Proposals for reform will evolve in line with the results of future research.

We recognise that some small island economies and certain less developed countries are heavily dependent on harmful tax practices arising from tax competition, and that such economies may suffer significant reductions in investment and economic growth. To the extent that these factors impact negatively on the general population in such countries, we propose multilateral support to assist with re-structuring.

Wealthy vested interests will oppose progress, but we entirely reject the economic arguments by which tax exemptions for the rich are presented as beneficial to us all. Experience demonstrates that tax cuts usually lead to increasing inequalities between rich and poor.

Increases in government revenue may only deliver progress for ordinary citizens where broader society is democratically engaged in spending decisions.

1. The reasonable privacy of citizens must be distinguished from regimes of financial secrecy, from which only the wealthy and the dishonest benefit at substantial cost to the majority. Taking into account the concerns expressed above, we demand an immediate end to all regimes of financial secrecy, in every territory and state, in favour of open, honest and accessible publication of information as detailed in annex 1. This will:

increase the data available to authorities, researchers and policy-makers;

discourage corrupt capital flight;

expose criminal fortunes;

increase current global tax revenues.

1. In the past decade, efforts to tackle harmful tax practices have frequently consisted of attacks by industrialised countries on smaller tax haven economies. Such initiatives have not fully recognised that tax competition is also deeply embedded within the financial structure of the industrialised countries themselves, and therefore we look beyond the narrow concerns of industrialised governments. We propose the immediate initiation of a democratic global forum, to consist of representatives from governments and from citizens' groups across the world. We call for improved international tax co-operation and widespread debate on these issues, in particular to consider the appropriateness of policies such as those detailed in annex 2.

2. We propose that as citizens and as social movements from around the world, we intervene wherever and however we can, to promote awareness and debate of these issues, and to develop practical solutions. Our active participation is essential to fight for global tax justice.

Annex 1: Immediate Measures Proposed

(i) Public Disclosure of the following information, in all states and territories:

all tax laws and treaties; detailed national statistics for financial services activity and public accounts data; audited accounts for all significant business entities and trusts, specifically disclosing turnover and tax paid with a breakdown for each entity and in each territory or tax jurisdiction, and other improvements to disclosure; beneficial ownership of all business entities, trusts, bank and investment accounts, property, and any other form of asset.

(ii) Development of comprehensive and automatic information exchange between all tax authorities:

to facilitate both assessment and collection of taxes, including imposing obligations on states to obtain information from financial institutions, lawyers, accountants, auditors, and other relevant intermediaries

(iii) The provision of funding:

for substantial research into the extent of, the effects of, and solutions to, tax competition, tax havens, cross-border tax evasion, and tax avoidance by wealthy individuals and large corporations; for representatives from citizens' groups and developing countries to engage in this debate with sufficient expertise to promote their interests in this process.

(iv) The initiation of a democratic global forum:

to consist of representatives from governments and from citizens' groups across the world; to improve co-operation, to encourage debate, and to increase citizens' influence in the democratic control of taxation.

Annex 2: Additional measures to be urgently considered for improved international tax co-operation:

(i) Taxation of transnational corporations on the unitary basis, allowing tax authorities to effectively reverse the false shifting of profits to low-tax jurisdictions.

(ii) Universal application of the residency principle for corporate taxation.

(iii) States at comparable levels of economic development, and states geographically close to each other, should co-operate to eliminate destructive effects of tax competition between themselves.

(iv) Harmonisation of tax rates and tax bases for highly mobile capital such as that controlled by large corporations and wealthy individuals.

(v) The possibilities for establishing regional and global tax authorities that can represent the interests of citizens.

Drafted by Raphael Calvelli, John Christensen, Pete Coleman, Sven Giegold, François Gobbe, Pierre Guindja, Bruno Gurtner, Andreas Missbach, Juan Hernandez Vigueras

March, 2003

The Newhaven Declaration[103]

Human rights and international financial integrity are intimately linked. Where poverty is pervasive, civil, political, and economic rights often go unrealized. Today, large outflows of illicit money – many times larger than all development assistance – greatly aggravate poverty and oppression in many developing countries.

Illicit money leaves poorer countries through a global shadow financial system comprising tax havens, secrecy jurisdictions, disguised corporations, anonymous trust accounts, fake foundations, trade mispricing, and money-laundering techniques. Much of this money is permanently shifted into western economies.

Reducing these illicit outflows requires greater transparency and integrity in the global financial system. Achieving this is a prerequisite to creating an economic framework that is open, accountable, fair, and beneficial for all.

We call upon the United Nations, the G8, G20, WTO, IMF, World Bank, and other international fora, as well as on national governments, world leaders, faith groups and civil society organizations to recognize the linkage between human rights and financial transparency. We further call for decisive steps to ensure that developing countries can retain their resources for sustainable growth and poverty alleviation, which they must achieve if the human rights of all people are to be realized. The undersigned individuals and organizations shall be working together in the coming months to pursue this agenda and look to add additional voices to this effort:

Amnesty International, Human Rights Watch, Oxfam, Global Financial Integrity, Center for Applied Philosophy and Public Ethics, Open Society Institute Justice Initiative, Asia Initiatives, Basel Institute on Governance, Task Force on Financial Integrity and Economic Development, Tax Justice Network, Christian Aid, National Council of Churches, Harrington Investments, Inc., Asociación Civil por la Igualdad y la Justicia, Thomas Pogge, Yale University Robert Hockett, Cornell University, Frank Pasquale, Seton Hall

January, 2010

The Nairobi Declaration on Tax and Development[104]

We, the undersigned organisations and networks, having shared extensive research on the problems facing sub-Saharan African countries at the inaugural Pan-African Conference on Taxation and Development held in Nairobi, 25-26 March 2010:

(a) recognise the common threat to political progress, sustainable economic development and to poverty eradication that results from the unacceptable domestic and international obstacles to effective taxation for development.

(b) affirm that effective and equitable taxation and is critical to the independence of African countries; and to the strengthening of channels of political representation and government accountability.

(c) commit to work together for reform in the areas of domestic taxation, revenues from natural resource extraction and international taxation.

1. Domestic taxation

Having regard for the importance on tax compliance and accountability for tax revenues and expenditure we:

(a) call on African governments to commit to full transparency on tax revenues and tax expenditures.

(b) call on African governments to remove tax exemptions for multinational corporations and wealthy individuals and elites.

(c) call on revenue authorities to simplify the tax code and reduce the compliance burden, particularly for small businesses.

(d) call on fiscal research institutes to investigate the feasibility of land Value taxes in urban areas to funding of local infrastructure provisions, and to conduct analysis into the benefits of Export Processing Zones to African countries.

(e) agree to work within civil society to promote taxpayer education and compliance and call on other civil society organisations to do so.

(f) commit to ongoing research and advocacy with regard to the impacts of tax policy on men, women and vulnerable groups.

2. Revenues from natural resource extraction

Having regard for the importance of strong governance to ensure African governments benefit from natural resource extraction we:

(a) note the power and information asymmetry between African governments and multinational companies in negotiating fair contracts and the lack of capacity to determine appropriate prices.

(b) question the lack of transparency in mining contracts across the continent which increase potential for bribery and corruption and undermine accountability.

(c) call on African governments to audit natural resource bases before signing mining contracts.

(d) call on African governments to strengthen legal provisions relating to contracts, possibly including measures to over-ride stability agreements that prevent future governments from re-negotiating contract provisions, possibly including limits to length of the contracts.

(e) call on African regional bodies to explore regional coordination and harmonisation of fiscal regimes, and information exchange to challenge harmful tax competition in the mining sector.

(f) call on African regional bodies to commit to South-South learning of successful tax practices in relation to mining.

(g) call on African governments to sign on to the Extractive Industry Transparency Initiative (EITI), and to ratify the United Nations Convention Against Corruption.

(h) call on aid donors to build the capacity of civil society in monitoring the activities of mining companies.

(i) affirm that if it is not possible to arrive at a fair contract that, resources should be left in the ground for exploitation by future generations.

3. International taxation

Having regard for the leakages which undermine the tax bases of African countries we:

(a) note that developing countries lose more as a result of international tax evasion and avoidance than they receive in foreign aid.

(b) note the need for policy coherence among aid donors to take steps at the national and international level to challenge international tax dodging.

(c) affirm the need for international and regional tax cooperation to challenge harmful tax competition and stop tax leakages.

(d) challenge the widely held assumption that low tax rates encourage economic growth and development.

(e) call on the UN, IMF, World Bank and OECD to include civil society in international processes to challenge tax leakages.

(f) call on the G20 to involve African countries in international processes with regard to tax cooperation.

(g) having regard for the need for greater transparency among multinational companies, we call on the International Accounting Standards Board (IASB) to adopt a country- by – country reporting of key financial information for all listed companies

(h) having regard for the corrosive impact of financial secrecy in offshore financial centres we call on the G20 and the UN to move towards a multilateral agreement for the automatic exchange of tax information between jurisdictions, particularly developing countries.

(i) call on African regional and pan African bodies to initiate effective multilateral programmes for exchanging tax information to combat tax evasion.

(j) call on African governments to introduce legislation to make tax evasion a predicate offense under existing anti-money laundering provisions.

(k) call on aid donors to invest in strengthening the capacity for revenue authorities and to provide technical expertise in monitoring large taxpayers, in particular, transfer pricing issues.

(l) commit to research the impact of current tax regimes and campaign for reforms at the international level to ensure that the taxing rights of African countries are not undermined by abusive international tax practices

Signed

Alvin Mosioma Kenya Tax Justice Network-Africa, Sandra Kidwingira Kenya Tax Justice Network-Africa, John Christensen United Kingdom Tax Justice Network, Dereje Alemayehu Kenya Christian Aid- East Africa, Jack Ranguma Kenya Tax Justice Network-Africa, Attiya Waris Kenya University of Nairobi, Wakaguyu Wakiburi Kenya Tax Justice Reference Group, Semkae Kilonzo Tanzania Policy Forum, Jane Nalunga Uganda SEATINI, Alex Cobham United Kingdom Christian Aid, David McNair United Kingdom Christian Aid, Katrin Mc Gauran Netherlands SOMO, Aldo Calieri USA Rethinking Bretton Woods Project/Centre of Concern, Soren Ambrose Kenya Action Aid, Charles Chivweta Zambia Norwegian Church Aid, Samuel Fakile Nigeria Covenant University of Ota, Nara Monkam South Africa Africa Tax Institute, Chilufya Chileshe Zambia Jesuit Centre for Theological Reflection, Abdoulaye Doudou Sarr Mauritania Publish What You Pay, Silvana Toska USA Cornell University, Jean Marie Bolika DR Congo ILDI, Michael Otieno Kenya NTA, Jean Mballa Mballa Cameroon CRADEC, Steve Manteaw Ghana ISODEC, Alradjé dono dédengart Chad N'Djamena University, Kennedy Masime Kenya Centre for Governance & Development, Joanne Carpenter United Kingdom PANOS, Fiona Chipunza Zimbabwe AFRODAD, Vitus Azeem Ghana Integrity Initiative, Jean Luc Muke DR Congo Avocats Verts, Julien Tingain Côte d'Ivoire Publish What You Pay, Manyewu Mutamba South Africa IDASA, Rebecca Tanui Kenya BEACON, Vera Mshana South Africa Africa Tax Institute, Kiama Kaara

Kenya KENDREN, Isaack Otieno South Africa Institute for Security Studies, Marjolein Brouwer Netherlands Oxfam Novib, Lina Sjaavik Tanzania Norwegian Church Aid, Dennis Eliashifie Tanzania Norwegian Church Aid, Savior Mwambwa Zambia Centre for Trade Policy & Development, Mathias Kafunde Malawi Centre for Social Concern, Peter Kioko Kenya Institute of Certified Public Accountants-Kenya, Saviour Mwambwa Zambia Centre for Trade Policy & Development, Evariste Munyampunda Tanzania GTZ- East Africa

March, 2010

The Tunis Declaration: Tax Justice to End Inequality, World Social Forum 2015[105]

The prevailing international tax rules and practices, as well as the failure of governments to cooperate on international tax matters, continue to undermine the ability of governments in the Global South and the North to ensure that corporations and wealthy individuals pay their fair share of taxes. The recent 'Luxembourg Leaks' has confirmed that multinationals continue to dodge taxes with impunity. This is the latest in a long list of corporate tax scandals involving major brand names including Glencore, Google, Amazon, Starbucks, Caterpillar, Deutsche Bank, Zara, McDonald's, Associated British Foods and many more. Similarly, the recent 'Swiss Leaks' has revealed that wealthy individuals hide untaxed fortunes in hidden Swiss bank accounts.

At the same time, many governments themselves act in the interest of corporations, liberally providing tax incentives and signing tax treaties that enable huge outflows of public revenues. As a result, ordinary people all over the world carry a disproportionately heavy burden of raising tax revenues – while public services lack adequate resources to meet the needs of citizens. The continuing imposition of austerity measures and the increasing debt burden aggravate poverty and inequality within and between countries, making the need for tax justice more urgent than ever. Meanwhile, governments are compensating for the lack of available public funding in various ways such as incurring more debt and by entering into risky public--private partnerships with the very same multinational corporations that are dodging taxation. Privatization of vital social services, where profit principally drives service delivery and overrides basic human needs, is rationalized by the need to raise domestic revenues.

Instead of cooperating to solve the problems, the world's governments continue to invent new tax incentives for multinational corporations and wealthy individuals as part of a global race-to-the bottom. Meanwhile, rigged global tax rules fail to protect the tax bases of the world's poorest nations against erosion driven by international tax dodging. These global rules, which undermine global cooperation and ignore the interests of the poorest, continue to be negotiated and decided in closed forums of rich nations.

Continuing the tradition of the World Social Forum, which at the WSF in Porto Alegre in 2002 issued a 'Universal Declaration on the right to tax justice as a component part of social justice', and at the WSF in Tunis in 2013 issued a declaration on 'Tax Justice for Social Justice', we demand the following from our governments:

International cooperation for global solutions

Establish an inclusive and well--resourced intergovernmental body on tax matters under the auspices of the UN, which can initiate and lead negotiations on a new UN framework convention on international cooperation in tax matters as a first step in the reform of international tax rules.

Automatic information exchange and tax transparency for multinational corporations

Adopt a common UN standard of multilateral, automatic exchange of tax information with the option of non--reciprocal information exchange for countries with low capacity.
Eliminate secrecy of beneficial ownership worldwide through public registers of beneficial owners.
Ensure financial transparency by implementing annual public country-by-country reporting by multinational corporations.
Ensure that tax administrations are well resourced.

Progressive tax policies to tackle inequality within countries

Reduce inequality by adopting a full range of progressive taxation measures. Tax policy design and implementation must actively seek to reduce income and gender inequality.

Make it the highest priority commitment to invest tax funds in the vital human development related public services and public infrastructure (e.g., health, education, water, housing, sanitation, transportation), sustainable development, adequate social protection floors and to reverse climate change.

Provide the means for citizens to make their voices heard and hold governments accountable on their tax policy and how revenue raised is spent.

Ensure fiscal policies are gender sensitive. This should include assessing and tracking the impact of regressive taxes, such as VAT, and the tax burden, and implementing measures to shift the burden away from poor women and men.

Adopt and implement a financial transactions tax.

Fair international tax rules that make multinationals pay their share

Ensure the review of Double Taxation Agreements to bring them fully in line with sustainable development and financing for development needs and agenda.

Develop solid alternatives to the dysfunctional Arm's Length Principle.

Remove policies and treaties that erode the tax base of other countries.

To promote the tax justice agenda, we commit ourselves to:

(a) Continue and strengthen our advocacy and campaign to influence and increase the pressure on decision makers for tax justice. This includes public mobilization and political advocacy to ensure our government leaders deliver vital tax justice decisions in the UN Financing for Development summit in Addis Ababa this July and beyond.

(b) Enhance our efforts to create strong social movements locally and globally to force governments and challenge multinationals to end tax dodging. This includes new campaigns to make multinational corporations pay their share of taxes. We will march this May Day under the banner "Working people pay taxes – corporations must pay their share" and mobilize across civil society for global tax justice action days, including this June 23, World Public Services Day.

(c) Promote gender justice as a key element of tax justice. This includes engaging at the national level to challenge discriminatory tax laws and ensure that tax policies recognize the invisible and unpaid care work of women.

(d) Advance tax justice as a means to deliver climate justice by generating financing, including for adaptation and mitigation.

(e) Work together to transform the current economic system that privileges corporations and the wealthy, drives inequality and hurts our environment. Our vision entails progressive redistributive taxation polices that fund the vital public services, end inequality and poverty, address climate change and lead to sustainable development.

We welcome that Global Alliance for Tax Justice, owned and driven by major regional networks in Africa, Asia, Latin America, North America and Europe, has invited wide civil society engagement and pledged at this World Social Forum in Tunis 2015 to collaborate and build global synergy for advocacy and campaigns and peoples' mobilizations for tax justice.

March, 2015

Lima Declaration on Tax Justice and Human Rights[106]

We come together as a broad-based community of experienced advocates, practitioners, activists, scholars, jurists, litigators and others committed to advancing tax justice through human rights, and to realizing human rights through just tax policy.

Tax revenue is the most important, the most reliable and the most sustainable instrument to resource human rights in sufficient, equitable and accountable ways. The realization of all human rights, likewise, is a core raison d'être of government. It is through respecting, protecting and fulfilling civil, political, economic, social, cultural and environmental rights that the state earns its legitimacy to tax. Taxation also plays a fundamental role in redistributing resources in ways that can prevent and redress gender, economic and other inequalities and reduce the disparities in human rights enjoyment that flow from them. Moreover, a just system of taxation can cement the bonds of accountability between the state and its people, fostering governments to be more responsive to the rights and claims of those to whom they are answerable. Tax policies can likewise counteract glaring market failures and protect global common goods – not least a healthy environment within planetary boundaries.

Yet many countries struggle to collect sufficient tax revenue to adequately fund the realization of human rights, all of which come with some financial cost. In parallel, unjust tax systems at the national and global levels continue to fuel rising inequality and widening disparities in human rights enjoyment, shifting the burden of financing public services onto society's least well-off, weakening the provision of existing services and concentrating wealth in the hands of a privileged few. Regressive fiscal policies being pursued in many countries across the globe from North to South are a serious threat to the economic and social rights of already disadvantaged groups. This basic injustice is fuelling deeper economic, gender, and political inequalities, eroding trust in government institutions, which are perceived as more accountable to transnational economic elites than to their own people.

Tax policy is public policy, and so can no longer be treated as a matter of mere technical engineering or be left entirely to the often unaccountable discretion of government. Instead, we call on governments to cultivate transformative social and fiscal compacts, and empower citizen watchdog institutions that have the purpose of subjecting tax policy to the most rigorous standards of transparency, public participation, and meaningful accountability in line with internationally-recognized human rights principles.

Existing human rights standards provide a normative justification for a capable and well-resourced state. In order to comply with their obligations to protect and progressively realise economic and social rights, states must use and generate the maximum available resources (especially through sufficient and sustainable taxation) in equitable, non-discriminatory ways.

Tax laws, policies and practices must work to end structural discrimination rather than entrench growing inequalities of all kinds, including gender, ethnic, and economic disparities. Indeed, taxation is a key instrument for addressing discrimination against women and ensuring their substantive equality. Regressive revenue-raising measures (including those which effectively impose a disproportionate fiscal burden on the most disadvantaged within and between households and disregard individual ability to pay) as well as socially-useless tax incentives and relief for business and the wealthy that have the effect of shifting the tax burden to those less able to pay while relieving those more able to pay, are inconsistent with the human rights principles of non-discrimination and equality. We call on governments to conduct impact assessments of the human rights and equality implications of tax laws. Likewise, we urge governments and statistical agencies to collect individual, household, and corporate data that enables decision-makers to accurately evaluate the human rights and equality impacts of all fiscal policies.

Today's international corporate tax system – put in place when the nature and composition of the global economy was fundamentally different – is thoroughly outdated, privileging the interests of multinational corporate groups, global financial interests and some advanced economies while preventing national governments from raising sufficient revenue in non-discriminatory and accountable ways. Rigorous, evidence-based scrutiny of the impacts tax laws, policies and practices have on human rights and equality abroad should replace the all-too-often unsubstantiated assumptions about the economic benefits of maintaining the prevailing international tax system. Grounded on states' existing legal duties to take steps individually and through international cooperation and assistance to achieve the full realization of human rights, we call for the rewriting of global tax rules under the auspices of a legitimate, fully inclusive and democratic United Nations global tax body.

A state implementing tax policies or practices that erode the capacity of other states to resource human rights (whether by means of preferential tax rulings, preferential corporate tax regimes for internationally mobile forms of capital, or any other means) may be in violation of this international legal duty to cooperate. Further, states which purposefully obstruct tax information exchange, as well as banks and law firms that exploit secrecy arrangements to the detriment of the public purse, are foreseeably depriving other states of the resources needed to meet their human rights obligations. We therefore call on states to conduct human rights impact assessments of the spill-over effects of their tax policies on other countries, to take immediate action to halt any harmful practices, and to provide effective remedy where harm is done. Likewise, we call on states to enact legislation to regulate transfer pricing mis-practices, and to curtail financial and banking secrecy so as to enable governments to effectively combat tax abuse.

Business behaviour – and tax advice – that place tax revenues at risk may well deprive states of the resources they need to realise human rights. Therefore, the tax behaviour of business can no longer be treated outside the purview of the corporate responsibility to respect human rights. In order to implement their obligations in accordance with the United Nations Guiding Principles on Business and Human Rights, we call on governments to develop legal and regulatory frameworks which safeguard against the human rights risks of business tax behaviour. We also call on governments to provide effective remedy for any harmful conduct stemming from tax behaviour. In parallel, we urge companies and corporate groups to assess and address corporate tax abuse, for example in their policy statements, due diligence and grievance processes. Starting from a clear recognition of the adverse human rights impacts of tax abuse, companies should then conduct their tax arrangements in transparent and accountable ways so as to not jeopardize government revenue collection, even when such arrangements are technically lawful yet contravene human rights principles. We especially call on suppliers of schemes which may put government revenues at risk (in particular tax lawyers, accountants and financial intermediaries) to avoid colluding in tax abuse, to recognize their particular human rights responsibilities, to conduct human right due diligence, and to redress any harmful activities. Further, we call on companies of all stripes to refrain from interfering in the public interest of tax policy-making, be that directly through special-interest lobbying or indirectly through provoking tax competition. We call on international institutions to support the reform of the broken global tax system by, amongst other things, integrating human rights standards into how they address corporate tax avoidance and the adverse spill-over effects of certain governments' tax policies. Likewise, international financial institutions which advise governments on their tax and fiscal policies should, above all, respect those governments' human rights obligations.

Rather than be an obstacle, the law should be transformed into an instrument of tax and fiscal justice. We urge the legal profession (including human rights and tax lawyers, judges and the judiciary at large) to consider its particular responsibilities to oppose unjust tax policies that impede the realization of human rights.

One of the human rights community's most urgent challenges is to ensure states are accountable for equipping themselves with the material means for the fulfilment of human rights. We therefore call on the human rights community at large (e.g. advocates, lawyers, academia, women's rights organizations, NGOs, trade unions, national human rights institutions, treaty bodies and regional commissions) to actively examine how tax practices affect their missions, and develop capacities and practices to advance human rights through closer monitoring and review of tax policy. Whistleblowers and other tax justice advocates who work in the public interest to expose blatant tax-related human rights abuses, meanwhile, should be considered human rights defenders, and protected accordingly.

Finally, we call on the tax justice and development communities at large to integrate human rights into their research and advocacy, so as to harness the power of invoking human rights discourse, norms and accountability mechanisms in the pursuit of just taxation and sustainable development. The undersigned organizations endorse this Lima Declaration on Tax Justice and Human Rights, 1 and pledge to continue collaborating to advance tax and fiscal justice through human rights.

Signatories (as of 23 June 2015):

1. Academics Stand Against Poverty, Italy 2. ActionAid, International 3. Alliance Sud, Switzerland 4. Asia Initiatives, USA 5. Asian Peoples Movement on Debt and Development, Philippines 6. Asociación Civil

por la Igualdad y la Justicia, Argentina 7. Association For Women's Rights in Development (AWID), Global 8. Association of Canadian Financial Officers (ACFO-ACAF), Canada 9. Attac-Ireland, Ireland 10. Brazilian Society of Bioethics, Brazil 11. British Columbia Government and Service Employees' Union, Canada 12. Business & Human Rights Resource Centre, International 13. CCFD-Terre Solidaire, France 14. CEICOM, El Salvador 15. Center for Economic and Social Rights (CESR), International 16. Center for Women's Global Leadership (CWGL) at Rutgers University, USA 17. Centre for the Enforcement of Human Rights International, Austria 18. Centro Bonó, República Dominicana 19. Centro de Documentación en Derechos Humanos "Segundo Montes Mozo S.J." (CSMM), Ecuador 20. Centro de Estudios de Derecho, Justicia y Sociedad -DeJuSticia, Colombia 21. Centro de Estudios para el Desarrollo Laboral y Agrario (CEDLA), Bolivia 22. Centro de los Derechos del Campesino, Nicaragua 23. Christian Aid, UK 24. Christian Aid Ireland, Ireland 25. Comision Justicia y Paz Madrid, España 26. Comisión Nacional de Enlace (CNE), Costa Rica 27. Community Hope Project, USA 28. Compassionate Revolution, UK 29. Concejo Ecuménico Cristiano de Guatemala, Guatemala 30. Cristina Escarmis Homs, España 31. Development Alternatives with Women for a New Era (DAWN), Global South 32. EcoProsperity, UK 33. Ecumenical Association for Sustainable Agriculture and Rural Development (ECASARD), Ghana 34. Education International, Global 35. EDUCON, Czech Republic 36. Egyptian Center for Economic and Social Rights (ECESR), Egypt 37. EOS – Associação de estudos, desenvolvimento e cooperação, Portugal 38. Ethical Consumer Research Association Ltd, United Kingdom 39. European Federation of Public Service Unions (EPSU), Europe 40. European Network on Debt and Development (Eurodad), Belgium 41. Federación Internacional de Fe y Alegría, Colombia 42. Feminist Legal Studies Queen's, Canada 43. Forum Solidaridad Perú, Peru 44. Fundación para el Avance de las Reformas y las Oportunidades – Grupo FARO, Ecuador 45. Fundar, Centro de Análisis e Investigación, México 46. Giving What We Can, United Kingdom 47. Global Alliance for Tax Justice, Global 48. Global Initiative for Economic, Social and Cultural Rights, USA and Switzerland 1 The Lima Declaration emerges from the international strategy meeting, "Advancing Tax Justice through Human Rights," held in Lima, Peru in 2015, convened by the Center for Economic and Social Rights, the Global Alliance for Tax Justice, Oxfam, Red Latinoamericana sobre Deuda, Desarrollo y Derechos (LatinDADD), Red de Justicia Fiscal de América Latina y el Caribe and the Tax Justice Network. 49. Global Policy Forum, Germany/USA 50. Grupo de Trabajo Contra la Corrupción, Perú 51. Grupo Nacional de Presupuesto Público, Perú 52. Hoover Chair of Economic and Social Ethics, Belgium 53. IBIS, Denmark 54. IndustriALL Global Union, Switzerland 55. Initiative for Social and Economic Rights (ISER), Uganda 56. Institute for Economic Research on Innovation, South Africa 57. Institute of Global Responsibility (IGO), Poland 58. Instituto Centroamericano de Estudios Fiscales, Centroamérica 59. Instituto de Estudos Socioeconômicos – INESC, Brasil 60. Instituto Justiça Fiscal, Brasil 61. International Bar Association's Human Rights Institute, United Kingdom 62. International Federation of Musicians, France 63. International Trade Union Confederation (ITUC), Global 64. JONCTION, Senegal 65. Kairos Europe, Belgium 66. Kenya Human Rights Commission, Kenya 67. Labour, Health and Human Rights Development Centre, Nigeria 68. Lawyers for Better Business, UK 69. Methodist Tax Justice Network, UK 70. Movimiento Unificado Francisco Sánchez-1932, El Salvador 71. Natural Resources Alliance of Kenya (KeNRA), Kenya 72. Oxfam International, International 73. Oxfam Novib, Netherlands 74. Plataforma Global El Salvador, El Salvador 75. Plataforma Interamericana de Derechos Humanos, Democracia y Desarrollo (PIDHDD), Ecuador 76. Plateforme Paradis Fiscaux et Judiciaires, France 77. Promocion de Derechos de adolescentes en riesgo social (FUNPRODE), Nicaragua 78. Public Services International, Global 79. Red Activista El Salvador, El Salvador 80. Red de Justicia Fiscal de América Latina y El Caribe, Latin America and the Craibbean 81. Red de Organizaciones de Managua, Nicaragua 82. Red Latinoamericana sobre Deuda, Desarrollo y Derechos – LATINDADD, Latinoamerica 83. Red por la Justicia Tribuaria en Colombia, Colombia 84. Réseau Foi & Justice Afrique Europe, France 85. Right to Education Project, United Kingdom 86. Southern and Eastern African Trade, Information and Negotiations Institute (SEATINI), Uganda 87. SUPRO-Campaign for Good Governance, Bangladesh 88. Tapea, Paraguay 89. Tax Justice Network, International 90. International

Tax Justice Network, Africa 91. Tax Justice Network – Norway, Norway 92. Tax Justice Network-Far East Chapter, South Korea 93. Tax Research UK, UK 94. The Engage Network, United States 95. Transparency International France, France 96. Tunisian Observatory of Economy, Tunisia 97. UNI Global Union, Switzerland 98. United Food and Commercial Workers International Union, United States 99. Uniting Church in Australia, Synod of Victoria and Tasmania, Australia 100. Water Governance Institute, Uganda 101. WEED – World Economy, Ecology & Development, Germany 102. 11.11.11 – Koepel van de Vlaamse Noord Zuidbeweging, Belgium

Notes

1 Adam Smith, *The Theory of Moral Sentiments* (London: Penguin, 2010), p.xx

2 Thomas Piketty, 'A Practical Vision of a More Equal Society', *New York Review of Books*, June, 25, 2015

3 A 2010 article in *Private Eye* about Vodafone's tax affairs had already been credited with inspiring UK Uncut, a direct action group that attracted significant public support in the winter of that year.

4 www.taxhistory.org/

5 http://www.ctj.org/pdf/corpfed90san.pdf

6 www.citizenworks.org

7 Center on Budget and Policy Priorities at www.cbpp.org

8 Africa All Party Parliamentary Group, 'The Other Side of the Coin', March, 2006, archived online at http://www.taxjustice.net/cms/upload/pdf/other_side_of_the_coin_PDF.pdf

9 Tax Justice Network in written evidence to the AAPPG, quoting from *Capitalism's Achilles Heel* (2005).

10 Dr Patrick Darling in written evidence to the AAPPG.

11 This essay is a review of *Capitalism's Achilles Heel* by Raymond Baker (Wiley, 438pp, £16.99, September 2005, ISBN 0 471 64488 9. It first appeared in the *London Review of Books* on 6th October, 2006.

12 First published in the *Guardian*, November 6, 2007.

13 The Lawrence-Griffiths article was one of the first of its kind in the UK press. It was part of a shift in coverage of the offshore system that became more pronounced after the financial crisis of 2007-8. A few years later both Bloomberg and Reuters were publishing investigations into the tax affairs of multinational companies.

14 McKinsey Global Institute, 'Mapping Global Capital Markets: Fourth Annual Report', 2008.

15 Lane P and G Milesi-Ferretti, 'The External Wealth of Nations Mark II: Revised and Extended Estimates of Foreign Liabilities 1970-2004', IMF Working Paper, 2006.

16 European Network on Debt and Development, 'Addressing Capital's Black Hour: Regulating Capital Flight', 2008.

17 See Alex Cobham, 'The Tax Consensus Has Failed', on page xx of this collection.

18 Mick Moore and Nardia Simpson, 'How Tax Affects Governance', TJF Second Quarter 2007, Vol. 3, Issue 2, 2007.

19 Nicholas Shaxson, *Poisoned Wells: The Dirty Politics of African Oil* (Basingstoke: Palgrave Macmillan, 2007), p.95.

20 Patrick Wintour, 'Labour candidates challenge City bankers' elite that runs Square Mile', *Guardian*, February 6, 2009.

21 UK Revenue and Customs provided a clear outline of the main forms

of trusts, archived in June 2009 at: http://webarchive.nationalarchives.gov.
uk/20140109143644/http://www.hmrc.gov.uk/pdfs/ir152.htm

22 http://www.taxjustice.net/cms/upload/pdf/European_Union_Savings_Tax_
Directive_March_08.pdf

23 http://taxjustice.blogspot.com/2009/07/secrecy-havens-new-us-
congressional.html

24 http://www.taxresearch.org.uk/Blog/2006/06/15/jersey-passes-law-allowing-
%E2%80%98sham%E2%80%99-trusts-for-use-by-tax-evaders/

25 See also http://www.taxresearch.org.uk/Blog/2006/10/02/jersey-shoots-
itself-in-the-foot/

26 [Missing note]

27 One of these companies describes its services at http://www.trustamsterdam.
nl/services/

28 The author would like to thank Paul Sagar and John Christensen for their
advice on this article.

29 Liam Murphy and Thomas Nagel, (2002), *The Myth of Ownership: Taxes and
Justice* (OUP), p. 9.

30 Liam Murphy and Thomas Nagel, (2002), *ibid.* , p. 9.

31 Liam Murphy and Thomas Nagel, (2002), *ibid.* , p. 8.

32 Oates, Wallace and Schwab, Robert (1997) 'The Impact of Urban Land
Taxes: The Pittsburgh Experience', *National Tax Journal.*

33 First published in the *London Review of Books* in April 2011 as a review of
Treasure Islands: Tax Havens and the Men who Stole the World by Nicholas Shaxson
and *Winner-Take-All Politics: How Washington Made the Rich Richer – and Turned Its
Back on the Middle Class* by Jacob Hacker and Paul Pierson.

34 More precisely, 'source countries' are those whose total real accumulated
net unrecorded private capital outflows are positive for the period 1970-2010 (or
whatever period is available for the particular country.) Equivalently, it is those
countries whose private citizens have accumulated positive net unreported/untaxed
financial wealth abroad.

35 This is a rather homogenous group, the large majority of which are low-
middle income countries, but it includes some 'rich non-OECD' countries like
Saudi Arabia and Kuwait, as well as a few 'developed' countries like Hungary and
Korea. Our criterion was that a) external debt data was available, and b) they are
'source' countries: that is, those countries whose private citizens have accumulated
positive net unreported/untaxed financial wealth abroad.

36 World Bank/IMF data (2012), author's analysis.

37 See James Henry, *The Blood Bankers, tales from the global underground
economy*, October 2003, for an investigative inside look at the intestines of the
global private banking model in developing countries.

38 See *The Price of Offshore Revisited*, Appendix 3, p.55 for more details.

39 See *The Price of Offshore Revisited*, Appendix 3, p.54.

40 Section 4 of *The Price of Offshore Revisited* explores this in more detail.

41 HMRC, Measuring Tax Gaps 2011, An Official Statistics Release, 21st
September 2011: http://www. hmrc.gov.uk/stats/mtg-2011.pdf

42 TUC (2010) The Corporate Tax Gap, London: TUC, http://www.tuc.org.
uk/extras/corporatetaxgap.pdf

43 Goodall, A. (2012) HMRC staff 'know' that Richard Murphy is not overstating the tax gap, says PCS, *Tax Journal*, 22 May, 2012 http://www.taxjournal. com/tj/articles/hmrc-staff-know-richard-murphy-not-overstating-tax-gap-46681

44 National Equality Panel, An Anatomy of Economic Inequality in the UK. London, Government Equalities Office, 2010, Figure 2.19b http://sticerd.lse.ac.uk/case/_new/publications/NEP.asp

45 National Equality Panel, ibid, Figure 2.18

46 National Equality Panel. Ibid, Figure 2.17

47 Picketty, P., Saex, E. and Stantcheva, Taxing the 1%: Why the top tax rate could be over 80%, Vox: Research-based policy analysis and commentary from leading economists, December 2011, http://www.voxeu. org/index. php?q=node/7402

48 Murphy, R. Tax havens report. London: PCS, www.pcs.org.uk/taxhavens, 2011, p.33. Quoting Haig Simonian from March 23rd, 2009 in the FT: http://www.ft.com/cms/s/0/2ed5ef86-17e3-11de-8c9d- 0000779fd2achtml

49 Congressional Budget Office (2011) 'Trends in the Distribution of Household Income Between 1979 and 2007', US government Printing Press: Washington DC. Available online at http://www.cbo.gov/ftpdocs/124xx/doc12485/10-25-HouseholdIncome.pdf and Piketty, Thomas and Emmanuel Saez 'Income Inequality in the United States, 1913-1998', Quarterly Journal of Economics, 118(1), 2003, 1-39, series updated to 2008 in July 2010, online at http://elsa.berkeley.edu/~saez/

50 The World Top Incomes Database (F. Alvaredo, T. Atkinson, T. Piketty, and E. Saez), online at http://g-mond.parisschoolofeconomics.eu/topincomes/

51 Piketty, Thomas, Emmanuel Saez, and Stefanie Stantcheva 'Optimal Taxation of Top Labor Incomes: A Tale of Three Elasticities', NBER Working Paper No. 17616, November 2011, online at http://www.nber.org/papers/w17616

52 Piketty, Thomas, Emmanuel Saez, and Stefanie Stantcheva, op. cit.

53 Piketty, Thomas, Emmanuel Saez, and Stefanie Stantcheva, op. cit.

54 Özgür Orhangazi, *Financialization and the U.S. Economy* (Cheltenham: Edward Elgar Publishing, 2008)

55 This is the introduction to Nicholas Shaxson and John Christensen, *The Finance Curse: How Oversized Financial Sectors Attack Democracy and Corrupt Economies* (Margate: Commonwealth Publishing, 2013).

56 See the Kilburn Manifesto: 'After neoliberalism?' by Stuart Hall, Doreen Massey and Michael Rustin. http://www.lwbooks.co.uk/journals/soundings/manifesto. Also in *Soundings*, 53, Spring 2013, pp. 8 – 22.

57 For a fuller analysis see Doreen Massey, *World City* (Cambridge: Polity Press, 2010).

58 See *World City* and Nicholas Shaxson and John Christensen, *The Finance Curse* (Margate: Commonwealth Publishing, 2013)

59 See Kilburn Manifesto (note 28).

60 This is what I have begun to do in Doreen Massey (2013) 'Vocabularies of the Economy' at the Kilburn Manifesto site, and in *Soundings*, 54, Summer 2013, pp. 9 – 22.

61 See *World City*.

62 BBA summer lecture, 20 June 2012: author's transcript.

63 Miller and Dinan, Revolving Doors, Accountability and Transparency – Emerging Regulatory Concerns and Policy Solutions in the Financial Crisis,

a report commissioned by the OECD, May 2009: http://www.olis.oecd.org/
olis/2009doc.nsf/ENGDATCORPLOOK/NT00002B52/$FILE/JT03263841.
PDF

64 http://www.dailymail.co.uk/news/article-2333068/Goldman-Sachs-banker-
hand-picked-Osborne-job-new-finance-watchdog-gave-400-000-Tory-party.
html#ixzz2cSO6seie

65 Parkinson, M., Meegan, R.,Karecha, J., Evans, R., Jones, G., Sotarauta, M.,
Ruokolainen, O., Tosics, I., Gertheis, A., Tönkő, A., Hegedüs, J., Illés, I., Lefèvre,
C., Hall, P. (2012) 'Second Tier Cities and Territorial Development in Europe:
Performance, Policies and Prospects'; Scientific Report | Version 30/06/2012 for
the European Observation Network on Territorial Development and Cohesion
(ESPON), p.27. [online] http://www.ljmu.ac.uk/EIUA/EIUA_Docs/SGPTD_
Scientific_Report_-_Final_Version_03.10.12.pdf

66 See for example Nick Clegg: Regions 'can rely on City no more' http://www.
channel4.com/news/clegg-regions-can-rely-on-city-no-more

67 Froud, J., Johal, S., Law, J., Leaver, A., Williams, K. (2011) Rebalancing the
Economy (Or Buyer's Remorse), Centre for Research on Socio-Cultural Change
(CRESC) working paper 87, p.22 [online] http://www.cresc.ac.uk/sites/default/
files/Rebalancing%20the%20Economy%20CRESC%20WP87.pdf

68 The PFI is a form of Public Private Partnership (PPP) where public
infrastructure projects are funded, built and managed by the private sector to a
public specification. Generally PFI contracts last a minimum of 25 years, during
which the private sector receive payments in exchange for bearing the project
risk. Notionally private sector participants are paid only if services are delivered
according to the negotiated concession agreement.

69 CRESC (2009) 'An Alternative Report on UK Banking Reform', [online]
http://www.cresc.ac.uk/sites/default/files/Alternative%20report%20on%20
banking%20V2.pdf

70 For more detail on this, see Haldane, A. (2010) 'The $100 Billion Question',
comments given at the Institute of Regulation & Risk, Hong Kong, 30 March 2010
[online] http://www.bankofengland.co.uk/publications/Documents/speeches/2010/
speech433.pdf

71 This article is based on an article entitled "The Six Trillion Dollar Question"
that appeared in the IBA's *Global Insights* magazine in October 2013: http://
www.ibanet.org/Article/Detail.aspx?ArticleUid=E2915C5C-B70B-4A64-9D85-
A0613827DF33. The IBAHRI Task Force's publication can be accessed at: http://
www.ibanet.org/Article/Detail.aspx?ArticleUid=4A0CF930-A0D1-4784-8D09-
F588DCDDFEA4.

72 Universal Declaration of Human Rights, article 25.

73 Boston Consulting Group, *Global Wealth 2013: Maintaining Momentum in
a Complex World* (2013), pp. 4 and 11. www.bcg.de/documents/file135355.pdf

74 Martin Hearson and Richard Brooks, 'Calling Time' (Action Aid, 2010
[April 2012 Update]), available at: www.actionaid.org.uk/doc_lib/calling_time_on_
tax_avoidance.pdf.

75 Dev Kar and Brian LeBlanc, *Illicit Financial Flows from Developing
Countries: 2002-2011* (Global Financial Integrity, December 2013), pp. iii, vii, x.
http://iff.gfintegrity.org/iff2013/2013report.html.

76 http://mdgs.un.org/unsd/mdg/SeriesDetail.aspx?srid=569&crid=

77 Christian Aid, *False Profits: Robbing the Poor to Keep the Rich Tax-Free*

(Christian Aid, March 2009), p. 3. https://www.christianaid.org.uk/Images/false-profits.pdf. There are many pressures toward improving current government spending patterns in poor countries, which are often distorted by corruption, bloated security apparatuses and indifference to the poor. Insofar as such efforts are succeeding, additional revenues would have an even larger human rights impact than Christian Aid is calculating.

78 An example are the 'tax holidays' periodically granted by the US Congress, such as the *American Jobs Creation Act* of 2004, which enabled US-based MNCs to repatriate profits accumulated in tax havens at a discounted 5.25% (instead of the usual 35%) tax rate. Without the prospect of such tax holidays, US MNCs have little to gain from shifting their profits from poor countries into tax havens.

79 Even the OECD's new landmark model agreement on automatic exchange of financial information is likely to exclude many less developed countries from its benefits because they lack the resources to set up the data collection arrangements required to qualify as a reciprocating partner.

80 For more on human rights and tax justice, see International Bar Association's Human Rights Institute (IBAHRI) Task Force on Illicit Financial Flows, *Tax Abuses, Poverty and Human Rights*, www.ibanet.org/Human_Rights_Institute/TaskForce_IllicitFinancialFlows_Poverty_HumanRights.aspx.

81 See http://www.ohchr.org/EN/Issues/Poverty/Pages/Fiscalandtaxpolicy2014.aspx

82 M. Sepúlveda, 'Report of the Special Rapporteur on Extreme Poverty and Human Rights: Mission to Paraguay' (3 April 2012) UN Doc A/HRC/20/25/Add.2, para. 43.

83 Ortiz, Chai and Cummins, 'Identifying Fiscal Space: Options for Social and Economic Development for Children and Poor Households in 182 Countries', UNICEF, 2011, p. 242.

84 Center for Economic and Social Rights, 'Spain Factsheet', 2012: http://cesr.org/article.php?id=1285.

85 Based on the International Energy Agency's 2014 World Energy Outlook -http://www.worldenergyoutlook.org/publications/weo-2014/ and the OECD's 2015 database - http://www.oecd.org/tad/agricultural-policies/producerandconsumersupportestimatesdatabase.htm

86 Global Subsidies Initiative, "Untold Billions Fossil-Fuel Subsidies, Their Impacts and the Path to Reform. A Summary of Key Findings", 2010

87 OCI and ODI, *The fossil fuel bailout: G20 subsidies for oil, gas and coal exploration*, 2014. Retrieved from http://www.odi.org/sites/odi.org.uk/files/odi-assets/ publications-opinion-files/9234.pdf

88 Stefanski, R., *Dirty little secrets: Inferring fossil-fuel Subsidies from patterns in emissions intensities*, 2014. Retrieved from http://www.oxcarre.ox.ac.uk/files/OxCarreRP2014134(1).pdf

89 Coady, D. Parry, I. Sears, L. and Shang, B. May, 'How Large Are Global Energy Subsidies?', IMF, 2015 https://www.imf.org/external/pubs/cat/longres.aspx?sk=42940.0

90 *Guardian,* 'Fossil fuels subsidised by $10m a minute, says IMF' 18 May, 2015.

91 Merrill, L. Harris, M., Casier, L., Bassi. M. A, 'Fossil-Fuel Subsidies and Climate Change: Options for policy-makers within their Intended Nationally Determined Contributions', 2015.

92 *GSI 2015, infographic 2015* http://www.iisd.org/gsi/sites/default/files/FFSR_and_climate_infographic_snd10-12_0.jpg

93 Merrill, L., 'Financing the sustainable development goals through fossil-fuel subsidy reform: Opportunities in Southeast Asia, India and China', Geneva: Global Subsidies Initiative, International Institute for Sustainable Development, 2014

94 IMF (2013), "Energy Subsidy Reform: Lessons and Implications" 28 January 2013. Available at: http://www.imf.org/external/np/pp/eng/2013/012813.pdf

95 Commander, S. (2012). *A guide to the political economy of reforming energy subsidies* (IZA Policy Paper No. 52). Retrieved from http://ftp.iza.org/pp52.pdf

96 Commander, S., op. cit.

97 'The wild frontier: Smuggling in Venezuela', August 16, 2014. *Economist*. Retrieved from http://www.economist. com/news/americas/21612186-border-colombia-closed-crackdown-contraband-wild-frontier

98 Arze Del Granado, J., Coady, D., & Gillingham, R. (2010). *The unequal benefits of fuel subsidies: A review of evidence for developing countries* (IMF Working Paper 10/22). Retrieved from http://www.imf.org/external/pubs/ft/wp/2010/wp10202.pdf

99 Ohaeri, V., 'Fossil-Fuel Subsidies: The Reality of Reform', 2014 *http://www.iisd.org/gsi/csos/docs/Ohaeri%20Spaces%20for%20Change%20Nigeria.pdf*

100 Beaton, C., Gerasimchuk, I., Laan, T., Lang, K., Vis-Dunbar, D., & Wooders, P. (2013). *A guidebook to fossil-fuel subsidy reform for policy makers in Southeast Asia*. Geneva: GSI. Retrieved from http://www.iisd.org/gsi/sites/default/files/ffs_guidebook.pdf

101 McGlade, C. & Ekins, P. (2015, January 8). The geographical distribution of fossil fuels unused when limiting global warming to 2°C. *Nature, 517,* 187–190.

102 Lunden, P. L. & Fjaertoft, D. (2014). Government support to oil and gas in Russia. Retrieved from http://www.iisd.org/gsi/sites/default/files/ffs_awc_russia_yamalprirazlomnoe_en.pdf

103 In December 2009 Global Financial Integrity and the Illicit Financial Flows project organized a conference at Yale University that brought together human rights advocates and campaigners for financial transparency. The New Haven Declaration was published the following on 7 January, 2010.

104 In March 2010 Tax Justice Network Africa hosted a Pan-African Conference on Tax and Development that focused on harnessing domestic tax policies for development, the taxation of extractive sectors; and closing the floodgates on illicit financial flows.

105 The Tunis Declaration was issued by the Tax Justice Convergence Assembly of the World Social Forum in Tunis on March 27, 2015.

106 The Lima Declaration was drawn up after the international strategy meeting convened in Lima, Peru by the Center for Economic and the Global Alliance for Tax Justice, Oxfam, Red Latinoamericana sobre Deuda, Desarrollo y Derechos (LatinDADD), Red de Justicia Fiscal de América Latina y el Caribe and the Tax Justice Network. The meeting took place on April 29-30, 2015.